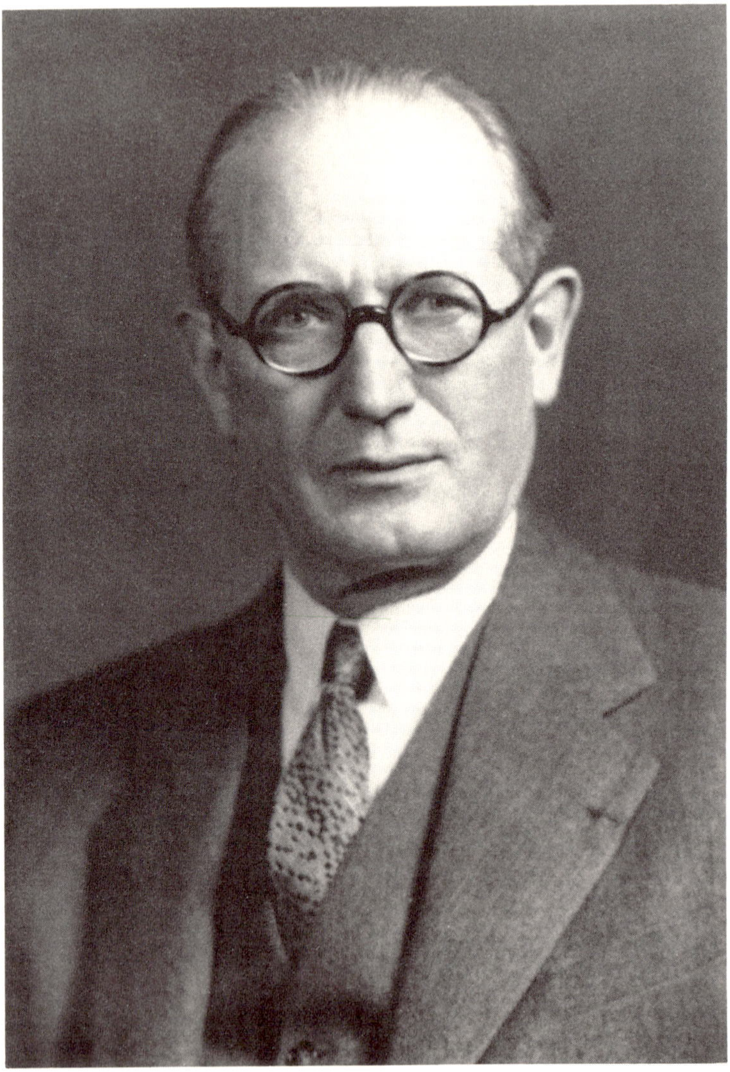

The GREATEST of GREATNESS:

The Life and Work of Charles C. Williamson (1877–1965)

by
PAUL A. WINCKLER

The Scarecrow Press, Inc.
Metuchen, N.J., & London
1992

Frontispiece: CHARLES C. WILLIAMSON, prior to 1940, at Columbia University. *Courtesy of Genevieve H. Williamson and Charles S. Watson*

British Library Cataloguing-in-Publication data available

Library of Congress Cataloging-in-Publication Data

Winckler, Paul A.
　The greatest of greatness : the life and work of Charles C. Williamson, 1877-1965 / Paul A. Winckler.
　　p. cm.
　Includes bibliographical references and index.
　ISBN 0-8108-2447-7 (alk. paper)
　1. Williamson, Charles C. (Charles Clarence), 1877-1965.
2. Library administrators—United States—Biography.
3. College librarians—United States—Biography.　I. Title.
Z720.W465W65　　1992
.25.1′092—dc20
[B]　　　　　　　　　　　　　　　　　　　　　　　91-30441

Copyright © 1992 by Paul A. Winckler
Manufactured in the United States of America
Printed on acid-free paper

*This book is dedicated to
my mother and father
with loving thanks.*

CONTENTS

	Acknowledgments	vii
	Preface	xi
1.	Early Life, Education, and Work (1877–1897)	1
2.	Teacher, Principal, Secretary, and College Student (1897–1904)	18
3.	The Graduate Student in Economics (1905–1907)	32
4.	The Young Professor at Bryn Mawr College (1907–1911)	51
5.	The New York Public Library (1911–1914)	70
6.	The Municipal Reference Library of the City of New York (1914–1918)	83
7.	The Carnegie Corporation of New York and the Americanization Study (1918–1919)	102
8.	Back to the New York Public Library (1919–1921)	107
9.	Librarianship and Library Education	127
10.	The Carnegie Corporation of New York and the Williamson Report	137

11.	The Rockefeller Foundation (1921–1926)	176
12.	Columbia University in the City of New York (1926–1943)	186
13.	Related Professional Activities	253
14.	Personality and Interests	275
15.	Retirement and Death (1943–1965)	289
16.	Life and Contributions in Retrospect	296
	Published and Unpublished Works of Charles C. Williamson	301
	Bibliography	309
	Chronology of Williamson's Life and Career	327
	Index	335

ACKNOWLEDGMENTS

THIS ACCOUNT OF THE LIFE and work of Charles C. Williamson required the assistance of many people who were helpful in providing information, source materials, ideas, criticism, and encouragement. The original idea for the biography developed at New York University as the theme of my doctoral dissertation, and the present book is based on that document.

Without the cooperation and support of Dr. Williamson, who gave permission for the writing of this biography, and his wife, Genevieve H. Williamson, this book would not have been possible. In late 1964 the author visited Dr. Williamson at his home in Greenwich, Connecticut, and during two visits discussed various aspects of his life and obtained the loan of a number of source materials. The author made use of many other documentary materials now located in the Charles C. Williamson Papers in the Rare Book and Manuscript Library at Columbia University in the City of New York; the items which Dr. Williamson loaned the author were eventually deposited in that collection, as a gift of Mrs. Williamson. After Dr. Williamson's death, in early 1965, his widow continued to encourage the author by providing ongoing assistance. The research for this book is based on these primary source materials, in the seemingly endless search for relevant data. From that plethora of materials has emerged this biography.

Additional materials and data were obtained from relatives, friends, and colleagues, including Mr. and Mrs. Alfred Williamson and Miss Grace Richards of Salem, Ohio, for information on Dr. Williamson's early life. My thanks to Miss Florence Anderson, former Secretary of the Carnegie Corporation of New York for permission to quote from the 1922 Report of the Advisory Committee on Training for

Library Work. Thanks to Dr. Sarah K. Vann for giving permission to quote from statements and correspondence she had with Dr. Williamson; Mr. Robert Hall and Mr. Edward di Roma of the New York Public Library; Mr. John Fall and Miss Ella Struska of the Public Affairs Information Services; Mr. Eugene Bockman and Miss Thelma Smith of the Municipal Reference and Research Center of the City of New York; and Mr. David Clift, former Executive Director of the American Library Association.

Administrators and faculty at Columbia University were most helpful, including Dr. Jack Dalton, Dr. Richard Logsdon, Mr. Ralph Baugham, Mr. Kenneth Lohf, Dr. Maurice Tauber, Dr. Carl White, and Dr. Phyllis Dain. Columbia University also permitted use of the Charles C. Williamson Papers and gave permission to the author to quote from documents owned by the university. Quotations not referenced in the Notes are taken from materials in that collection.

Authorities in the field of librarianship, library education, and library history provided information in answer to a questionnaire sent to them for their comments. Many of these people also were friends, colleagues, or had worked with Dr. Williamson. This includes Dr. Leon Carnovsky, Miss Lucy Crissey, Dr. J. Periam Danton, Dr. Robert B. Downs, Professor Bertha Frick, Miss Alice Jewett, Dr. Keyes D. Metcalf, Dr. L. Quincy Mumford, Professor Miles Price, Professor Ernest J. Reece, Mr. Paul North Rice, Dr. Jesse H. Shera, Dr. Louis Shores, Dr. Joseph Wheeler, and Dr. Louis Round Wilson.

My special thanks goes to the administration, faculty, and staff of the Palmer School of Library and Information Science of Long Island University for help and encouragement. I also want to thank the library staff of the C. W. Post Campus Library and of the Palmer School Library for assistance.

The author received two grants providing funds for research expenses from the Research Committee at the C. W. Post Campus of Long Island University and a Grant-in-Aid from the Grolier Foundation. The author is grateful to Long Island University for the granting of a

Acknowledgments

sabbatical leave which provided time for completion of this book.

I also want to thank Patricia Garvey for her editorial assistance, and Deborah Whelan for the typing of the manuscript.

No acknowledgment would be complete without special thanks to the members of my family who were intimately and continually involved, bearing the constant burden of cooperation and understanding. To my late wife, Anne, and to my children, Mark, Christopher, Karen, Patrick, and Pamela, my sincere thanks.

That the writing of such a work is long and arduous, no one can deny; that it is exciting and challenging, the author feels is reflected in a deeper knowledge and understanding of the man and his times; and that it will be of interest and value to the library world, only time will tell.

> PAUL A. WINCKLER
> Palmer School of Library and
>   Information Science
> Long Island University
> Brookville, New York

PREFACE

THE LIFE AND WORK OF Charles C. Williamson is the story of professional librarianship and library education in the United States during the first half of the twentieth century.

Williamson's work, contributions, and ideas about library service helped to shape the structure of library education and librarianship today. As a university librarian he was concerned with professionalism in library work, while as a library educator he was involved in teaching that professionalism. He was both a librarian, occupied with the professional quality of his staff, and an educator, engaged in the professional education of librarians. This dual role was clear in Williamson's mind, but he had to exert much effort and energy to make it clear to others. It is to his credit that they were achieved at all. Professional librarianship in the twentieth century is indebted to his efforts. Whatever pattern librarianship takes in the future, whatever becomes of the traditional concept of the librarian, Williamson's standards and goals will always be remembered.

Williamson set extremely high standards for himself and others. At times few people were able to meet those standards. He was, however, certain about his goals and how to achieve them. In 1931 he remarked: "In my talking and writing about library service and training for library service I have sometimes been accused of being dogmatic. Perhaps there is ground for the accusation, but I am inclined to adopt Chesterton's defense for being dogmatic," relating the story that "somebody complained to Matthew Arnold that he was getting to be as dogmatic as Carlyle. 'That may be true,' said Arnold, 'but you overlook an obvious difference. I am dogmatic and right, and Carlyle is dogmatic and wrong.' "[1]

Williamson was dogmatic and he was often right. This fact is established today, for his ideas of library service continue to point out many of the needs and problems of librarianship. Certainly Williamson will be remembered as one of the great ones of librarianship, not only for his own work but for his ability to view critically the problems of the library profession.

To some people Williamson seemed aloof, cold, unapproachable, and rather formidable, but they really did not know him. To those who knew him well he was considerate, thoughtful, interested, even if always precise and meticulous. Williamson was human in his personal shortcomings and strengths. He was demanding of others because he demanded perfection of himself. Those who met these demands obtained his continued help and support. The names of his students and protégés make an impressive roster. Those of his students who continued in his footsteps upheld his desire that the profession of librarianship take its place with other professions.

Dr. Frank Bradway Rogers stated, "Dr. Williamson's contribution to librarianship and library education has been widely recognized . . . he was the right man, in the right place, at the right time." Williamson's death brought "to a close the career of a man of high standards, goals, and achievements."[2] Miles Price eloquently summed up Williamson's place: "He was a giant, with some of the giant's vices, but overwhelmingly with a giant's virtues."

The late David Clift observed that Williamson was surely "one of this country's greatest librarians. The real history of library education begins with him," and with his death an era in the history of librarianship came to an end.

This book is an attempt to recreate that time and to examine Williamson's role and contributions to this era in the history of librarianship and library education.

NOTES

1. Charles C. Williamson, "The Place of Research in Library Service," *Library Quarterly* 1 (January 1931), 2.
2. Frank Bradway Rogers, *Librarianship in a World of Machines*, p. 1.

1
EARLY LIFE, EDUCATION, AND WORK (1877-1897)

WILLIAMSON'S BACKGROUND

IN ORDER TO UNDERSTAND Charles Williamson, it is necessary to have an idea of the land, environment, and people that were influential in forming and developing the child, the boy, and the young man.

> The early culture of the Middle West is found to derive its genesis from the road, the tavern, the church, and the school, the court, and the press and to express its products through these same institutions. But a study of these monuments convinces one of nothing so impressively as the significance of the men who were responsible for them. In no period of American history, in no region, in no social group, has the worth of the individual man so strongly asserted itself.[1]

In 1877 Charles Williamson was born at Salem, Ohio, into an environment and cultural milieu that encouraged hard work, perseverance, endurance, heroism, courage, energy, and resolution. The Middle Westerners were people with definite ideas about life and the worth of the individual; theirs was a tradition born of the pioneer spirit of aggressive individualism. These ideas and ideals strongly affected Charles Williamson.

The land around Salem was first settled by pioneers who traveled along the Old Salt Springs Trail and made camp at New Lisbon. Later, explorers pushed on along the trail to the upland section which was to become Salem. They established camps then settlements, usually at twenty-mile intervals, since this was about the distance covered in a day's journey. As these early settlements spread, new trails grew and the

Old Conestoga extended west, entering Salem from the north. Towns prospered in the Ohio wilderness; the old horseback trails had to be widened for wagons carrying pioneer settlers and traders.

In 1787 Ohio became part of the Northwest Territory. This land was established as a free territory from which slavery was forever excluded. Many members of the Society of Friends (Quakers), seeing an opportunity to escape the social systems of Virginia, Maryland, and the Carolinas, undertook the long and arduous journey to the new territory. These pioneers found that the natural resources and fertile soil of Ohio compensated for leaving their homes and farms.

The story of Salem began in 1801 when "Elisha Schooley came from Virginia, and located where a few years later Salem was to become a thriving village. . . . Jacob Painter, who had seven children, also came from Virginia to make his cumulative effort to the new settlement."[2] In 1803 sturdy members of the Society of Friends, coming west from Pennsylvania, New Jersey, Maryland, and Virginia, settled in this area. In 1804 John Straughan, Abram Warrington, and Jacob Cook also settled there, and in 1806 Zadok Street, Sr., who had, in the winter of 1805-1806, come out with his family from Salem, New Jersey, purchased a portion of land and located upon it. Salem village was "laid out in 1806, the first plat of lots being recorded on May 6 of that year. . . . The village received its name from Salem, New Jersey, from which town the Street family had come."[3]

Life in Salem in the early years was primitive; the residents were frugal from necessity. Clothing, furniture, and tools were made at home. Social life centered on "log-rollings," when neighbors gathered to help each other set the logs in place for building their cabins. These were festive gatherings with a hearty supper as reward.

> The hospitality of the people was proverbial. No one ever appealed in vain for food, in any emergency, whether he were a neighbor or a stranger, and nothing would give greater offense than to offer to pay for the same. The latch-strings always hung on the outside, and the stranger or wayfarer always received a generous and hearty welcome. In their friendships they were firm, constant and true.[4]

Early Life, Education, and Work

Into this environment moved a slow but steady stream of pioneers. As the village of Salem grew, mechanics and artisans settled there, as well as millwrights, bricklayers, blacksmiths, cabinetmakers, carpenters, hatters, tailors, and shoemakers. In 1833 the stage route was established from Wellsville on the Ohio River to Fairport on Lake Erie; in 1835 another stage route was established from Wellsville to Cleveland. Both routes passed through Salem. In 1852 the railroad arrived, bringing an increase in business and the advantages of faster, more direct transportation. The Salem Post Office was established on April 6, 1807; John Street, Salem's only merchant, was the first Postmaster.

Through the years Salem continued to grow. In 1806 the population of the town was about 100, and by 1842 the population totaled 1,000. However, the largest period of growth took place between 1887 and 1906 when the town grew from a population of 4,500 to 10,000. It was during this time that Charles Williamson was a boy and a young man, living and working in Salem, Ohio.

The earliest education offered in Salem was the teaching of the three R's to the youngsters of this wilderness settlement. Private homes and the Friends Meeting House served as makeshift classrooms.

Salem's first school opened in 1804. In 1810 the citizens built a schoolhouse of hewn logs. A new brick schoolhouse built in 1828 was financed by the Friends under the direction of the Monthly Meeting. In 1853 the dominance of the Society of Friends over Salem's educational activities came to an end. The citizens voted a tax levy to establish a public school, called the Chestnut Street School. This move instituted the union school system, unifying classes in one building and grading pupils according to age.

The following statement reveals the educational philosophy of the mid-nineteenth-century Salem school system:

> The High school of Salem was organized immediately after the adoption of the graded system in 1853. Previous to its organization, select schools of a higher grade had been very extensively patronized by the town and surrounding country. In these the higher branches of mathematics seem to have occupied a prominent place, and continued to do so after the

change. As a rule, the classics and studies relating to languages have found less favor among the Friends, who were the early settlers and the fashioners to a great extent of public sentiment in Salem, than mathematics and the natural sciences. The High school from its earliest days maintained a higher order of excellence, both in discipline, and acquirements, its pupils were taught to think, to compare, to judge for themselves; to regard the education of the schoolroom as a means rather than an end.[5]

From 1850 to 1900 the Salem public schools slowly assumed the shape and pattern which would continue into the twentieth century.

In 1853 "the pupils spent one year each in grades one through eight. However, they remained in ninth grade for three years, making eleven years preparation for high school. Salem students who elected to continue their studies in high school averaged seventeen years of age, and this maturity contributed to a high degree of educational attainment on the high school level."[6] These standards explain the fact that Charles Williamson graduated from high school at twenty years of age, and how, with only his high school diploma, he worked as a teacher in the district school of Mahoning County, Ohio.

As Salem grew, new school buildings were needed. The Chestnut Street School served the system from 1853 to about 1870; the first Fourth Street School was built in 1860; the Columbia Street School was erected in 1880. Williamson was principal and taught at the Columbia Street School.

Quakers were the first religious group to settle in Salem; their ideas and views set the pattern for the community. Even with the division of the Friends into the "Orthodox" and the "Hicksite" groups in 1828, their influence remained strong.

> Among the early settlers were the Friends, or "Quakers" as persons of the persuasion were then sometimes and are yet frequently called, predominated. They were then—and they retain the characteristics still—a God-fearing, peace-loving and altogether most estimable people, of whom almost the worst that could be said—and which was in later days considered bad enough—was that they were averse to going to war, to fight in a good cause, although the sacrifices to

Early Life, Education, and Work

which they gladly devoted themselves in their efforts to free their fellowmen from abject bondage proved that their hearts were in the right place.[7]

In this environment of tolerance and acceptance of the beliefs of others, Charles Williamson lived and practiced his own belief. His family was Quaker in origin, but early in his life Williamson became a loyal attender with his family at the Sunday services of the Bunker Hill Methodist Church, located about three miles from their home. According to his brother, Alfred Williamson, Charles "was quite active for some years, later after he was away at college—he became a doubter." In part, the various religions represented in Salem indicated the variety of foreign cultures which were established and prospered in that city.

Ohio's first permanent settlers were central Europeans who settled the towns of Zoar and Gnadenhutten. Their coming doubtlessly influenced others from those sections of Europe to migrate to the Ohio wilderness. The people who settled in Salem selected the town presumably because it was "not a rowdy town of the then raw West. Salem was a good town, and the good Friends were friends as well, and welcomed all good people as equals, no matter what their origin. Here a stranger could belong and help found a community."[8]

Blacks were the first to follow the original Anglo-Saxons, Celtic, and Pennsylvania German settlers to Salem. The underground railroad and abolitionist movement brought many to Salem; although some used the town as a place of passage en route to freedom, many stayed and settled there. "Their diligence and progress during times when vestiges of intolerance and ignorance remained, does them even greater credit."[9]

Others among the early settlers were Germans, Italians, Transylvanian Saxons, Slovenes, Greeks, Romanians, Czechoslovakians, and Poles. "These Salem people are representative of those from other lands who have brought color and new traditions to the community. Their industry and civic pride have also contributed materially to the growth of Salem, and in making their town one of which to be proud, they have added new facets to brighten it."[10]

Williamson's Ancestry

The information on Charles Williamson's ancestry was provided by his niece, Margaret (Williamson) Gerlach. She prepared a family tree that although incomplete does provide a picture of the genealogy of the Williamson and Mather families (see pages 8-9).

It is not possible to identify with certainty where the families came from originally, but family members were living in Maryland, Delaware, New Jersey, and Pennsylvania before the American Revolution. Margaret Gerlach comments that "rumor has it they came from Wales, 1st to Maryland, then to Penna., on land granted by Wm. Penn. However there is no verification of this." In a letter to the author on December 6, 1967, she observes, "I guess all this boils down to the fact that Chas. Williamson came of pioneer, early settler stock."

Among the early Ohio settlers was Gilbert Williamson, who was born in 1787 and died in 1865. He had originally settled in New Jersey but moved in 1818 to Elk Township, Columbiana County, Ohio, with his wife Elizabeth Rouncevel. They had four children: Lewis, Lambert, Mahlon, and Lavina.

Lewis Williamson was born on June 7, 1811, and died on June 23, 1873; he lived all his life in Salem, Ohio. His first wife, whose maiden name was McConnell, died about 1840; the two children who were born of this marriage died before 1860. Lewis had nine children by his second wife, Jane Adams: Loando (born in 1843), Nora (1849), Clarence (1853), Zorenda (1856), Lizzie (1858), Effie (1859), Florence (1861), Elaner (1862), and Herbert (1863). Jane Adams was born on March 10, 1823, and died on October 18, 1877. She was the daughter of James Adams and Eliza McDonald of Utica, Pennsylvania.

Clarence Williamson was born in Salem on June 10, 1853, and died there on November 5, 1945. He was a sawmill

Early Life, Education, and Work

operator, following the same trade as his father. Later in life Clarence took up the trade of carpentry in addition to working his farm; he spent six years working without pay to learn the carpentry trade. Clarence married Lizzie Keturah Mather on March 9, 1876. Lizzie Mather was born on October 22, 1855, and died on June 10, 1910. She was the daughter of Benjamin Mather and Lavina Cook.

WILLIAMSON'S BIRTH AND EARLY LIFE IN OHIO

Charles Clarence Williamson was born on January 26, 1877, the eldest of Clarence and Lizzie Williamson's three children. At that time the family lived on a farm in Goshen Township, Mahoning County, Ohio. Williamson spoke of his humble beginnings: "I was born and raised on a small farm in northeastern Ohio and attended a one-room country school. My parents themselves had only that kind of country school education and were poor, even by the rural Ohio standards of the 1890s."[11] Even though they lived in rather modest circumstances, the Williamsons were a happy and closely knit family.

Clarence Williamson purchased a fifteen-acre farm on Goshen Road. Charles Williamson lived in the small farmhouse with his parents, his brother Alfred, and his sister Mary. Alfred was two years younger and Mary five years younger than Charles. These children spent their early life on the farm, experiencing the problems, joys, sorrows, and activities of the young. In correspondence with the author, Alfred Williamson recalled those early childhood days,

> playing "follow the leader" and one time when Charlie led him to a log laying across the creek which ran through their farm and started to walk across with Alfred following and being solicitous of his little brother's welfare turned around and cautioned him to be careful not to fall—and with that he [Charlie] slipped and fell into the water, much to Alfred's amusement.
>
> Walking on stilts was a favorite pastime among the "kids" of their day. So Charlie made a pair of stilts for himself and

ANCESTORS OF

Clarence Williamson
B June 10, 1853
M March 9, 1876
D November 5, 1945
R Salem, Ohio

Lewis Williamson
B June 7, 1811
M
D June 23, 1873
R Salem, Ohio

Gilbert Williamson
B 1787
M
D 1865
R
- B
- M
- D
- R

Elizabeth Rouncevel
- B
- D
- B
- M
- D
- R

James Adams
B August 15, 1795
M
D August 2, 1880
R Utica, Pennsylvania

James Adams
B October 30, 1770
M
D August 8, 1851
R Mifflin County, Pennsylvania, moved to Utica, Pa.

James Adams
B October 30, 1734
D September 18, 1825
R Mifflin County, Pa. (Soldier of the Revolution)

Isabelle Weldon
B September 22, 1736

(spouse)
- B
- D

Eliza McDonald
B June 29, 1799
D January 31, 1884
- B
- M
- D
- R
- B
- D

Jane Adams
B March 10, 1823
D October 18, 1877

CHARLES C. WILLIAMSON

B January 26, 1877
D January 11, 1965

Thomas Mather
B July 2, 1809
M November 30, 1831
D June 16, 1890
R

John Mather*
B September 30, 1783
M October 16, 1814
D March 10, 1855

Catherine Smith

Benjamin Mather
B September 22, 1832
M June 8, 1854
D March 23, 1892
R Salem, Ohio

Elizabeth Wright
B August 28, 1811
D October 30, 1849

Joseph Wright**
B December 21, 1777
M April 26, 1799
D August 30, 1867

B March 20, 1782
D October 12, 1863

Rebecca Bunting
B 1781   D 1853

Lizzie Mather
B October 22, 1855
D June 10, 1910

Joel Cook
B
M
D
R

Lavina Cook
B December 4, 1834
D November 17, 1872

B
D
M
R

B
D

B
D
M
R

B
D

KEY TO GENEALOGY

B-Birth M-Marriage D-Death R-Resided
*This record goes back two more generations.
**This record goes back five more generations.

Genealogical table by Margaret Gerlach

also a pair for Alfred. Again Charlie told him to follow him across the creek, on stilts this time. All went well until one of Charlie's stilts slid off a stone in the bottom of the creek and again he fell into the water.

This incident is typical of the small episodes which fill a child's life; Charles behaved very much like all small boys. Childish pranks furnished some diversion in an otherwise stern and hard world. Alfred also recalls that "Charlie was quite a 'tease' and teased him a great deal—but was not allowed to tease their little sister Mary."

The community in which Charles grew up consisted mainly of farmers who were quiet, hardworking, peace-loving Quakers. Charles worked on many of their farms and by all accounts was a good worker. During this time he went to work for the Richards family at Nutwood Farm.

The Williamson children were taught to persevere in whatever they did. Charles did the farm chores because he had to, but never really liked to care for animals. Alfred and Charles both helped with these duties, while Mary assisted with the household work.

The life of the Williamson family was that of any family living in a rural community dependent on farming for part of its livelihood and for food to supplement its income. Their economic circumstances could be described as poor, although they "were highly respected." The children were responsible for certain tasks and performed them because it was a necessity if all the daily routines were to be completed.

Farm life in rural Ohio at the end of the nineteenth century was arduous. The work was no matter of choice for the Williamson family; it was essential. Farm life, with all its problems, difficulties, hardships, and sacrifices, was the environment in which Charles grew up; it would have an effect in molding his character and personal traits. The Williamsons taught their children to "be honest, truthful, kind but firm for what was right and to be industrious." Charles always appreciated the virtues of hard work, thrift, and self-reliance.

Throughout his life, Charles Williamson was reserved and quiet. Alfred observes: "He seemed deeply in thought

Early Life, Education, and Work

most of the time. He was never given to sports or athletics. He could be considerate of the feelings of others but he could be stern."

Clarence Williamson taught his sons to use carpenter's tools, and while still a boy Charlie made several small articles of furniture in his spare time. In June, 1898 Charlie came to help out when the Richards' family barn was struck by lightning and burned to the ground along with two other two-story buildings. Making use of his father's training, he worked high in the rafters and assisted the carpenter whom Mr. Richards had hired to rebuild the barn.

In the Williamsons' modest but neat home, Lizzie Williamson also helped supplement the family income. She made liquid yeast which she sold to the neighbors for two cents a pint. As was customary in those days, she taught her daughter Mary sewing and other homemaking tasks. Lizzie Williamson was a dressmaker and made many of her children's clothes even after they attended the district school.

According to Grace Richards, "Charles, Alfred, and Mary were bright children and eager to learn." In later years Mary became a deaconess of the Methodist church and taught printing at a boy's school in Quincy, Illinois. Alfred owned a fruit farm, and his choice apples and peaches won prizes at many fairs.

The libraries of the time did not offer children much in the way of books or other matters of interest. Not until Charles was in high school was a public library established in Salem. Reading was limited to textbooks and some books at home, mostly children's magazines. The Williamson household was a poor one, and the amount that could be spent for books and magazines was limited.

Williamson commented on the reading materials of his youth.

> We had some books in the home, but these were all for adults, none for children or young people, either at home or in the school. (*Youth's Companion* and *St. Nicholas* magazines certainly did something to compensate for lack of suitable books.) The school textbooks were pretty dull, though many of the selections of McGuffey's series of readers I found

interesting and even exciting. Many of them I still recall vividly.[12]

The Williamson boys continued with carpentry work, which for Charles developed into a lifelong hobby. Alfred Williamson recalls Charles' versatile and practical talent.

> Charlie was also an inventor of sorts. In those days there was no central heating, no gas or electric cook stove. There was a woodburning cook stove in the kitchen of their home and a woodburning heat stove in the living room. The rest of the house was cold.
> In order to save their mother (who was not strong) having to get up in a cold house to make breakfast it was agreed that the boys get up and build the fire (they were around 12 and 14 yrs old). However, mother still had to get up in a cold house—walk across the living room and kitchen to the stair door to call the boys, who slept upstairs—their bed being directly over the parents bed. So Charlie got a "bright idea!" He fastened a bell of some sort to the head of his and Alfred's bed with a string attached to it which he put through a hole in the floor to the parents bed below so that mother needed only to pull the string to ring the bell to waken the boys, who then got up, and started the fires.

Although carpentry work interested him, it was not so great a love as gardening. Until the end of his life, gardening was his favorite pastime. He loved to grow plants indoors and out; "artificial flowers disgusted him." Both Charles and Alfred "each year, helped to make a 'hot bed' where they raised early plants and vegetables and some flowers. Tomato, cabbage, pepper and sweet potatoes were raised, each year—some to sell and others to transplant in their own garden, for they raised most of their living."

The three Williamson children went to the district school in Goshen Township, Mahoning County, Ohio. This was a one-room country school for the first seven grades. Charles walked the mile to and from school each day. There he learned, in addition to the three R's, a little geography and history and how to get along with people. When he finished seventh grade he decided to go to the Salem School

Early Life, Education, and Work

three miles away, walking both ways for his eighth grade work and high school.

In commenting on his early education, Williamson stated that

> through some influence which I cannot now trace—it may have been one of the teachers in the country school—I decided one October day when I was nearly seventeen that it would not be worth while to go back to the country school that winter only to cover the same ground I had already covered at least twice before; that instead I would try to gain admission to the graded schools in the nearest town, about three and one-half miles from my home, by unimproved country roads.
>
> An interview with the pompous Irish superintendent of schools led to admission to an eighth-grade class. Though I missed several weeks of the fall term I never missed a day after getting started and had the satisfaction of graduating at the head of the class. Walking those three and one-half miles to school every day in all kinds of weather, winter, and summer, would be fatal to most seventeen-year-olds today, I fear, but I survived it and even enjoyed it except when the snow or mud was knee deep. At all events, I knew well before finishing the eighth grade that I had to go on to high school, located in the same antiquated building, and that I did for four years, graduating as valedictorian.[13]

To pay the tuition to attend this school, he earned part by selling vegetables and part by doing various tasks at school. He stated that "in my spare time I ran a market garden to meet my expenses."

About the age of twelve, Charles lived at Nutwood Farm, owned by Daniel I. and Emma F. Richards. Grace Richards commented on this part of his life.

> This was a larger farm almost a mile from their home. He was to help with all the farm tasks, staying at night, but returning to his father's home on Sundays. He was treated as a member of the Richards family, as their children—Herbert, Lola, Grace, Lewis, Samuel and Tom—in due time, arrived.
>
> Daniel I. Richards was Justice of the Peace for many years and often Charlie was present at the lawsuits held in the living room, at Nutwood Farm, where many lawyers from Salem

and even from Youngstown, would come. Charlie helped with all kinds of farm tasks and chores—gathering the sap to make maple sugar, in season, as well as helping care for a vegetable garden, raising both Irish and sweet potatoes for sale; caring for milk cows and calves, working in hay fields, bunching the clover in hand stacks to cure, hoeing corn, etc., etc. In all these tasks he worked cheerfully and willingly.

In the summertime, after a busy day's work, Charles enjoyed the swimming hole down in the pasture at a branch of the Little Beaver Creek. In later years he was present occasionally when the minister at Bunker Hill Methodist Church baptized parishoners at the swimming hole as they sang, "Let Us Gather at the River."

Daniel Richards, on whose farm Charles worked, was a Quaker, a Hicksite Friend, and it was he who taught Charles many lessons in their faith. Charles became a most honorable, obedient, and conscientious helper and friend. A few years later he obtained a testimonial from Mr. Richards which stated that "the bearer Chas. C. Williamson sustains a good moral character."

In addition to other tasks on the Richards' farm, Charles cut wood to fill the woodbox and kindling for the cookstove. Each year he helped Mrs. Richards care for the flowering plants. Even with all this work, his education was not neglected. Grace Richards observes: "He was always a good student, loved books and reading. Had an insatiable appetite for learning. As a child was read to a lot by his mother."

Joseph Cessna of North Jackson, Ohio, was a classmate of Charles Williamson in the eighth grade and in the first ten weeks of high school. Cessna said that Charles was "serious from start to finish . . . our teacher [said] a short time after [Williamson] entered our room that we would have to do our best to keep him from heading the class." Cessna stated that while in school, Charles had no interest "in anything but excelling in his studies" and was "serious beyond his years."

Charles was well liked by his teachers. There often developed a warm and friendly relationship between teacher and pupil. An early indication of this is seen in a letter written to "my dear Charlie" by Mr. C. S. Barnes. This letter

Early Life, Education, and Work 15

of February 4, 1895, reveals a warm, simple, and honest expression written by a teacher to a former pupil, who was eighteen years of age at the time.

> Let me stop long enough in the midst of my work to thank you very sincerely for your kind remembrance of me in your little poem. If you do so well with such a poor subject, what may you not do with a lofty theme? Good, I may say for a "starter." Shall I entertain hopes for you of a future Holmes? Whether so or not I know you will not disappoint me in achieving the greatest of greatness, and that which is possible to all—that of being pure, and true and strong. . . .
> Remember me most kindly to your friends among the pupils. I miss you all, perhaps more than you miss me. I have no one to take your place.

Williamson's course of study in high school was that usually followed by students of his day who took what was called the Latin Course.

The transcript of a "Certificate of Standings" records his academic work at Salem High School. The certificate is signed by Mr. Myron E. Hard, Superintendent of Schools, who certified "that the foregoing is a correct statement of the work of Chas. Williamson, and that he is of good moral character."

Williamson was an A student in high school. The course of study was strenuous, including the usual courses: English grammar, history, mathematics, science, language, and literature, but in addition included descriptive and physical geography, history of the United States, history of Greece, history of Rome, botany, astronomy, physiology, geology, Latin (including Caesar, Virgil, and Cicero), and German.

Charles graduated as valedictorian, first in his class of six girls and six boys—two of the latter being black, and was listed in the graduation program as Class President. His oration at graduation was entitled "Wanted—A New Man." According to the statement in the Board of Education minutes, "The following named pupils were granted diplomas on graduation from Salem High School—Latin Course, Charles Williamson . . . June 17, 1897."

The development of reading and the interest in books,

which was to figure so prominently in his later career, had humble beginnings. Williamson considered his early introduction to reading rather unusual.

> The high school had no library. Students were not encouraged to read beyond their textbooks and the standard texts in English literature required for admission to college. I judge that our high school teachers had not read much more widely, though they were all college graduates—one a graduate, I think of Trinity College, Cambridge University, England. A real taste for reading was acquired if at all somewhat by accident. And such accidents did happen. I recall one that led to my introduction to Dickens.
>
> The janitor of the old-time school building, the top, or third, floor of which was occupied by the high school (thus literally justifying its name), was a fairly recent graduate of the high school and may have had an unusual home background. In any case he liked to read. I recall clearly now, some sixty years later, the day when I stood watching this Mr. Young alternately pulling down and then releasing the rope that rang the large bell in the tower. How the subject of reading happened to come into our conversation that day I do not know, but he asked me if I had ever read any of Dickens. I had not. He said I should and that he would recommend I begin with *Bleak House*. I did forthwith, was thrilled by it, and went on to read several more Dickens' stories at that time.
>
> Many times in these sixty years it has come home to me that the formation of reading habits is apt to be somewhat adventitious in their inception. I would say that in my school days love of reading did not originate very often in the contact between teachers and pupils, and I doubt that it does even today to any great extent, but perhaps the last person to expect a high school student to have as his reading adviser would be the school janitor.[14]

Charles was fortunate in being able to obtain the books he wanted from the new public library that had been established in Salem, even though he did not use the library as a bona fide subscriber.

> There was no public library in the small town, but during my high school days a group of public spirited citizens, some of

Early Life, Education, and Work

them college graduates and others of some cultural pretensions, got together and organized a subscription library. The high school principal and some of the teachers had a hand in it. The fees were no doubt modest enough but, even so, they were out of reach of a poor high school boy. Fortunately some of the teachers found a way to give me the privileges of the library without payment of fees and that meant a great deal to me and may have had much to do with my later slightly bookish career.[15]

NOTES

1. James M. Miller, *The Genesis of Western Culture: The Upper Ohio Valley, 1800-1825*, p. 163.
2. William B. McCord, *A Souvenir History of ye Old Town of Salem, Ohio*, p. 2.
3. *Ibid.*, pp. 5-6.
4. *Ibid.*, p. 13.
5. *Ibid.*, p. 33.
6. Thomas R. Howett and Mary B. Howett, editors, *The Salem Story, 1806-1956*, p. 76.
7. McCord, *op. cit.*, p. 7.
8. Howett and Howett, *op. cit.*, p. 108.
9. *Ibid.*, p. 107.
10. *Ibid.*, p. 111.
11. Sarah K. Vann, "Statement Prepared for the Use of Miss Sarah K. Vann," by Charles C. Williamson, June 27, 1955, p. 1.
12. *Loc. cit.*
13. *Ibid.*, pp. 1-2.
14. *Ibid.*, p. 2.
15. *Loc. cit.*

2
TEACHER, PRINCIPAL, SECRETARY, AND COLLEGE STUDENT (1897-1904)

Teacher in Ohio

When Williamson became aware that a teacher was needed for the winter term in District 6, he wrote to the Board of Education of Goshen Township, Mahoning County, Ohio: "I beg leave to be considered as an applicant for the position at $35 per month. I enclose testimonials from my Superintendent, and Principal. Should you see fit to choose me, I shall discharge the duties to the best of my ability, and, I hope to your entire satisfaction." This application was made two months before he graduated from high school; he did not plan to go to college at that time but wanted to teach and earn money to pay for his college education. He comments on this phase of his life:

> What with the school work and the two hours or more a day of getting back and forth to school, spare time was spare indeed. But I had summers and weekends and with some help from my father and mother, especially on the marketing end, I did manage to cover expenses and save up a little money toward starting a college course. Even before I finished high school I managed to pass the examinations and get a certificate for teaching in the schools of the county in which I lived.[1]

The two testimonials which were included with the application were from Mr. M. E. Hard, Superintendent of Schools of Salem, Ohio, and Mr. W. H. Maurer, Salem High School Principal. Both documents attest to the academic standing and the high esteem in which these men held the young Williamson. Maurer wrote that Williamson "has easily stood first in his class during the four years with us. One seldom meets with so good, thoughtful, earnest and worthwhile a student in a High School." Maurer continues that he had the "highest regard for his ability and I am confident he will prove eminently successful as a teacher in any school for which he may apply. . . . Confidence cannot be misplaced in Mr. Williamson and I commend him most earnestly to any Board of Education who may want a faithful, earnest and conscientious teacher." Hard was as praiseworthy of Williamson's character and abilities. His testimonial of April 29, 1897, states that Williamson "has been at the head of all his classes." Hard considered the young man to be a "most careful and painstaking student,—few have ever graduated from our Schools who have stood higher in scholarship," and concludes that the young man is "kind both in manner and speech—a requisite so essential to a successful teacher. I can heartily commend him to anyone seeking a good teacher."

In order to qualify for this teaching position, Williamson was required by Ohio State Law to take a series of examinations conducted by a board of three people called the County Examiners, named by the Board of County Commissioners.

Williamson took the examination and on May 8, 1897, was granted Mahoning County Teacher's Certificate No. 277 to teach grade 4, class 4, for one year. On March 12, 1898, he was granted Certificate No. 115 to teach grade 3, class 4. The examinations were in the fields, or branches, required by law to be taught in the common schools of Ohio. He was examined in orthography, reading, penmanship, arithmetic, English grammar, theory and practice, U.S. history, physiology, civil government, and the harmful effects of narcotics.

In the fall term of that year, Williamson returned as a teacher to the one-room school, working there for the 1897-1898 academic year. Williamson recalled that "the pitifully small teacher's wages added a little to my savings."

The Richards children were taught in their home by an aunt who was a teacher. Grace Richards states, "We then started to the public school, as our friend, Charlie, was our teacher." Perhaps as a gesture of warmth, Williamson gave a photograph of himself to each of his pupils.

Again in the summer of 1898 he worked for Daniel Richards. It was during this time that he helped rebuild the barn which had been struck by lightning. He returned to his usual method of earning some money by raising "vegetables to sell."

In June 1897 he was offered a full scholarship at Ohio Wesleyan University, but he did not accept the offer at that time, probably because he found it difficult to save enough money to cover the expenses of living away from home. One year later, however, he accepted the scholarship, left his teaching job, and went to Delaware, Ohio, one hundred miles away, to begin his college career. In the fall term of 1898 he was registered in the Classical College Preparatory Course at Ohio Wesleyan University.

College Student at Ohio Wesleyan University

When Williamson decided to attend college, leaving Salem for Delaware and the campus of Ohio Wesleyan, Mrs. Richards purchased a silver napkin ring for the five Richards' children to give Charles as a gift. He wrote to tell the family that "he felt very proud of it, as he was the only one at his table who used a napkin ring."

Williamson's first year at college was not very successful; he did not particularly like Ohio Wesleyan.

> By waiting on table and tending furnace I managed to finish the freshman year. On the whole it was an unprofitable year. The instruction was mediocre and the courses uninteresting—Latin, Greek, English, and Mathematics, plus military drill which I disliked especially. To gain full freshman standing it was necessary to take an extra course in Latin, three Latin courses in all . . . At the end of the year my funds were exhausted and I knew I would never go back to that college.[2]

In those days, Ohio Wesleyan offered three courses of study: Classical, Scientific, and Literary. Each course led to the corresponding course in the College of Liberal Arts. The Classical Course Williamson was to embark on was a program that

Teacher, Principal, Secretary, College Student

> embraces three year's work, the minimum of which is the same as the requirements for admission to the Freshman Class. . . . The studies are arranged with a view to give the students a thorough and symmetrical mental development, and to fit them for admission to the Classical Course of any college.[3]

This was a period of uncertainty for him, one aggravated by financial problems as well as his growing dislike for the school.

A letter from M. E. Hard of Septemper 24, 1898, declared: "I am glad you are at last at Delaware. I trust you . . . will reflect credit upon your old teacher. . . . Let me hear from you soon as to your success."

Williamson did find the college library:

> The one bright spot that year was the college library. Though I suppose the book collection was only what could have been expected in a small denominational college, it far excelled anything I had ever dreamed of and was housed in what seemed to me a splendid new building. Since I did not care for my courses, I did only enough work on them to get by and then spent the rest of my time in the library reading widely and purposelessly in hitherto unknown subjects and authors.[4]

By June 1898 he had made his decision not to return to Ohio Wesleyan in the fall:

> At this point I believe I made a wise decision. Instead of trying to find a job and earn money for another year of college somewhere, I decided to study stenography and typing at a local business college. By working on a farm I could earn enough to pay the tuition. At the end of a short summer course I was very far from being a skilled stenographer, but the little skill I had, together with my good record in the high school, brought me the position of assistant to the superintendent of schools. This involved many kinds of clerical work and substitute teaching in every grade from one to eight. It was a strenuous year. For the following year I was made principal of a graded school, teaching the eighth grade, taking the place on her retirement of a much loved teacher who had been in the school system for many years.[5]

Return to Teaching

While still a student at Ohio Wesleyan, Williamson investigated the possibility of working in the Salem Public Schools. He had letters of recommendation from Superintendent Hard and Mr. W. H. Kirtlan, Secretary of the Board of Education, Goshen Township, Mahoning County, Ohio, praising him as "one of the best students I have ever known" and saying that "he possessed exceptional ability to manage and control a school." Both men felt Williamson was a "true gentleman in every sense of the word."

Williamson evidently had indicated to Ohio Wesleyan University that he did not plan to return and left the University by choice. He was able to obtain a letter of recommendation from Dr. W. F. Whitlock, Dean and Professor of Latin at Ohio Wesleyan, stating that his academic ability was of a high grade and that he was "equal to the demands of a responsible position."

On June 16, 1899, Williamson was hired by the Salem Schools for the position of substitute teacher. From September 1899 to June 1900 he was involved in what he considered a "strenuous year." His work involved a number of clerical duties, as well as helping the Superintendent and doing some substitute teaching if and when needed. Williamson was secretary to the superintendent of the Salem Public Schools during this time. The duties of such a position included just about "everything, on occasion, from the starting of the engine, in an emergency, to visiting the schools and criticising the methods of teaching."

He was working in a different school district than the one he had worked in from 1897 to 1898. The Salem Schools were in Perry Township in Columbiana County, while his former teaching position was in the school district in Goshen Township in Mahoning County, Ohio. There was no official connection between these two school districts at the time.

Appointment as Principal

The "Minutes, 1900," of the Board of Education of Salem state: "Charles Williamson was employed as principal and eighth grade teacher at Columbia Street School, Salary $630.00 . . . September, 1900."

Although he was now employed he still thought of returning to college and was encouraged to do so by friends and acquaintances. Grace Richards stated, "Our father advised Charlie to continue his education by attending college, though his own parents did not insist he should."

Mr. Hard also encouraged Charles and wrote on April 22, 1900, offering him a teaching position but hoped he really did not want it because "I hope to hear that you are going to college next year."

Possibly as a result of these pleas, Williamson did not accept this new teaching job and finally decided to return to college. An undated letter from Superintendent Hard's successor, Mr. W. P. Burris, then at Harvard University, states, "I was greatly delighted to hear of the prospect before you and am sure you can now go on with your college courses without interruption."

At this time Charles was involved in intellectual, spiritual, and philosophical probing. He was a reflective young man, prone to introspection, analysis, and inquiry. He considered ideas and thoughts challenging and supportive of his own personal ideas and convictions. This is revealed in a letter from Burris: "I hope Dewey has captured you before breakfast and that you may have some wholesome spiritual food." Referring to these philosophical and theological problems, Burris continued:

> I cannot spring these in a letter, for it took 6000 words to tell what is meant by one of them the other day, but we will hope to talk it over some day. I wish you could be here. At any rate you must think your way through certain problems that I know to be pressing upon you. Royce's *The World and the Individual* would help on both the religious and metaphysical problems that you are sure to keep meeting and a book that I can commend to you.

While a schoolteacher, Williamson went to the Chautauqua (New York) Summer School and took two courses with Dr. John Dewey, probably in the summer of 1899 or 1900. Williamson's recollection was not clear, and he had no documentary evidence; however, he did recall taking a course in psychology and another on some pedagogical subject.

SECRETARY AND COLLEGE STUDENT AT WESTERN
RESERVE UNIVERSITY

Although his first attempt at a college education had not been successful, he decided to complete his work by obtaining a degree from another institution. Williamson received a letter from President Charles F. Thwing of Western Reserve University in response to his inquiry of April 23 [1901], which states: "By all means let me see you in Cleveland as soon as is to your convenience. Please let me know a day or two in advance of your coming that we may be able to meet in the easiest possible way. I know we can offer you some work at least." This resulted in Williamson's starting work on June 1, 1901, at Western Reserve University. He was to work in the president's office as stenographer and secretary and describes this new development.

> Toward the end of my first year as principal of the Columbia Street School I was offered the position of Secretary to President Charles F. Thwing, of Western Reserve University, Cleveland, with the understanding that I could fit my secretarial work into a full-time program of study in Adelbert College, the undergraduate college for men, the oldest and the key unit in the University. Of course, I accepted, and reported for work.[6]

Adelbert College of Western Reserve University was founded in 1828 and had a tradition of a faculty of scholars. In 1904 the total enrollment was about 250 male students, with a freshman class of under 100.

Charles F. Thwing was born in New Sharon, Maine, in 1852 and died in Cleveland, Ohio, in 1937. He went to Phillips Academy and obtained his A.B. from Harvard in 1876. He also studied at the Andover Theological Seminary in the fields of history and philosophy. He graduated in 1879 and was ordained a Congregationalist minister. In 1890 he accepted the presidency of Western Reserve University and at that time was the youngest university president in the United States. He continued as President until his retirement in 1920, becoming President Emeritus. He wrote extensively in the fields of education, religion, and administration. Thwing brought about rapid expansion of the university, which grew from a student body of 246 to well over 2,000, while the faculty increased from 37 to 415. He was progressive in his educational thought, yet conservative in his administration and management of the institution. Thwing was well liked by the students and his peers. He was a "large man of great energy, cheerful, and friendly . . . Among the cardinal qualities of a college president he held patience to be a necessary component likely to be overlooked. By nature sympathetic toward the desires of others, he was inclined to encourage hopes beyond the range of eventual attainment."[7] His influence on the young Williamson was evident in the fact that their friendship continued until Thwing's death.

The somewhat vague arrangement of his duties and responsibilities as secretary to President Thwing soon led to confusion and conflict. Although he was hired mainly as a stenographer, his job gradually came to include other responsibilities. Harry W. Haring had been Thwing's secretary and had been promoted to the position of secretary-treasurer; Williamson was his replacement. Haring attempted to clarify Williamson's duties and wrote on September 3, 1901:

> I have been wondering about another item in our arrangement. What we desire, second only to having a good stenographer, is to have some one on whom we may depend present in the office during the afternoon. Either President Thwing or I, usually both of us, are at the College during the morning hours, but it often happens that we are both out all the afternoon. . . . I have been wondering, therefore, whether you could arrange to spend your afternoons at the office.

In a letter of January 6, 1905, to Professor Richard T. Ely of the University of Wisconsin, Williamson described his work as secretary to President Thwing.

> My function here is to a large extent that of keeping many things in order. I keep the alumni catalogues of all departments up-to-date and attend to the mailing of all publications. The annual report of the President and Faculties I edit and publish during the summer without assistance. For the last eight or nine months I have served as Secretary of the College of Dentistry and have edited the catalogue of the current year. For almost two years Dr. Thwing has not read or signed the letters dictated by him. Even now, when I do not take the dictation, I sign practically all of his letters. I have also taken care of a considerable part of the correspondence on ordinary matters, both of the Secretary's and President's Office, without their attention to any part of it. Mail addressed to the University or to the Secretary, Registrar, etc., usually comes to my desk for reply. I mention these things, you will understand, merely to show that I am accustomed to assume responsibilities of various sorts.

His financial problems caused him to ask Thwing for better financial arrangements, and in a letter of July 20, 1902, he apologizes for bringing up such a small matter, confessing that he tries in everything to "put money considerations last,—one has to if he hopes to achieve success in any kind of work for human betterment. Yet . . . such considerations do have a legitimate place, even in the humblest kind of educational work." He was requesting a remission of the tuition fee of $27.50 for the first half of the coming year, and goes to great lengths to establish his request. He discusses his own financial position stating that with the $30 a month he received as secretary and $230 which he had left at the end of the summer from savings of two years previous, "I got through the year, a little behind, though, it is true. I was careful, I thought; but my typewriter payments, insurance premiums, and the little help that I was prompted to give to one of the poorer college boys, together with my personal expenses and the college fees, took my last cent, and a little more." The letter continues in this apologetic tone and seems to go beyond the needed request for tuition remission, reflecting that probably there were other problems.

> Moreover, I have tried to be a good secretary first, a fair student second, and a college man last of all. I cannot say that

I have more than partially succeeded, unless it be in the last named: but I have tried and tried hard. I ought to have done better in every way. The fact that I have not done better makes me feel I am not in the right place, or that nature ran short of material or forgot some important element in my makeup. I am convinced that this must be so, for I have been reminded again and again that others have done the work that I do, and yet were students, carrying a full college course and being real college men.

Williamson was becoming dissatisfied with his job and work as a student. He carried a heavy schedule; the combination of full-time college work in addition to his duties as secretary to the President was too much for the young man, and this letter expresses his frustration. There is no evidence of an answer from President Thwing, although it can be assumed that the matter was settled to Williamson's liking, since he continued for several years as a full-time student and secretary.

The relationship between Thwing and Williamson was a good one which continued after the latter left Western Reserve. Thwing never forgot his secretary and wrote letters from 1902 until his death in 1937. The correspondence concerned business matters, yet over the years it was filled with personal references, sharing of events, and problems. Thwing was concerned about Williamson's career, and his letters offer advice, admonitions, congratulations, guidance, and warnings. The letters showed a growing feeling of mutual admiration, confidence, and concern. It is evident from these letters that the young man whom Thwing had taken under his personal charge became more than a secretary; their correspondence is a testimony to friendship.

One letter pointed out the warm relationship which existed between the two men. In this letter of August 31, 1907, written shortly after Williamson's marriage to Bertha Torrey, Thwing rejoiced at their new life together.

Dear Mr. & Mrs. Williamson:

It seems odd when addressing you as I do but I believe it is pleasanter than odd, and odd enough it is. For the relation of each of you to me and my relation to each of you has been intimate and prolonged. . . .

I believe I never had quite the time for personally saying to you how happy I am at your marriage. I have a right to say that—haven't I? For are you not each, in a sense, my son and daughter.

Mrs. Thwing joins me in heartiest salutations; and believe me,

> my dear friends,
>
> As ever, and ever, yours,
> Charles F. Thwing

Williamson expressed his appreciation of Thwing's concern in a letter of October 23, 1929: "One of the nicest things about these little honors is that you always take note of them and write me generously about them." This remark referred to Thwing's congratulatory letter on Williamson's being awarded the Legion of Honor by the French government. Thwing did much to develop the young man. He and Professor Richard T. Ely of the University of Wisconsin were most influential in molding Williamson's character.

Williamson's work for Thwing did not end with graduation, for the President, most reluctant to let him go, encouraged him to continue graduate work at Western Reserve. Williamson remained at the college and continued to work as the President's secretary until February 1905.

Thwing was interested in having Williamson pursue a career which would be suited to the young man's abilities and talents, since his own "thirst for knowledge . . . made him distinctly a scholar and a supporter of scholarly attainments throughout his life."[8] He became concerned when Williamson was at the University of Wisconsin working with Professor Richard T. Ely. Thwing writes to Williamson on February 27, 1905: "Saturday night Dr. Arbuthnot and I had a conference about you. He told me that your work so far has largely been that of Librarian. I am most deeply interested in all that interests you. You must not be a Librarian or a Secretary. You are to be a scholar and a teacher." At this time Thwing did not think too highly of librarianship for his protégé, advocating a career as an economics scholar.

From 1901 to 1904 Williamson combined his work as secretary to the President with a full-time schedule of courses working toward his baccalaureate degree. He majored in economics at Adelbert College of Western Reserve University, obtained his A.B. degree, magna cum laude, in June 1904, and was elected to Phi Beta Kappa. Williamson was always a good student and maintained an excellent academic record while an undergraduate. He reflected on his decision to enter the field of economics, "Sometime during my second year at Cleveland I had decided after much advice-seeking to prepare myself to teach economics in college."[9] His decision may have been partly influenced by President Thwing's attitude.

His genuine interest in the field of economics was evident during this time of his life. His advice seeking reflects his usual thoroughness. While still at Adelbert, he sent what he called "A Circular Letter of Inquiry" to eminent United States economists asking questions about the choice of economics as a career. The questionnaire, sent on July 24, 1903, concerned the demand for teachers of economics and the advantages and disadvantages of the work. There were many replies; some were brief and to the point, while others stated that it was hard to answer such involved questions without some knowledge of their author's background. Not content with this, Williamson also prepared a twenty-five page document entitled "The Results of a Circular Letter of Inquiry" in which he tabulated and organized the results of this questionnaire. The project gives evidence of the traits of thoroughness and detail which were to last throughout his life. The consensus of the questionnaire was that economics was a just-emerging field which a young man certainly should enter. This was satisfactory to him and possibly helped him reach the decision to embark on a career in that field.

In order to obtain some idea about Williamson's character and personality as a college student, the author sent letters to a few of the alumni of the Class of 1904 of Adelbert College. Their replies provide interesting if brief recollections about Williamson in those days.

Noyes Prentice of Cleveland Heights stated, "I knew . . . Williamson but not well." He was a "very good" student, and got along "very well" with teachers and fellow students. Prentice describes him as a "very nice fellow but rather reserved."

Jonathan F. Oberlin, also a member of the Class of 1904, maintained:

> Dr. Williamson, as indicated by the year of his birth (1877), was older than most if not all of his classmates. He furthermore served, throughout his college courses, as private secretary to Dr. Charles F. Thwing, President of the College and University. By reason of the foregoing, he did not participate in normal student activities, athletic or otherwise, although he was a member of a college fraternity, Phi Gamma Delta.

W. H. Heinmiller, a classmate, remembered him as "a congenial person. He was several years older than the majority of his classmates. He impressed me as a serious student."

Another classmate, Carl Vitz, became a librarian and served as Director of the Toledo (Ohio) and Cincinnati (Ohio) Public Libraries, and President of the American Library Association from 1944 to 1945. Vitz knew Williamson from 1904 until his death in 1965. His recollection during the time at Adelbert was slight but he stated: "I am sure that he was quietly congenial. He was thoughtful and considerate. Did not take part in athletics or student organizations." Vitz felt his personal habits were "of the best" and he "probably had to earn to make college possible. I judge this because he was older than most of his classmates and because he worked as the President's personal secretary." According to Vitz, there was no doubt of his dedication.

Williamson did not have the usual undergraduate education. He was older than the rest of his classmates and had to assume unusual responsibilities and authority. When he came to Western Reserve, he already had gained experience as a teacher and principal; therefore, he brought a maturity to his work as the President's secretary, to his classwork, and to his relationships with his fellow students.

His major interest in ecomomics began during this time at Western Reserve University and continued for several years to come.

NOTES

1. Sarah K. Vann, "Statement Prepared for the Use of Miss Sarah K. Vann," by Charles C. Williamson, June 27, 1955, pp. 2-3.
2. *Ibid.*, p. 3.
3. Ohio Wesleyan University, *Fifty-fifth Catalogue*, p. 58.
4. Sarah K. Vann, *op. cit.*, p. 3.
5. *Loc. cit.*
6. *Ibid.*, p. 4.
7. *The Dictionary of American Biography*, vol. 22, p. 663.
8. *The National Cyclopaedia of American Biography*, vol. 28, pp. 16-17.
9. Sarah K. Vann, *op cit.*, p. 6.

3
THE GRADUATE STUDENT IN ECONOMICS (1905-1907)

THE UNIVERSITY OF WISCONSIN

ALTHOUGH WILLIAMSON GRADUATED from Adelbert College in June 1904, he remained at Western Reserve University as secretary to the President and assistant in economics until February 1905, when he went to the University of Wisconsin to accept a scholarship and undertake graduate study in economics.

Fellows and Scholars at Wisconsin in those days were expected to perform service of some kind in return and my recollection is that they usually gave to the University far more than the value of their stipends. It was nothing short of a system of exploitation of graduate students, an evil that persists to this day in some places. But I did not object to that system for the first year at least. I lived as a member of the family of Professor Richard T. Ely, head of the large department of economics, and one of the best known economists of the day. In this way I was able to meet many interesting people.

To earn my stipend I was to serve as Professor Ely's personal assistant, and since I was known to have library interests my work tended to center on his large and personal library and the economics department of the University library. I carried a full program of courses in history, economics, and political science through the second semester of 1904-5, the 1905 summer session and the following year. When a fellowship was offered me for the year 1906-7 I declined to accept it, because by that time I saw clearly it would take me several years to get my degree under the Wisconsin system of exploiting graduate students who held fellowships. Without consulting Professor Ely or any member of the Wisconsin faculty I applied for a Columbia University fellowship which carried a much larger stipend and required no service in return. Receiving the Columbia fellowship, I came to New York in September, 1906 and by very hard work met the residence requirements, wrote and published a thesis, passed all examinations and received the degree in June, 1907.[1]

At Adelbert College Williamson worked under Dr. A. A. Young of the Economics Department. Young was concerned about Williamson's future and had written to Professor Richard T. Ely about him. As a result Ely wrote to Williamson:

> I have just received a letter from Dr. A. A. Young in which he tells me something about your thoughts for the future. I shall be very glad to discuss your plans with you at Chicago if you attend the meeting of the A.E.A. If you could spend a few days in Madison looking over the ground that might be well worth your while. I do not know how freely Dr. Young wrote to you. The ideas which he expressed concerning your future certainly commend themselves to me as sound.

Williamson was pleased with the suggestion that he continue his studies at Wisconsin under Ely's sponsorship and guidance. It was quite an honor for him to be invited to work with a man of Ely's stature.

Richard T. Ely, Ph.D., LL.D. was considered one of the greatest economists of his day. He was

> distinguished, not only for his writings on special subjects in political economy, but also for the spirit he has infused into the science in this country for the development of theory along various lines, for the many well-known American economists trained by him—he has probably trained more than any other one teacher—and for the remarkable revival of popular interest in the science, with which he is doubtless more to be credited than any other one man.[2]

He was born at Ripley, New York, in 1854 and died in 1943. He went to Dartmouth College, but transferred to

Columbia University in the City of New York, where he graduated in 1876. He obtained a fellowship and continued his studies in Europe, where in 1879 he received the degree of Ph.D. summa cum laude, from Heidelberg University. He started teaching at Johns Hopkins University in 1881 and the following year became Professor of Political Economy and Director of the School of Economics, Political Science, and History at the University of Wisconsin. This "event . . . was looked upon as marking the beginning of a new era in the history of that institution."[3] Dr. Ely's influence was strongly felt in the development of economic science in the United States. He was a prolific writer in the field of economics and sociology, including such works as *French and German Socialism in Modern Times* (1883), *Past and Present of Political Economy* (1884), *Recent American Socialism* (1885), *The Labor Movement in America* (1886), *Taxation in American States and Cities* (1888), and many more. He worked for the United States Department of State. Theodore H. White commented: "Wisconsin professors had a national impact on progressive tax and labor legislation in the early 1900's . . . Professors on University Hill in Madison . . . were only a mile away from the politicians on Capitol Hill."[4]

The invitation to the University of Wisconsin at Madison came in a letter dated January 3, 1905, from Professor Ely together with the suggestion that Williamson might be interested in working as Ely's private secretary while pursuing a full program of study toward the doctorate. In this long letter Ely advised the young man to continue for his doctorate and tentatively offered him a position.

> This raises in my mind the question if it is not possible for us to make a mutually satisfactory arrangement for the second semester. I take it that you are not getting a great deal from your present position, as you lack the associations which are especially valuable. The time evidently could be put in more advantageously for you. I believe that you are expecting to take the master's degree at the close of this year, but even if you have to give that up, it does not cut much of a figure provided you expect to go on and take the Ph.D. You could of course, take the master's degree here after a year, should that

be desirable. I do not, however, recommend those to take the master's degree who expect to take the Ph.D. Another question is whether or not you can secure a release at Cleveland. From what you told me I should not think that this ought to be difficult.

I have wished to have a secretary entirely free from any other University work, but it may be that we can arrange things satisfactorily during the second semester. I think you could perhaps take my two courses and also the economic seminary. . . . At the same time it should not require a great deal of time after the thing is well started provided one has the natural capacity and the training, and without the natural gift the thing is hopeless anyway. I should like to know how you feel about this matter. I must say you impressed me as a person who has far more than usual gifts in this direction. Have you ever kept books? I have a limited amount of bookkeeping and in this accuracy is absolutely necessary. Will you also tell me what knowledge you have of French and German? It is important that my secretary should be able to take responsibility and answer certain classes of letters without troubling me except for my signature. This I take it you have been accustomed to do in the office of President Thwing. . . . I cannot today make what I have suggested a definite offer, but if you will let me know how my suggestion strikes you, I think I can let you know very soon after I receive your reply.

Although Williamson was pleased to go to Wisconsin and work with Ely, he was reluctant to leave Thwing. In a letter of January 6, 1905, to Ely he stated, "While I realize to some extent, I hope, the greatness of the opportunity you open to me through your letter of January 3rd for the carrying out of cherished plans, and although I heartily appreciate your kind thought to me, I find it very difficult to decide to leave my present place before next September." However, later in the same letter he stated that he could leave, if he wished, and was "willing to accept your tentative proposition."

Williamson was torn between desire to pursue "his cherished plans" and reluctance to leave Thwing. His description of his duties and responsibilities indicate that Thwing relied heavily on him to carry out a great range and variety of work and trusted him completely. In addition, Williamson now had some experience at the job, and Thwing could leave many troublesome and time-consuming details to his secretary. Thwing was reluctant to let Williamson go but was also concerned about the young man's future.

Williamson, realizing the opportunity afforded him to work with Ely, stated in the same letter, "The end of the whole matter seems to be that if you still think I can serve you acceptably, and I have a correct understanding of what is expected of me, I am willing to come to you almost any time after February 1st, and stay until the end of the semester, on the conditions you state."

Ely did not want to put Thwing to any inconvenience, but he felt Williamson's experience to be "precisely the kind to fit you to do many things which it is important for me to have done."

There was some correspondence between Ely and Thwing about Williamson. In an undated and unsigned letter to Ely, Thwing expressed his appraisal of the young man in glowing terms.

> I have found my heart a little reluctant to write to you regarding my friend and associate Mr. Williamson, for my heart does not easily bring itself to the conclusion that he is to leave this association. But in my own sense of regret my heart is also eager to convey to you a message of congratulations upon your wisdom in asking Mr. Williamson to come into association with you. For he is one of the best of men, able, faithful, tireless in endeavor, gracious of accomplishment, and of noble spirit. I have for years put absolute confidence in his ability, integrity, and good taste. He has proved to be a comfort as well as a noble co-worker. I am glad for you, my friend. Let me also add that I am glad for him. For myself alone I am sorry.

Thwing realized that he could not keep Williamson, that the offer for the young man to work with Ely was too great an opportunity and that Thwing would be selfish if he insisted that Williamson remain as his secretary. The young man's future was at stake, and Thwing fully realized this when he wrote Williamson on June 17, 1905, "We expect great things, my friend."

The 1905 spring term started on February 20 with Williamson in attendance as a graduate student at the University of Wisconsin at Madison. He was beginning his work toward the Ph.D. and had accepted a scholarship from the university. His friend Dr. C. C. Arbuthnot of Western Reserve wrote on February 19, 1905, "I am glad to learn that you have found yourself so soon and at a kind of work that is congenial."

The terms of agreement between Richard Ely and Charles Williamson were stated in Ely's letter of January 3, 1905:

> A further point which I should mention is that it seems desirable that my secretary should live in my home. I like, however, to separate the payment for board from the remuneration. The board matter is arranged with Mrs. Ely who receives twenty-five dollars a calendar month, which is no more than others would be glad to pay for the same accommodation. In fact, I have reason to think that if we were willing to take in others we could receive considerably more. What I would suggest is that I let you take the two courses of study and the seminary and pay you fifty dollars a month for four months beginning somewhere around the tenth of February. This would take us through the second semester. This would be experimental and would enable both of us to determine about the desirability of the continuance of the arrangement. It would also enable you to tell whether or not you would care to continue your studies in Wisconsin.

Ely stated of himself: "One of the most important things for me is what may be called perhaps a gift for order. This means far more than an ability to follow a routine. It means the ability to organize order. It is by no means easy to keep the kind of order that is important for me." Williamson was expected to take dictation, do a limited amount of bookkeeping, answer letters, and type.

Their businesslike relationship was that of professor and student. In fact, Ely even went to the trouble of drawing up a rather formal "Agreement" between "Richard T. Ely, Party of the First Part, and C. C. Williamson, Party of the Second Part." This stipulated the working arrangements, the stipend, extent of work, and vacation, all for the "sake of clearness and the avoidance as far as possible of opportunity for misunderstanding." As the years passed, the relationship between Ely and Williamson grew friendlier and continued after Williamson left Madison. Ely constantly tried to get Williamson involved in research and writing in the field of economics; frequently he offered advice on professional matters. Over the years a friendly personal relationship developed, with Williamson often writing Ely for advice.

The University of Wisconsin, especially the Department of Political Economy, was involved in many activities of national significance, and the campus was the heart of this political and social ferment. Williamson, as a neophyte economist in this milieu found himself directly involved as Ely's secretary.

Although he worked for Ely as private secretary and jack-of-all-trades, Williamson's main reason for being at the University of Wisconsin was to obtain his doctorate in economics. The formal "Agreement" of May 9, 1905, stated:

> It is understood that the primary purpose of said C. C. Williamson is to carry on his studies in the Department of Economics, History, and Political Science, and that the aforementioned duties as private secretary will not interfere with his taking full work, and such courses as he chooses, in the Summer School of the University of Wisconsin.
>
> The said C. C. Williamson, for his part, while laying the primary emphasis on his studies and looking forward to taking the degree of Ph.D. in the University of Wisconsin, or other university, in the summer of 1907, and desiring to do as much more than the minimum amount of work required for this degree as possible, agrees to assist the said R. T. Ely in such ways as he may be able.

The registrar's office of the University of Wisconsin Graduate Department has on file an application for graduate work which Williamson filled out on September 23, 1905. He had already taken courses at Wisconsin in the 1905 spring and summer terms. This application indicates his candidacy for the degree of Ph.D. with a major in economics, a first minor in political science, and a second in history.

The Graduate Student in Economics

The university *Catalogue* gives some idea of the kind of work Williamson was doing at Wisconsin in its statement of the aims and objectives of the Department of Political Economy and the requirements for the degree:

> The purpose of the department is to afford superior means for systematic and thorough study in economics and social science. The courses are graded and arranged so as to meet the wants of students in the various stages of their progress, beginning with elementary and proceeding to the most advanced work. . . . Capable students are encouraged to undertake original investigations, and assistance is given them in the prosecution of such work through seminaries and the personal guidance of instructors. . . .
>
> Among the special facilities which Madison affords to students in political economy mention should be made of the various libraries elsewhere described. The library of the University of Wisconsin is especially rich in economic works, while the Wisconsin Historical Library has valuable collections helpful in research and investigation. The materials for the study of history described in connection with the work of the Department of History are especially helpful to students working in the field of political economy at a time when political economy is giving so much attention to historical investigation. The University library has complete sets of the most important economic and statistical journals, while the State Historical Library has important files of labor periodicals and valuable collections of documents relating to social movements.
>
> The studies offered by the department are elective in all the courses of the University. The graduate work of the department may lead to the master's degree in not less than one year, and to the doctor's degree in not less than three years.
>
> The work of this department has the following distinct but related aims:
>
> 1. To provide instruction in economics and sociology for undergraduates in all the courses of the University.
> 2. To provide advanced and graduate work in the studies falling within its field.
> 3. To assist and encourage the development of these studies.
> 4. With the co-operation of other departments, to pro-

vide special training courses for various practical pursuits.
5. To supplement the work of the College of Law. . . .

All such candidates will be expected to be familiar with the history of economic thought, the elements of statistics, and the principles of political economy as presented in advanced modern treatises.

Each candidate must have also made an intensive study of at least one of the following special fields: economic theory; economic history; sociology; labor; public finance; money, banking, and private finance; transportation. In the special field or fields selected, the candidate will be expected to exhibit not only thorough knowledge of the literature, methods of study, and social bearings of the subjects included, but also ability to prosecute research.[5]

In the spring term of 1905 Williamson studied exclusively with Professor Ely and took three courses: History of Economic Thought, the Distribution of Wealth (part 1), and the Economic Seminary. In the summer session, he took four courses: Elementary Sociology, Elements of Public Finance, Elements of Money and Banking, and Economics 6 (not listed in the *Catalogue*). This was followed by additional courses in the 1905-1906 terms: Distribution of Wealth (part 2); Philosophy of the State; Medieval Civilization; and the History of the U.S. from 1816 to 1837. In his last term at Wisconsin, he took Political Economy 53 and another Economics Seminary with Professor Commons (Ely was on leave of absence for the first semester of 1905-1906). Williamson also took Municipal Government, and Public Finance. He passed the French Language Examination on September 29, 1905, and the German Language Examination on February 21, 1906.

This record testifies that Williamson had excellent background training in the field of economics. In spite of his heavy course load, he was an A student throughout his graduate work at Wisconsin.

He definitely was interested in the field of economics and at this time planned to make it his life's work. Later developments would change this intention, but during his graduate work he gained a solid background in his chosen field and took his course work with some of the most illustrious economists of the day.

By December 1905 Williamson had begun to think about leaving Wisconsin to continue his doctoral work elsewhere. On December 8, he wrote to Professor H. R. Seager, secretary of the faculty of political science at Columbia University in New York City stating that "I am much inclined to finish up my work at Columbia, and that my ability to do so will depend on being a successful candidate for one of your fellowships." He states three reasons for leaving Wisconsin and wanting to go to Columbia:

> (1) By the end of the present year I shall have had practically all the advanced courses offered in Economics here. (2) My thesis is a study in municipal finance, "The Financial History of Cleveland." It will be well in hand by the beginning of next year, and I feel that I should be especially fortunate could I enjoy the advice of Professor Seligman and Professor Goodnow in putting it in its final shape. (3) The stimulus of a new environment, of new instructors, and especially the year's residence in New York City, it seems to me would offset what I might lose by the change.

By February 1906 Ely was aware of Williamson's interest in continuing at Columbia. Williamson wrote to him on February 21, 1906:

> The question of next year is still before us. I shall be in Wisconsin or Columbia, which I do not know.... Following the plan which I have discussed with you once or twice I am now applying for a fellowship in Columbia, and I feel that if you were willing to recommend me I shall make a pretty strong candidate.
> ... The Columbia people know that I am happy and well pleased here; that I am not seeking a change because Wisconsin is tired of me or because I am tired of Wisconsin. ... My feelings are not unmingled when I ask you to do that which may take me away from Wisconsin. Yet even if I am not to be here next year the favorable conditions under which

I have spent the two years will undoubtedly cause the Wisconsin associations to be more lasting than any other.

At this time Williamson played his first active role with regard to libraries. In a letter of April 14, 1906, to Dr. Frederic C. Howe, of Garfield, Howe and Westenhaver, Attorneys and Counselors at Law, of Cleveland, Ohio, he suggested the establishment of a legislative reference department to be associated with the Cleveland Public Library. The former would be headed by a "properly trained and efficient man to make a really serviceable collection of books and materials and constantly serve legislators and government officials in their use of it." This idea was credited partly to Dr. Charles McCarthy, Librarian of the Legislative Reference Library, Wisconsin; in fact, Williamson suggested that McCarthy speak to groups in Cleveland to stimulate their interest. Shortly after this, McCarthy offered him a job. "At the time I left Madison I was on the point of taking up work with Dr. McCarthy, as he advised me to do, and becoming a legislative reference librarian. The Columbia Fellowship turned me aside from that purpose."

President Thwing wrote several letters to Columbia on behalf of Williamson's candidacy for the Columbia fellowship. Williamson was most grateful: "It is very, very good of you to do so much in impressing my candidacy upon the Columbia Faculty. . . . I am quite sure that if some one else gets the appointment it will not be for the reason that his friends took a greater interest in his case."

Professor Henry R. Seager of Columbia wrote Williamson on April 12, 1906, "It is my pleasure to advise you privately and unofficially that you have been recommended for one of the fellowships in Economics for next year." On April 17, 1906, the official notice informed him he had been appointed a "University Fellow in Political Economy in Columbia University for period from July 1st, 1906 to June 30th, 1907 with a stipend of $650.00 per annum."

Upon hearing from Seager, Williamson immediately wrote to Thwing: "It gives me great pleasure to tell you that I have received notice of provisional appointment to the Columbia fellowship. . . . I am naturally gratified over the result of my year in Madison. The year in New York should be better."

He also notified Professor Ely.

> I received yesterday morning from Columbia notice of provisional appointment for the fellowship. It becomes final of course, after I have given assurance that I will not resign to accept a similar appointment elsewhere. This assurance I have given and have withdrawn my application at Wisconsin. I do not like the idea of leaving Wisconsin, for it has meant much to me. There is some consolation in the feeling that I am making way for some good man who deserves the Wisconsin appointment more than I do. And on the other hand I feel my efficiency will be the greater for a year's study and experience in New York.

While Williamson was working with Ely he became involved in recommending books for purchase by the University Library in the field of economics, economic theory, and history of economic thought. He was constantly examining catalogs and bibliographies for books of a general and special nature of sufficient importance to warrant their purchase.

He expressed his appreciation to Ely in a letter of June 1, 1906, thanking him for this opportunity: "In this my last formal report I wish to thank you for giving me the opportunity of trying my hand at the difficult task of sifting the existing mass of economic literature. It has been invaluable to me, and I trust of some value to the Library equipment." The value of this experience in contributing to his knowledge of the economics field would stand him in good stead at Bryn Mawr College and lead eventually to his first library position as Chief of the Economics Department of the New York Public Library.

The Experience at Columbia University

An authorization form issued on October 1, 1906, by Columbia University to C. C. Williamson indicates that he was "duly registered as a candidate for the degree of Ph.D.

and is hereby authorized to pursue courses for the academic year 1906-07. R. Tombo, Jr., Registrar." During an exhausting year in New York City, Williamson finally met the requirements for the doctorate at Columbia.

At this time Williamson was working on a paper dealing with the financial history of Cleveland. He started this at Wisconsin and continued it at Columbia University; it was to become the basis for his doctoral dissertation, "The Finances of Cleveland." He discussed the project in a letter of March 10, 1907, to Professor Curtis of Western Reserve.

> My dissertation, as you may know, is a critical and historical study of the finances, organization, and administration of municipal corporations in Ohio, with special reference to Cleveland, under the title "The Finances of Cleveland." The work is now completed and is being published in the Columbia Studies in History, Economics, and Public Law. It has turned out to be a book of some 230 to 250 pages and I think it will be useful for reference and especially helpful for anyone who wishes to get an acquaintance with municipal affairs in Cleveland. Professor Bemis, Mr. Orr, Mr. Stockwell, Mr. Cooley and Mr. Leslie have read and commended the parts which deal with their respective departments. Mr. Newton D. Baker, with whom I have consulted freely all along has, at his own suggestion, read the entire manuscript and has just written to me a letter in which he says: "It gives me a great deal of pleasure to say that you have surprised me beyond measure with its excellence and that I shall want and shall constantly use a copy as soon as it comes from the printer." Professor Gardner of Brown University has read it and commented favorably upon it. But more important to me just now is the fact that it was promptly accepted by the Faculty of Political Science here, not only for publication as a thesis, but for publication in the Series.

In the same letter Williamson commented on his course of study at Columbia.

> I am taking Economic Theory with Professor Clark; History of Economics, Taxation and Public Finance with Professor Seligman; and Trust Problems with Professor Seager. All these I regard as reviews, having already had similar courses.

My reading I am doing along the courses given by Professor Giddings, taking all the work he offers in the Graduate School, and Professor Dunning and Goodnow, the former in Political Theories and the latter in Municipal Government. It was city government that I took with Dr. Sparling in Wisconsin, but as my thesis is in this field I felt it was worth while to follow Goodnow too.

At that time Newton D. Baker was the City Solicitor of Cleveland, Ohio. Williamson sent him the manuscript for examination, suggestions, and comments. That he was still concerned about the dissertation is revealed in a letter sent on February 20, 1907, to Baker.

I want to thank you for taking the time to read my dissertation. . . . Although I have gone over the whole thing with great care, I hesitate to print it without more study and verification. Until it is printed, I cannot receive my degree. Let me thank you also for the expression of your favorable opinion of my maiden effort at book making.

The dissertation was accepted by the Faculty of Political Science of Columbia University. On Friday, May 24, 1907, from 2 P.M. to 5 P.M., Williamson was examined for the Ph.D. degree in the field of economics. His examiners were Professors Dunning, Giddings, and Goodnow. On June 5, 1907, the following notification was mailed to Williamson:

I am authorized to say that, upon the recommendation of the University Council, the President will confer upon you at Commencement, June 12, 1907, the degree of

DOCTOR OF PHILOSOPHY

The diploma may be obtained from the Registrar, Room No. 109, Library building, when you have completed all requirements.

Respectfully,

Rudolf Tombo, Jr.
Registrar

The degree was awarded at the 153rd annual commencement of Columbia University, held on June 12, 1907. The name of Charles C. Williamson is listed on page 26 of the commencement program. Professor William Henry Carpenter, Secretary of the University Council, presented the candidates.

Ten days after receiving the doctorate, Williamson married Bertha Torrey whom he had met at Western Reserve University.

DEVELOPMENT OF A NEW INTEREST

Up to this point in his career Williamson was deeply involved in the field of economics. He had studied with the leading economist of his day, Richard T. Ely, and continued this interest at Columbia University. There can be no doubt that he was sincerely interested in the field. He had committed himself to assist Ely in the revision of his classic, *Taxation in American States and Cities*, and was active in the professional organizations. That he was competent in this field is evident. However, his change in interest to the library field was not so drastic as it first appears, since his first library appointment in 1911 was as Chief of the Economics Department at the New York Public Library. Certainly his knowledge of the literature in the field eminently qualified him for this position.

It would be unfair to ignore Williamson's research in the field of economics, since it did consume part of his professional work and continued into his first library position. For several years after his entry into librarianship, he continued to write for professional journals on economics and taxation.

A background in economics was useful to Williamson in the library field. His writing in the field of librarianship reflects scientific training, accuracy, thoroughness, and an ability to evaluate and criticize—characteristics that developed during his undergraduate and graduate training in economics.

Shortly before receiving his doctorate, Williamson became concerned about his future work and about obtaining a position. On February 4, 1907, he received a letter from President Martha Carey Thomas of Bryn Mawr College: "We are anxious to appoint an economist next year and, as usual, we have consulted Professor John B. Clark of Columbia University. He has mentioned several names to me, and, among others, your name." President Thomas asked Williamson to meet her in New York to discuss the position of "Associate with a seat in the faculty, the term of appointment to be for two years, the salary, $1,200 for the first year, and $1,500 for the second year." In the final contract the salary was increased to $1,500 for the first year. Williamson was interested; although he received other offers, the position at Bryn Mawr interested him the most.

At about this same time, Williamson also received a letter from William Howard Brett, Librarian of the Cleveland (Ohio) Public Library, offering him a job in their Reference Department with the opportunity of attending Library School. The arrangement would be that Williamson "would work six hours daily, in the Reference Department, for the first year and do the work which may seem worthwhile in the Library School. The tuition in the Library School would be free."

Somewhat interested, Williamson wrote Brett:

> As I have already said to you, however, the idea of developing and making useful a collection of books along the lines of sociology, economics, and political science appeals to me. One thing that causes me to hesitate just now is the fact that through my residence in the University of Wisconsin and Columbia University I have been fortunate in making the acquaintance and securing the good will of many of the most eminent scholars in my chosen field, and at the same time have made the acquaintance of a large number of young men who are to devote themselves to this work; I do not want to get completely out of touch with these men by settling down to work in which they have little or no interest and work which would not enable me to keep abreast of the scientific work or, perhaps, take a hand in it.

Although Williamson indicated he might be interested in library work, he decided at that time to remain in his chosen field of economics. He was definitely committed; therefore, the offer of a teaching position at Bryn Mawr appealed to him. He did not consider the offer to work at the Cleveland Public Library an impossibility, but Bryn Mawr and teaching had the greater appeal at this time in his career. Williamson concluded his letter to Brett, "For the present I am not ready to decide in favor of library work, though I am glad to be able to keep the question open a little while longer."

On March 20, 1907, Williamson received another offer, this time from President Thwing, asking him to teach at Western Reserve in Adelbert or the College for Women and also to serve as assistant to the President. Thwing stated: "Your teaching would represent six hours. . . . Your chief work, however, be it said, would be executive." Thwing also stated his feeling that Williamson had a "special facility in executive work." Williamson was not interested. "The salary seems to me quite inadequate for the work expected; the appointment as instructor would be even more unsatisfactory. The combination of the two positions would be a distinct disadvantage in every way, it seems to me. These are the main reasons which have appealed to me in not accepting the offer."

ACCEPTANCE OF POSITION AS COLLEGE PROFESSOR

Through this period of having to make a decision on his future career, Williamson continued in the field of his first choice, that of a teacher of economics. He informed President Thwing on March 26, 1907:

> You will be interested to know that I have decided to accept the place of Associate in Economics at Bryn Mawr College. The appointment is for two years; with the prospect of the full professorship if I wish to remain. I shall be head of the department, there being one instructor besides myself. I shall never be asked to teach more than twelve hours a week, and it will probably be less. The facilities for my study and teaching are admirable. The salary begins at $1,500 which you see is for less than nine months, and I find that living expenses

are not essentially higher than in Cleveland. The professional advantages of being at Bryn Mawr and in the East—twenty minutes from Philadelphia and two hours from New York—I need not enumerate.

Although Thwing regretted that Williamson would not return to Western Reserve, he was gracious.

> I am very glad to know that, if you are not to come to us, that you are to have that honorable place in Bryn Mawr. The salary is good, the environment is beautiful, your associates will, I know, have much happiness in you and you in them. The whole opportunity is rich. I am very glad for you. . . .
> I did not really expect that you would accept my offer, but I knew it was right for me to make it to you.

On March 25, 1907, Williamson received a letter from President Thomas: "It gives me great pleasure to tell you that the Directors of Bryn Mawr College have today appointed you Associate in Economics for a period of two years beginning September 1, 1907, at a salary of $1,500 a year." President Thomas continued: "It gives me very great pleasure to think that you will be a member of our College Faculty next year. Professor Mussey tells me this morning that his talk with you was very satisfactory, and he feels as I do, that his classes in economics will be in good hands next year." This letter contained an enclosure of a "Memorandum of Agreement Between the Directors of Bryn Mawr College and Charles C. Williamson," which gave the term of employment and salary.

Charles Williamson was ready to start on a new phase of his career, settling with his new bride at Bryn Mawr College as an Associate Professor of Economics.

NOTES

1. Sarah K. Vann, "Statement Prepared for the Use of Miss Sarah K. Vann," by Charles C. Williamson, June 27, 1955, pp. 7-8.
2. *The National Cyclopaedia of American Biography*, vol. 9, p. 200.

3. *Loc. cit.*
4. Theodore H. White, "Scholarly Impact on the Nation's Past," *Life,* June 16, 1967, p. 62.
5. University of Wisconsin, *Catalogue, 1905-1906,* p. 123-125.

4
THE YOUNG PROFESSOR AT BRYN MAWR COLLEGE (1907-1911)

Teaching Experience at Bryn Mawr College

Williamson wrote to President Thomas on March 26, 1907, commenting on his impression of Bryn Mawr and the prospects before him: "Even my anticipations were exceeded by what my eyes saw of Bryn Mawr. My fiancée and I are looking forward with the utmost pleasure to our life and work in an environment so congenial and beautiful in every way." The relationship between Williamson and Thomas was friendly, and he thanked her "for these courtesies, and especially for your personal hospitality."

Martha Carey Thomas was President of Bryn Mawr College from 1894 until her retirement in 1921, when she became President Emerita. She was born in Baltimore, Maryland, in 1857 and died in Philadelphia, Pennsylvania, in 1935. She graduated from Cornell University in 1877 and was a member of Phi Beta Kappa. She studied Greek at Johns Hopkins University and then went to Germany to continue her studies at the University of Leipzig. Although she spent three years there, she was refused the doctorate because she was a woman. She then went to the University of Göttingen, which also refused to grant her the doctorate. She consequently applied at the University of Zurich, passed a most brilliant examination, and was awarded the doctorate, summa cum laude, in 1882.[1] Thomas also studied for a time at the Sorbonne.

On her return to the United States, she was appointed dean and professor of English at Bryn Mawr College. In 1894 she became the second president at Bryn Mawr. There she had the opportunity to put many of her ideas into practice, and she gave the college "a wide reputation and made it a leader in the movement for higher academic standards in American education."[2]

She was active in the fight for equal suffrage and in the movement for international peace. She traveled extensively and has been described as "a person of indomitable physical and intellectual energy, who made a deep and instantaneous impression on the college student body, on the audiences she addressed, and in fact, on nearly everyone she met."[3]

There is no doubt that President Thomas ran the college with a firm hand and had been accused of being autocratic and dictatorial. However, she "never deviated from her original purpose of maintaining the highest possible standards for the education of girls, and of ensuring their preparation for professional careers."[4]

At the beginning of his career as a college professor at Bryn Mawr, Williamson was very pleased about the appointment and his work there. After their marriage, Williamson and his wife, Bertha, lived in Cleveland during the summer of 1907, moving to Bryn Mawr around the first of October. He wrote to Ely on October 13, 1907, that he was enjoying his teaching and that he and Mrs. Williamson were "both more than pleased with our surroundings. We live in one of the College houses, on the campus, which is very pleasant." He also commented:

> In my elementary classes which meet five hours a week there are about sixty-five or seventy girls. Of post-majors (i.e., those who have had at least two years of economics and politics) there are about a half-dozen and I am giving them a course in Public Finance, three hours a week. With two graduate students I am about as busy as I should be.

During his early days at Bryn Mawr College, Williamson contracted typhoid fever, which left him extremely weak. He was so ill that he obtained a leave of absence at full salary for the 1908 spring semester. Ely wrote on March 7, 1908, that he was "sorry to learn that your health had not improved." However, Ely felt that the leave of absence at full pay was "strong evidence that you are doing good work that the Bryn

Mawr people are willing to make such generous arrangements with you."

In the summer of 1908 the effects of the illness were still felt and Ely wrote on July 21: "I am glad to hear from you but sorry that it has taken so long to recover your health and strength . . . Be careful about getting to work and take things easy at first." By the fall semester Williamson was back at work but still "not well yet, though better I think than a year ago." He remained under a doctor's care and was advised to do as little as possible during the remainder of the year.

In the fall term of 1908 Williamson taught new courses. Due to his illness he was permitted to repeat the finance course, although the policy at Bryn Mawr College did not usually permit an instructor to repeat a course in any consecutive term. He lectured to his largest class on Socialiam and Social Reform and also supervised three graduate students. He still was weak and confessed to Ely that work "absorbs all the strength I have left from the undergraduate courses, and even then I do but a fraction of what should be done." There is no question that this illness strongly affected his teaching.

Ely was trying to persuade Williamson to revise his *Taxation in American States and Cities*, originally published in 1888. Williamson had started to work on this revision, but the responsibilities of his new position and his illness prevented him from doing more than some preliminary study. The venture never was finished, although plans continued for several years.

On April 21, 1909, he was offered a reappointment as Associate in Economics at Bryn Mawr College for a period of two years, beginning September 1, with a salary of $1,700 the first year and $1,800 the second. President Thomas wrote Williamson that he was being offered a two-year reengagement rather than the usual three because "we feel that this will be sufficient time to enable you and us to judge the work at Bryn Mawr." A memorandum of agreement issued on the same day indicated that she wanted time to evaluate Williamson's teaching abilities without being held to a three-year contract.

Beginning of Dissatisfaction

The first indication of dissatisfaction appears in a letter that Williamson wrote Ely on May 18, 1909:

> President Thomas and I, however, I wish to say to you in confidence, are not altogether in harmony as to the content of my courses and the method of conducting them. I shall yield to her wishes as far as possible, but I am not at all certain that I can work out a solution. . . . There are other conditions here, also, which I should like to talk over with you. The total result is that I [have] been and am seriously tempted to try to find another place, or failing in that, to ask for a year's leave of absence and come to Madison and, awaiting some opening, to work with you on Taxation in American States and Cities. I should like very much to know what you think of that.

Ely was a little puzzled to know what to say. He felt there was some danger in breaking away from any position before securing another, but wrote, "You are however, young enough to make this comparatively safe and so many have left Bryn Mawr dissatisfied, and in fact the terms of office have been so short there, that it would not so likely injure you as it would be to leave another institution."

It is strange that no one seems to have warned Williamson about possible problems with President Thomas at Bryn Mawr College. According to Ely, many left Bryn Mawr dissatisfied, yet nowhere in the correspondence is there any word about this or even the slightest hint that Williamson might meet with difficulty.

The conditions and the relations that developed with President Thomas were far from ideal, although Williamson did state to Ely in a letter of May 18, 1909: "We like Bryn Mawr; I have been happy in my work. So that we should leave this place with keen regret. Still I am by no means certain that for the sake of the future it would not be better to make a change, if that opportunity should be presented." Although Williamson did not mention his desire to leave to President Thomas, he felt she would put no serious obstacle in his way.

However, he decided to remain for the time being and

follow Ely's advice to hold on. He confessed to Ely on June 27, 1909, that he also had other reasons for not wanting to leave at this time, primarily the thought that if he stood by his work, "President Thomas will be more likely to commend my work than if I leave her in the lurch," but he continued looking for a new position.

Most of the Thomas-Williamson correspondence dealt with daily problems of teaching, library budget, and regulations concerning conduct of examinations. Up to this time the relationship between the two seems to have been business like and pleasant. President Thomas even took the trouble to write to him on August 26, 1908, "I am very glad to hear from your letter . . . that you are nearly well again."

The problem over courses dealt mainly with his approach in teaching economics. In fact, there is an early indication of the core of the problem in President Thomas's letter to him of February 4, 1907: "Our work at Bryn Mawr . . . is rather on the theoretical side." Williamson knew this; in fact, one of the reasons he gave Ely for not working on the book on taxation was his feeling that the practical nature of the work would jeopardize his chance of getting the Bryn Mawr position. He fully realized the Bryn Mawr policy, as he told Ely on February 20, 1907:

> The work outlined at Bryn Mawr for next year is largely theoretical; they do not seem to wish to develop the practical lines of their work and I feared they might be influenced in the wrong direction by knowing that I am committed to the "practical" side of economics too thoroughly.

The Bowdoin College "Affair"

The conflict between Williamson and Thomas was never anything more than latent until the Bowdoin College "affair," when the situation changed and the animosity between them was revealed. On April 18, 1916, he stated in a letter, "While I would be glad to know exactly what happened, I feel no bitterness toward anyone." The correspondence, however, indicates otherwise. At the time, Williamson was furious at the treatment he felt he had received from President Thomas because of an offer he received to become Professor of Economics and Sociology at Bowdoin College.

The difficulty began on February 5, 1910, with a letter from President William DeWitt Hyde of Bowdoin College, Brunswick, Maine. President Hyde wrote letters to several other people in "order to find men who would be willing to make a change." The rank was that of full professor; the salary was $2,500, considerably more than Williamson was making at Bryn Mawr.

Williamson's concern about the effect of this appointment on President Thomas was well founded. In his answer of February 11, 1910, to Hyde, he wrote that he would "regard it as a great favor if you will not correspond with her unless other inquiries incline you to offer me the place. You will readily appreciate that I am reluctant to appear to be dissatisfied with Bryn Mawr."

Williamson wrote to Ely on February 7, 1910, and expressed his concern about the situation. He admitted frankly now that he was disappointed with President Thomas, although he did like Bryn Mawr.

> Other things being equal, I should prefer to remain here. But one is always on the tenter-hooks here, even after he gets his professorship, which, if Miss Thomas, happens to conceive a dislike for a man, will never come. You know that I do not feel secure here and that I have much reason to believe I am working at a great disadvantage. I like my students and I like the teaching. This semester I am lecturing to one class five hours a week, which contains nearly seventy students. I have trained myself to give a careful and systematic lecture straight from the shoulder without a scrap of note and it gives me the greatest satisfaction and it apparently satisfies the students also and I think the students are as critical here as anywhere. This I say in order to intimate that, whatever Miss Thomas might say, I feel that my teaching is a success. Parenthetically, I may say, that I do not know what Miss Thomas would say if asked what kind of work I have done. She has been known to knock a good man out of a good position for no other reason than a slight personal grudge.

The Young Professor at Bryn Mawr College

Williamson confided to Ely that he felt he should accept the Bowdoin position if it was offered. To his request that Ely write a letter of recommendation to Hyde, Ely replied on February 10, 1910, that he had written to "President Hyde recommending you." Ely was encouraging about the Bowdoin professorship. "It is an excellent one and I believe under all circumstances it would be wise for you to accept it should it be offered to you."

Williamson wrote Hyde on February 11, 1910, informing him of the difficulties of leaving Bryn Mawr College and the problems early in his appointment with his health and the effect of this on his teaching.

Williamson and his wife discussed the situation thoroughly. They enjoyed living at Bryn Mawr, which they considered a most charming spot, and they had a house on campus which they regretted having to give up. But, he wrote Hyde: "We have threshed it out and have come to the conclusion that on the whole we should probably find in Bowdoin an even better opportunity to do our best work than we have here. I am therefore prepared to assure you that I will accept your professorship of Economics and Sociology if offered to me." Probably aware of the reaction if and when President Thomas became involved, he cautiously informed Hyde: "But I must make one provision, namely, that my acceptance is to be contingent on the willingness of President Thomas to release me from my present contract which covers one more year. Until a definite offer is made me, and one which I am willing to accept, I do not think it would be wise to take the matter up with her." However, Hyde wrote to President Thomas; on March 4, 1910, she answered with an appraisal of Williamson and a statement of her position regarding his appointment to the Bowdoin College faculty.

At first Hyde was enthusiastic about having Williamson on the faculty. He received favorable accounts of the candidate from several sources, and it appeared that Williamson was destined for the Bowdoin professorship. Hyde notified Williamson on March 10, 1910, that he wrote to President Thomas asking whether he could be released and heard from her in a letter of March 4, 1910.

Dear President Hyde,

Doctor Williamson may feel free to take another position provided he gives us sufficient notice to enable us to fill his post satisfactorily. If you are thinking of calling him to Bowdoin I should be very glad if you would let me know at your earliest convenience, as it is getting late in the year to make appointments.

Doctor Williamson is a thoroughly nice man. He is an agreeable colleague, very much interested in his work and in his students, very faithful and painstaking and cooperates cordially, so far as I am able to judge, with the administration of the college. He is very well equipped in economics; his bibliographical knowledge in very many economic fields is extraordinary, and his reading is also wide. As a teacher I do not feel that we are yet able to judge him fairly because when he came to us he had not yet recovered from the effects of typhoid fever, so that he was unable to put the necessary energy into his teaching. Indeed he was so ill that we gave him a leave of absence during the second semester of his first year. This year he is, I think, well, but he has had to overcome the tradition caused in part, I believe, by his ill-health, that he was not a very inspiring teacher, so that I have felt it would probably not be fair for us to judge him as a teacher even this year, but during next year if he stayed with us we should be able to reach a conclusion. At the end of last year we renewed his engagement with the College for two years because we felt that we were not yet able to make up our minds. His teaching is the only thing that I am not quite sure about. In every other respect he is an excellent man.

As I must leave my office for the day I have asked my stenographer to sign this letter for me.

Very sincerely yours,

M. Carey Thomas [Signed]

Although certainly not a letter of high praise, it was a frank, truthful, and honest appraisal of his work, without malice on Thomas's part, yet hardly the type of letter to help Williamson secure the position.

Williamson, realizing that "something has occurred,"

wrote to President Hyde on March 15, 1910, withdrawing his nomination for the professorship at Bowdoin. Hyde answered seven days later:

> The testimony submitted to both the Faculty and the Committee was in the highest degree satisfactory, both as to personality and scholarship: all the testimony we were able to get, however, leaves some doubt as to your complete success as a teacher: it shows that partial failure the first year was probably due to ill health, and that there has been steady improvement since.

Hyde continued that although the faculty were "inclined to take a hopeful view of this evidence, the Committee, on the other hand, have always been inclined to insist that in taking a man from another institution, success there must have been complete and assured beyond all possibility of doubt." Hyde asked him to meet with the Committee on Wednesday, March 30, 1910, at nine-thirty, at the Parker House in Boston. This meeting was postponed, and Williamson met the Committee on April 9, 1910, at nine in the morning. The records do not reveal anything about this meeting. On April 11, 1910, Williamson was notified by Hyde, "It is a real regret that you are not to be with us next year."

Williamson was most concerned about the turn of events. He had written his predecessor, Dr. Mussey, on March 19, 1910, asking for advice.

> After writing [these] two letters [Hyde] apparently heard from President Thomas in reply to his letter asking her if I could be released, for he immediately wrote me hedging; suggested that there is no telling what the Committee of the Boards will do, etc., I suspected what had happened and wrote offering to withdraw. Yesterday his reply came and although he gives no names I think my suspicion is correct. Although he does not accept my offer to withdraw, it is clear that President Thomas had put plenty of wire in my lawn mower.

Mussey had answered on March 22, agreeing with him that his analysis is "entirely correct . . . it all has a familiar ring." Mussey had heard nothing from Hyde but in case he did, "I shall pull out all the wire I can."

On April 11, 1910, Williamson again wrote Mussey, informing him that he had not gotten the Bowdoin position. "In regard to the source and exact nature of the hitch I am still quite in the dark, except as I can guess." Williamson was concerned regarding this incident, which he stated in a letter to Ely on April 13, 1910: "I do not know why I was turned down after being virtually chosen."

As a result of this, Williamson became increasingly dissatisfied with Bryn Mawr. His friends sympathized with him, and Arbuthnot wrote on April 14, 1910:

> I have not been in such a helofa temper for a long time as has been in possession after getting your letter to-day. Of all the infernal outrages this takes the lead . . . I am glad to see that you are not letting the matter prey on your nerves. It takes grit to keep a cool head under such conditions but it is bad personal economics to do anything else. Deliverance . . . will come sooner or later.

Williamson's annoyance only increased when he learned that the man chosen for the Bowdoin position was a friend of his from Cornell by the name of Catlin, at a salary not over $1,500 as Assistant Professor, while his own negotiations had all been on the basis of a full professorship at $2,500.

Although Williamson remained at Bryn Mawr, he continued to look for another position. President Thomas wrote him a belligerent letter on December 10, 1910, in which she chastised him for discussing with his students what she regarded as a "confidential conversation between us." She protested angrily: "I hope very much that you will assist me in trying to let all the agitation die out of itself as it soon will. We do not wish a repetition of what must have happened in the case of the Bowdoin appointment if you hear of a post you really wish for." This letter confirmed his suspicion that it was she who had blackballed him. He became more eager than ever to leave Bryn Mawr.

The episode was a strange one, yet not uncommon at Bryn Mawr College under the administration of Martha

The Young Professor at Bryn Mawr College

Carey Thomas. She always was a controversial figure and had been accused of being dictatorial in her administration of the college. She was forceful and determined; nevertheless, she did much to change Bryn Mawr College from a girls' finishing school to a reputable college for women, and was certainly a leading educator and pioneer in the education of women. Much of this was accomplished in spite of seemingly endless internal struggles, especially with the faculty at Bryn Mawr.

Williamson probably was right that Thomas was angered in not having been advised of the discussion for the Bowdoin position. She may have been annoyed most of all at his possible appointment as full professor at a much higher salary, especially since she had criticized his teaching and believed he was not an inspiring teacher.

However, the animosity between them did not interfere with her awareness of his research ability and critical mind. Even after he left Bryn Mawr, she sought his assistance. In a letter in 1914 she asked for his help with an address she was to give on suffrage for women. He sent her a three-page report of his research.

End of Economics Teaching at Bryn Mawr

Williamson's contract for the following year was not renewed. On January 26, 1911, President Thomas wrote a letter of recommendation from Luxor, Egypt, at Williamson's request. She was away from Bryn Mawr College during the winter. In this letter she stated:

> Dr. Williamson has found himself to be a very conscientious and faithful teacher and has spared no pains to make his department successful. His relations with his fellow members of the faculty, with the executive of the college, and with his students have been cordial and pleasant in every respect. He is a sound scholar and exceedingly well read in his special field. His graduate students have frequently spoken to me of his bibliographical knowledge and his power to direct their investigations.

She continued, explaining why he was not reappointed, "As it is we have not asked him to renew [the contract] because we cannot promise him in the future the advancement in salary and position which he has a right to expect."

She hoped the fact that his engagement at Bryn Mawr College was not renewed would not, "stand in the way of his securing such a college position as his training and teaching experience deserve." She indicated that "his work with us has been on the whole so satisfactory and his relations with the College so pleasant."

Williamson's teaching career was rapidly coming to an end; library work would soon replace his work in the field of economics. How much the problems at Bryn Mawr had to do with his decision to change careers will never be known. One thing is certain: he was not reappointed at Bryn Mawr and therefore he did not have a job. The need to find a new position was crucial.

GROWING INTEREST IN LIBRARY WORK

On December 17, 1910, Williamson again wrote to Arbuthnot. "Yesterday I learned that I am being considered in connection with a job in New York City that requires economic training and a knowledge and a taste for book collecting in the field of economics. I am quite in the dark as to the precise nature of the position, but it seems to be something very attractive in connection with one of the great New York libraries."

Williamson, being dissatisfied with things at Bryn Mawr, had started to look for another position. He wrote to several people, including Dr. William D. Johnston of Columbia University, John Glenn of the Russell Sage Foundation, and Edwin Hatfield Anderson, Assistant Director of the New York Public Library. The letters provided information on his background, education, training, and interest in library

The Young Professor at Bryn Mawr College

work. These letters are most revealing in reflecting the change which was taking place regarding his career choice, and they help answer the question of why he left the field of economics teaching. The letter to Johnston of December 17, 1910, reveals how Williamson's library interest began.

> It was while I was President's Secretary in Western Reserve University that Mr. Carnegie founded the Library School. This brought me in touch with many librarians and increased the interest I had had for some time in library work. I read and studied library literature, such as the New York State Library Bulletin, studied various schemes of classification and the methods of cataloguing, and also became interested in bibliography and public documents. Most of this library interest was quite outside my college course and the duties of President's Secretary, and was due in considerable measure to the inspiration of Mr. E. C. Williams, then in charge of the Hatch Library.
>
> As Assistant to Professor Ely I recatalogued his private library, or supervised its recataloguing, and also classified and catalogued a large collection of economics pamphlets, clippings, etc. During the last year of my work with Professor Ely I was employed in collecting books in economics to strengthen the already extensive collection of the University of Wisconsin and the State Historical Society. This gave me greater familiarity with publishers and book dealers catalogues and facility in the use of trade bibliography, French, and German, as well as English.

The letter indicated that he had been offered various positions during this time including some in library work.

> When I finished my work at Columbia I had the choice to become Executive Secretary of Western Reserve University and Instructor in Political Science, or Reference Librarian in the Cleveland Public Library, or Associate in Economics in Bryn Mawr College. I chose the latter because the Cleveland Public Library position was that of general reference, while I had hoped to specialize, and although Mr. Brett urged the possibility of developing a special reference library I could see

no prospect of financial support in Cleveland for such a collection as I had in mind.

All the time that I have been in Bryn Mawr I have contemplated leaving teaching for library work of some sort. I shall certainly make a change next year and it was to talk over the nature of this change that I went up to New York yesterday to see Professor Seligman. This letter, of course, is not an application for any position, as I know next to nothing of what you have in mind; but I infer it is more or less in line with my training, experience and inclination.

Williamson gave another reason for wanting to change from teaching economics to library work in an undated letter to John Glenn of the Russell Sage Foundation.

I have been led to make the shift from the lecture room to the library for the reason that I like administrative work and take special delight in keeping touch with the literature of the social sciences, and also because I am convinced that at this juncture I can contribute more to the advance of social theory and practice through a great city library than through a small college.

Although the change from teaching economics to library work might appear abrupt, for him the change was gradual. His correspondence with members of the library profession reveals that not one of these people ever indicated that they did not feel him possessed of the necessary requirements for library work or indeed that he was not an extremely eligible candidate. His entry into library work was a perfectly natural and logical development. Librarianship in 1910 differed from most library positions today in that the requirements did not necessarily include formal library education. In fact, the "profession" of librarianship did not really exist; training was more of an apprenticeship and training on the job was not only acceptable but common.

Williamson was interested in becoming a special collections librarian in order to make use of his knowledge and training in the field of economics. He had a doctorate in economics from Columbia, his teaching experience was in this field, and he had excellent references from the foremost economists of his day. His interests covered a wide range, including political economy, economics, history, statistics, political science, public finance, taxation, public health, and municipal government, and he was well acquainted with the literature in these fields. He wanted a library position where he could make full use of his specialized background and subject interests.

Even President Thomas acknowledged this in her letter of recommendation of January 26, 1911: "He is a sound scholar and exceedingly well read in his special field. His graduate students have frequently spoken of his bibliographical knowledge." Williamson felt that he and President Thomas differed mainly "on questions of teaching method. So far as I know she never criticized my scholarship or general ability."

His qualifications for library work were far above those of most candidates of that time. Although he did not possess the educational background in library science or have any experience in library work, he did have a sound bibliographical knowledge of the literature of economics.

Williamson recalls his reasons for entering library work.

> You asked for my reasons for being interested in librarianship. I doubt that I ever went through any conscious reasoning process that led me in the direction of library work. It all seems to have come about through a chain of events in which the initiative was not mine, although I suppose at each fork of the road I must have given some thought as to which direction to take. But I doubt that my choices were ever based on adequate information or reasoning. When I say *chain* of events, I mean only that one event followed another in a time sequence covering a period of about fifteen years. It seems to me now that no one of these events had any traceable connection with the others.[5]

Williamson comments further on his choice of librarianship as a career:

> I seem never to have reasoned my way through library work. It came about through a series of unrelated circumstances and events. . . . Never before have I had occasion to review the various steps which seem, as I now look backward some sixty years, to have added up to a library career, of sorts. I am myself amused by the process as well as the result.[6]

In a letter to Richard R. Bowker, the publisher, on September 1, [1928], he observed: "I still recall with feelings of pleasure and gratitude a cordial and helpful letter you wrote to me twenty-five years ago in reply to some questions I as a college student had the temerity to put to you. You were then and still are an economist. I was hoping to be one. Had I succeeded our paths would probably never have crossed again. Instead I was drawn into library work, which meant of course that I should have the opportunity to know you personally and I count this one of the privileges that library work has brought me."

He gave credit for his early library interest to his experience at Western Reserve University at the time when their library school was established and when he was involved as Thwing's secretary. "The whole process of organizing a new professional school I found very interesting."

One of the individuals whom Williamson credited for his growing library interest was Edward C. Williams, Librarian of the Hatch Library at Western Reserve University. The two men met soon after Williamson began working for President Thwing and they remained close friends until Williams' death in December 1929. Williamson expressed his debt to Edward C. Williams:

> Mr. Williams was a Negro who had graduated from Adelbert College at the head of his class in 1892. Not only in scholarship, but in athletics as well he had made a distinguished record and was perhaps the most popular man in his

class. Two years after graduation he was appointed librarian of the College and in the summer of 1895 attended the Amherst summer school of library economy. The year 1899-[19]00 he spent at the New York State Library School, Albany, receiving an honor first-year certificate. I must have arrived at Adelbert College within a few days time Ed Williams got back from Albany with his full credentials as a trained professional librarian. But he was not a man to flaunt his scholarship or his credentials. He was more likely to conceal them, since he was extremely modest. He was never too busy to go to any length in helping a teacher or student, or to talk about books and libraries. . . .

I do not recall that Williams ever spoke of seeing in me a recruit for the library profession. We often talked about reference books which was one of his special interests, and about cataloging and many other aspects of library work, but I think we more often talked about books, new and old. I believe I said in that Fisk University address that Williams had more to do with my eventually going into library work than any other individual.[7]

DECISION TO CHANGE CAREERS

The sequence of events which finally led to Williamson's change in careers came when Dr. John Shaw Billings, Director of the New York Public Library, wanted to start a Social Studies Department in the new building of the New York Public Library, then being built. Billings instructed his assistant, Edwin Hatfield Anderson, to find a chief for this department. Anderson in turn inquired of Johnston, Librarian at Columbia University, who spoke to Professor Seligman, Professor of Economics at Columbia. Seligman had been Williamson's major adviser during his studies at Columbia. The result was that Seligman recommended Williamson for the position. Williamson's friends knew about the situation at Bryn Mawr College and that he was looking for a new position.

Many of these friends encouraged him to enter this new career and were pleased when he decided to make the change. He wrote Ely on December 17, 1910, "The problem of a satisfactory place for next year may be solved by an opening in connection with a position in one of the great New York libraries." Williamson continues to explain what he knew about the requirements of the new position:

> I know very little of the place as yet, but it requires economic training, a general knowledge at least of library work and methods, and ability to do book collecting in the field of economics. What else it requires I do not know, but I do know that it pays an initial salary higher than I can hope to get in teaching and that it has other advantages in the way of opportunity for study and writing that I do not find in my teaching thus far. If this place turns out to be what I infer it is, I shall certainly accept it if it is offered to me.

Ely strongly encouraged him to accept. "I am inclined to think that a satisfactory position in a great public library might prove the best thing after all."

Events moved rapidly, and within a week he was offered the position and accepted it. He writes happily to Arbuthnot on Christmas Eve of 1910 that he had accepted the position as Chief of the Economics and Sociology Divsion of the New York Public Library and was "delighted to leave these hovels in Bryn Mawr to dwell in a marble palace on Fifth Avenue New York . . . It would be impossible to give you an adequate idea of the pleasure I expect to have in this work and in the opportunity to live in New York." His elated state at the prospect before him is reflected in his observation that "of all the changes I have made . . . this seems to me to be the best." Within a period of four years the "congenial and beautiful" environment at Bryn Mawr had become a "hovel."

Friends congratulated him. He had decided to leave his chosen field as an economics professor to embark on a career as a special librarian. The unpleasant situation was over, he had a new position and was going to leave Bryn Mawr. He could now plan for this new career "in the marble palace" on Fifth Avenue in New York City.

NOTES

1. *The Dictionary of American Biography* (supplement 1), p. 684.
2. *Loc. cit.*
3. *Ibid.*, p. 685.
4. *Loc. cit.*
5. Sarah K. Vann, letter from Dr. Charles C. Williamson, May 23, 1955, p. 1.
6. Sarah K. Vann, "Statement Prepared for the Use of Miss Sarah K. Vann," by Charles C. Williamson, June 27, 1955, p. 1.
7. *Ibid.*, pp. 4-5.

5
THE NEW YORK PUBLIC LIBRARY (1911-1914)

WILLIAMSON, THE LIBRARIAN

WITH THE MOVE TO THE New York Public Library, Williamson felt he was definitely in his proper element. The Library had an excellent staff, and he was able to build up an interesting and worthwhile clientele for his department.

His letter of December 17, 1910, had been transmitted to Dr. John Shaw Billings, Director of the New York Public Library. Three days later, Billings wrote Williamson at Bryn Mawr College asking if he might be interested in the position as Chief of the Department of Economics and Sociology. Billings described his plans:

> We propose to establish a special department of sociology, including economics and applied sciences, in this library, to assign to it a large room in the new library building on Fifth Avenue, next to and communicating with the room devoted to public documents. At present we have about 25,000 volumes to be placed in this department, not including the public documents under the charge of Miss Adelaide R. Hasse, which number about 75,000 volumes. To the chief of this department, if a satisfactory person can be procured, the salary at first will be at the rate of $1,800 per year. We shall move into the new building and start this department some time in May next, but it would be advisable that the man who is to be the chief of this department should come here in February, in order to perfect the preliminary arrangements.
>
> If you feel like considering the possibility of taking this position, I should be glad if you would come to New York at your convenience, take a glance at our collection and at the room in which it is proposed to place it, and discuss with me

the organization which will be desirable to make this department of the greatest possible use to the public.

On December 23, 1910, Williamson had the interview with Billings in New York City; on the next day he wrote accepting the position. He also wrote to Edwin H. Anderson, then Assistant Director, "I have already decided to accept the offer which Dr. Billings made me yesterday and I am writing to him to that effect." Williamson was particularly pleased with the personal good wishes of Billings and Anderson and declared, "You will allow me to say that your personal desire to have me join your staff, so frankly and so cordially expressed, as well as your evident confidence in the value of the opportunity presented, had great weight with me in reaching this decision."

Williamson, however, was unable to obtain a release from Bryn Mawr College until June 1911. He wrote Anderson on December 24, 1910: "I much regret that I cannot come on in February instead of the first of June, but I shall be able in the intervening weeks to take a beginning towards getting things in hand. I find that even now I am looking forward with the greatest satisfaction to the first of June."

Billings, pleased at Williamson's decision to join the staff of the New York Public Library wrote him on December 27, 1910:

> I have your letter of December 24th and am glad to know you have decided to accept the offer of a position here.
>
> I quite understand that you will not be able to come here permanently until some time next June, but that you will come over and give advice with regard to the shelving of the collection, etc.
>
> In the meantime I will submit your nomination for approval of the Executive Committee, which meets January 6, 1911. This, however, is almost purely a matter of form.

Williamson wrote Ely the day after Christmas to explain the events of a busy holiday:

Two or three days after I wrote you last I was offered the position of Chief of the Department of Economics and Sociology in the New York Public Library and after looking into the matter carefully I have accepted it. They want me to begin in February, but the College will not release me from my contract until June; so that I shall have to go over to New York as often as I can and get the work organized while carrying my courses here.

In May the New York Public Library will move into its magnificent new building at Fifth Avenue and 42nd Street which has been now so many years in the course of construction. Special provision has been made in the new building for the department which I am to organize. I am promised a very free hand in making the collection in my field as valuable as possible for reference and research. In many respects it is even now unsurpassed, but its usefulness has been greatly limited by reason of the cramped conditions in the old Astor building.

I look upon the opportunity before me as much more valuable than any teaching position likely to be open.

Although it was a personal relief for him to find a position, there is no doubt he was sincerely interested in the prospect before him. This was not a stopgap until something better came along. Of course, he may still have been disappointed to miss the extremely attractive professorship at Bowdoin, but all in all, Williamson would be doing work for which he was highly qualified.

Billings and Anderson were disappointed that Williamson would be unable to start on a full-time basis until June, but they understood the problem at Bryn Mawr and were most cooperative. Anderson informed Williamson on December 27, 1910: "While I am sorry you cannot get here before June 1st, I hope that during vacation times you may be able to familiarize yourself with our collection of economics and sociology, and its needs. Whenever you are able to run over to New York we will see that you have every facility to familiarize yourself with the affairs of the department of which you will have charge."

Thwing, Ely, and Arbuthnot were pleased with Williamson's new job and all wrote him letters of congratulations. Thwing wrote on January 3, 1911: "I am very glad for you at this tremendous opening. I wish I might send a message of congratulations to everybody whom you will serve in these next years." He had changed his mind toward librarianship as a career for his protégé.

Ely also was happy about the change and wrote on January 11, 1911: "I wish to congratulate you heartily upon your appointment. I believe that you are going to like it and that the time will soon come when you would not exchange it for any professorship in the United States." Ely, although a prominent economist, confessed, "I am free to say if the position had been offered me, I should at least have given it a very careful consideration."

During the 1911 spring term Williamson continued to teach at Bryn Mawr, although his interests now were in New York City. He was able to go there on several trips and work with the library people in the planning and organizing of the Economics Division as well as the general preparation for the opening of the new library building. On January 4, 1911, he wrote to Harry Miller Lydenberg, then Reference Librarian at the New York Public Library, of his plans and the times he would be in New York. They discussed problems of the catalog, shelving, and other library matters, indicating he was familiar with the work. At this time he was pursuing his dual role at Bryn Mawr and the New York Public Library.

This dual role required traveling from New York City to Bryn Mawr and back for just a few hours each Saturday and must have been exhausting. Actually, Williamson was working full time at his teaching job and part time at the New York Public Library. The schedule at Bryn Mawr came to thirteen hours a week, plus student advisement, work with his graduate students, and preparation for lectures. Drawing up plans for the Economics Division was an added task.

Williamson revealed to Ely some of the hectic activity of these months in a letter of February 11, 1911:

> Most of the holiday period and the mid-year period I spent in New York getting the new work started, and I am glad to say I am more and more pleased with the outlook. With my

thirteen hours teaching, however, and the necessity of giving some time and attention to the library work I shall get little time on the book I fear. The first months in New York will be rather strenuous ones, too, I anticipate; but the book is always in my mind and nothing but my regular everyday duties will interefere with it.

The book was never completed; it had a long history of delay. Although Ely felt Williamson should be the person to revise his *Taxation in American States and Cities*, this never came about. Williamson was moving further and further away from the field of economics and becoming more and more caught up in the literature of economics and in his work as a librarian.

He spent a great deal of time considering and planning his future work as Chief of the Economics Division. He wrote constantly to Billings, Anderson, Lydenberg, and others, asking for information, drawing up memorandums, discussing policy, recruiting possible staff members for the department, and getting things in order.

Williamson immediately grasped the situation at the New York Public Library and the role of the Economics Division. One of his characteristics was the ability to examine a situation, get the facts, arrive at conclusions and ideas, and set forth a course of action.

On February 1, 1911, he wrote a four-page report to Dr. Billings which displayed a remarkable understanding of the Library, the division, and what could and should be done. His comprehension of the situation at such an early stage of his library work was unusual. Since there is no indication that Billings or anyone had requested the report, it seems to have been a spontaneous statement. Williamson observed:

> Since I decided to give up teaching and accept your invitation to take charge of the Department of Economics and Sociology in the New York Public Library my mind has naturally been a good deal occupied with plans for organizing this new department so as to make it of the greatest possible service to the public.
>
> I find that the Library has at present a very fair collection in Economics and Sociology—a collection that probably de-

serves to be better known and more fully used [than] it is. But I imagine that in the past students and scholars have sought to do their work elsewhere if possible because of the meager and inadequate facilities afforded in the Astor Building. The new building, however, both because of its location and equipment, will certainly tempt the scholar and investigator to turn to the Public Library in the first instance not as a last resort.

In other words, it seems to me we must anticipate a greatly augmented demand on the resources of the Library in the new location and I very much hope that we shall be able in the next few years, beginning with the fairly good collection of books we now have, to build up a reference library in Economics and Sociology that will be a Mecca for every person interested in any branch of social science. Such an opportunity is clearly presented to us; we should not fail to take advantage of it.

I am [strongly] impressed with the idea that an absolutely unique opportunity for a great social service is open to this department of the New York Public Library, and so far as I can see now there appears to be but one element of doubt as to our ability to make the most of this opportunity. I refer to the matter of funds available for the purchase of books. In our various conferences we have not taken up this point as I would like to. May I now tell you, therefore, how very keenly I feel that it is a matter of serious importance that we should enter upon this new era in the history of the Library with a fairly adequate amount of money which can be relied upon from year to year for the purchase, not only of current literature, but in order also to go back and fill up the gaps which have been left each year in the past.

Williamson requested "an unusually large annual appropriation, $25,000 or $30,000, I should say." This must have come as a shock to Billings, since in 1911 the total appropriation for books, periodicals, and prints for the entire Reference Department came to $66,000.

Williamson stated: "Neither do I suggest an amount that will enable us to purchase everything published. It is my idea that we should continue to select only the best, as has been the rule in the past, but that we should be able to acquire more of the best and, if possible, *all* of the best in the whole field of the social sciences."

Williamson then discussed the aims and objectives of the Economics Department.

American scholars and statesman are apparently more and more inclined to inquire what light the thought and experience of foreign countries will shed on our increasingly complex social, economic, and political problems. This tendency makes at once for conservatism and progress and should be encouraged, it seems to me, in every possible way. For this practical purpose, then, if for no other, there should be built up somewhere in this country an adequate collection of the official and unofficial literature of important foreign countries touching their social, economic, and political affairs. This is hardly the function of our university libraries, even if their resources permitted it, so that this important task falls to the leading public libraries of the country, and I feel certain that it is to the New York Public Library more than to any other that the whole country will look to perform this service.

His concept of the Library as a "service agency" was unusual for a novice, particularly as it related to the role of the library in society. His report continued:

In the various ways I have indicated, and in many others, I am very sanguine that with adequate support we shall be able to make this department of the Library a real factor in the solution of the distinctly local problems of the great city of New York, a force in the public affairs of the country as a whole, and the leading center for scientific research and investigation. I sincerely hope that the time will soon come when the student, the scholar, and the public official, will turn to the New York Public Library, each in full confidence that he will find there every important piece of information bearing on his particular subject of inquiry.

This document must have either impressed or irritated Billings, depending on his mood toward budget demands. Whatever reaction Billings may have had, surely he must have realized that he had hired a competent man who already gave much thought to his new position and possessed insight into library service. The new Chief-elect of the Economics Division thought of his own work and of the entire Library on a level in keeping with its evolving place as one of the largest research libraries in the world.

The new Central Building of the New York Public Library was dedicated on May 23, 1911. Ceremonies were held in the Fifth Avenue entrance hall in the presence of about six hundred guests, including Billings and Anderson; Andrew Carnegie; members of the Board of Trustees; and national, state, and city officials, including William H. Taft, President of the United States; John A. Dix, Governor of the State of New York, and William J. Gaynor, Mayor of the City of New York. On the following day the Library officially opened to the public; the conservative count was about 50,000 visitors for that one day.

Williamson could not be present at the dedication ceremonies; however, soon afterward he moved to New York. On June 1, 1911, he began his full-time work as Chief of the Economics and Sociology Division. At this time Williamson thought of himself as "a kind of special librarian."[1]

As first Director of the newly formed New York Public Library, Billings was devoted to the idea of developing a great institution in New York. Williamson liked him, and they got along well.

Billings died on March 11, 1913. He had served as a distinguished scholar and investigator in various fields, as well as the administrator responsible for laying the foundation of public service for the Library.

Most of Williamson's work at the New York Public Library came under the direct supervision of Assistant Director Anderson, who had served in that capacity since June 1, 1908. On May 14, 1913, he was elected Director and succeeded Billings. Anderson's policy was to hire competent people and give them the responsibility of running their departments.

Williamson's earliest venture into library education took place while he was at the New York Public Library. "A school for general professional training was opened in the New York Public Library in 1911, supported by a grant from Mr. Carnegie of $15,000 a year." Williamson commented on his role in the early days of this Library School.

> At the same time that I was organizing my new department Miss Plummer was organizing the New Library School for

which Mr. Carnegie had provided funds. I cooperated with her by giving her students practice work and even gave some lectures to her classes, but I am afraid I always had a rather dim view of the nature and quality of the instruction in that school, including especially my own little part in it. Later I found that the School at the New York Public Library had the reputation of being one of the best in the country.[2]

Keyes D. Metcalf, who knew Williamson at the very beginning of his library career, stated that Williamson "lectured before the first class of the library school . . . on the literature of economics, sociology, and government."[3]

One of the first personnel problems to face Williamson at the New York Public Library was his relationship with Adelaide Hasse, who was in charge of Public Documents at the time he assumed his job as Chief of the Economics and Sociology Division. Prior to Williamson's appointment, Hasse's domain also included the material in the fields of economics and sociology. The Public Documents Division, although adjacent to the Economics Division, was separate. Hasse was not particularly pleased with Williamson's appointment and the establishment of the new division. Conflict resulted, since the work of the departments of necessity was interrelated and a degree of cooperation, though not forthcoming, was essential.

Adelaide Hasse was a rather formidable person who had achieved a reputation as an authority on public documents; she let no one cross her path. The Department of Public Documents had been established in 1897 with Hasse in charge. Hasse was a strong-willed person; so was Dr. Williamson. She constantly criticized Williamson, the Economics Division, and his entire staff. An unsigned and undated memorandum for Anderson presented the following frank account of the situation:

> Dr. Billings told Dr. Williamson when he joined the staff of the library in December [sic], 1911, that he would find Miss Hasse a hard person to get along with; that she was disappointed in not being made Head of the new Division of Economics and Sociology which Dr. Williamson was asked to organize; and that she would be jealous and would probably

do things calculated to make it difficult for him. Dr. Billings especially requested Dr. Williamson to report any difficulty he might have with Miss Hasse. Dr. Billings prediction was more than justified, although the Chief of the Economics Division seldom made complaint about her.

Hasse treated Williamson and his staff "with a studied contempt which was amusing." Later Williamson commented that "he really had problems" with Hasse.

One particular case is typical of the situation. On September 6, 1912, a reader came to the Economics Division and asked for statistics of standing timber in the Northwest. Williamson knew a report had been issued by the United States Bureau of Corporations on this particular subject, so he sent the reader to the Documents Division to ask for the report. The Documents Division, unable to find the report, stated that it did not exist. The reader returned to the Economics Division without his report. Rather than disappoint him, Williamson sent his assistant, Mr. Seaver, to the Documents Division with instructions as to where he might locate the particular document.

Williamson stated, "This failure on the part of the Documents Division was almost a daily occurrence." The incident so enraged Hasse that she wrote in the Division diary: "Dr. Williamson did not draw a clear line between his division and this one, so Miss Hasse drew one for him." On September 6, 1912, she wrote the following letter to him, which bristled with animosity:

> I think we might as well come to an understanding now that the Documents Division is a separate and independent division and not an adjunct to the Economics and Sociology Division. Courtesy as well as business, since the work of the reference divisions is measured by the numbers of readers, would seem then to dictate that we be very fair about the use of our respective rooms. If, as in the case of the Oregon lumber inquirer yesterday (and which is not the first of its kind) you had no material to answer the question, and all the material had to be taken from this room, it would have been only fair to have sent the reader here. This was particularly annoying both because all the material was from temporary records and is open to the danger of not getting back

properly, and because your messenger had to be helped to get the material. I should much prefer not to have Mr. Seaver sent here to do reference work. If I had found him efficient in document reference work, he would not have been transferred.

The unsigned memorandum to Anderson also commented on "poor Mr. Seaver," whom Hasse treated so shamefully, stating that the principal reason for this was "apparently, that Mr. Seaver was a rival to her as a documents expert. Those who know Mr. Seaver best would probably agree with Dr. Williamson that he is, not even excepting Miss Hasse, the most competent document reference worker in the United States."

According to James Child, problems developed. "With the death of Dr. John Shaw Billings on March 11, 1913, the coming of a new director, and other changes such as the merger of Public Documents with the Economics Division, a situation was created in which Miss Hasse, with boundless energy and specialized experience, did not adjust."[4] In 1918 she went to Washington, D.C., and was involved in the bibliographical work of various agencies of the U.S. government.

WILLIAMSON'S CONTRIBUTIONS TO THE LIBRARY

From 1911 to 1914 Williamson did much to develop the Economics Division and its services. When he started, the division had about 25,000 volumes; by 1914 the collection had grown to more than 70,000 volumes. Williamson was able to draw on a large clientele of library users and bring economists, professors, and sociologists to the division, thus increasing its ever-widening use.

The Economics and Sociology Division of the New York Public Library was part of the Reference Department. During the time Williamson worked there the total reference collection continued its steady growth. In 1911 the total number of books and pamphlets came to 1,142,141, which had grown to 1,271,356 by 1914. When Williamson returned to the same position from 1919 to 1921 the Reference Department Collection had reached 1,427,178 items by 1919, and by 1921 the total was 1,468,521. When he finally left the New York Public Library, in 1921, this had become a major collection of close to a million and a half items.

In addition, the number of readers and volumes used increased substantially during this period. In 1911 there were listed 246,950 readers; ten years later the count was 1,157,275. Use of volumes also increased greatly, with 911,891 being used in 1911, and 2,684,192 in 1921. The opening of the new Central Building at Fifth Avenue and 42nd Street brought a tremendously increased number of users, which continued to grow annually.

The budget for the Reference Department always came from endowments, donations, and private funds; the Department operated as a separate unit within the New York Public Library. In 1911, $426,496.16 was spent on books, reprints, periodicals, and salaries, which had grown to $979,221.20 in 1921.[5]

Williamson's goals and objectives were to make the Economics Division "of the greatest possible service to the public." He was pleased with the Division, enjoyed his work, and felt he was making an important contribution to the field of economics. He still considered himself primarily an economist, only secondarily a librarian.

While Williamson was Chief of the Economics Division he prepared *A Reader's Guide to the Addresses and Proceedings of the Annual Conferences on State and Local Taxation*, which was published in 1913 under the auspices of the National Tax Association. This forty-one page pamphlet was Williamson's answer to the request of the association for "something between an annotated catalogue and an abbreviated index, which will tell public administrators, students and readers generally, everything that can be found on a given topic in the six volumes."

From 1912 to 1916 Williamson was Tax and Finance Editor of the *American Yearbook*, published by D. Appleton and Company. He compiled and wrote the section, "Public Finance, Banking, and Insurance," a survey of the past year's events in the area of public finance. He continued his interest and activity in the field of economics.

Williamson claimed he had played a part in the development of the *New York Times Index* in 1913, but no documentary evidence has been located to substantiate the fact or reveal the extent of his activities.

MOVE TO THE MUNICIPAL REFERENCE LIBRARY

By 1913 the establishment of a Municipal Reference Library of the City of New York had become a reality. Robert Campbell was the first Municipal Reference Librarian, but a crisis developed and he resigned. Anderson turned to Williamson for help in the situation. The Municipal Reference Library had been placed under the administration of the New York Public Library, which would appoint the staff. Anderson, knowing of Williamson's interest in the field of municipal reference services, asked him to assume the duties of Municipal Reference Librarian. On October 19, 1914, Charles Williamson began his new job as the second Municipal Reference Librarian of the City of New York.

NOTES

1. Charles C. Williamson, "My Contribution to the Special Library Movement: A Symposium," *Special Libraries* 23 (May-June 1932), 213.
2. Sarah K. Vann, "Statement Prepared for the Use of Miss Sarah K. Vann," by Charles C. Williamson, June 27, 1955, p. 9.
3. Keyes D. Metcalf, "Charles C. Williamson," *Library Service News* 11 (November 1943), 23.
4. James B. Child. "Hasse, Adelaide Rosalia." in *Encyclopedia of Library and Information Science* (New York: Marcel Dekker, 1973), vol. 10, p. 376.
5. Statistics are from Harry Miller Lydenberg. *History of the New York Public Library: Astor, Lenox, and Tilden Foundations*, pp. 540-542.

6
THE MUNICIPAL REFERENCE LIBRARY OF THE CITY OF NEW YORK (1914-1918)

The Beginning of the Municipal Reference Library

Williamson commented that the move to the Municipal Reference Library "was not of my own choosing. . . . Mr. Anderson felt he needed me there, and I have never regretted that move. In many ways it broadened my library interests and helped to prepare me for the various tasks I was to undertake later."[1]

Several groups in New York City were eager to have a Municipal Reference Library. A letter of November 20, 1908, from Edwin R. Seligman, Chairman of the Library Commission of the Merchant's Association of New York, to the Honorable Charter Revision Commission suggested the desirability of an adequate Municipal Library for New York City. Seligman recommended that the library (1) be supported by the City of New York; (2) be located in City Hall, Hall of Records, or the new Municipal Building; (3) come under the custody and administration of the New York Public Library; (4) become a depository for city documents, reports, and minutes; and (5) have each department send its materials to the Municipal Reference Library.

The Municipal Reference Library was established by the Honorable William A. Prendergast, Comptroller of the City of New York. It was officially dedicated on March 31, 1913, in quarters at 280 Broadway. At this time it had a collection of about 5,000 books and pamphlets—368 purchased, while the others were gifts for the new library from the Librarian of the Department of Finance.[2]

REORGANIZATION OF THE LIBRARY

On February 4, 1914, Williamson wrote to Henry Bruere, City Chamberlain, to confirm their conversation that "the present time would seem to me to be a most opportune time to establish in the Municipal building an adequate and efficient municipal reference library to serve all departments of the city government."

On March 6, 1914, the Board of Estimate by resolution authorized the New York Public Library to assume management and to operate it as a branch in the Municipal Building. By the first of April the Municipal Reference Library had moved from 280 Broadway into quarters on the fifth floor of the Municipal Building. Robert A. Campbell had been appointed Librarian to start work with the opening of the Library. However, he resigned seven months later and was succeeded on October 19 by Williamson who was taken from the post as Chief of the Economics Division of the Reference Department.

From 1913 to 1914 the Municipal Reference Library was part of the city government, but its facilities and services were extremely limited. The New York Public Library was asked to make it a branch of the library system. Williamson was involved in the beginning of the Municipal Reference Library as part of the New York Public Library. From its establishment, until 1969 the Municipal Reference Library functioned as a unit of the New York Public Library under the supervision of its trustees and director, but with its own librarian and staff. Many years later this changed to the Municipal Reference and Research Center, under the New York City Department of Records and Information Services, and headed by a commissioner.

Williamson wrote another letter to Bruere stating that the Municipal Reference Library should be placed in the hands of the Public Library, rather than any branch of the city government, in order to keep the library independent and free from being "more closely identified with one department of the city government than with the others."

Williamson gave some indication of Anderson's problem at the Municipal Reference Library in a letter of March

7, 1921, to Edwin R. Embree of the Rockefeller Foundation.

> In regard to my work in the New York Public Library for the last ten years, no one can speak as well as Mr. E. H. Anderson, the present Director. He sent me to take charge of the Municipal Reference Library after another man who had been put in the place had failed after three or four months service, because of a lack of executive ability and ability to meet a difficult political and personnel problem.

Williamson felt this library work was of great value to him because it brought him "into more or less intimate relations with people of quite varied interests."

Williamson's letter to Bruere also revealed some of his ideas about a municipal reference library and its plan of operation.

> Without attempting at present to suggest what in my opinion such a library ought to be and so do, I would like to mention just one thing suggested by our talk. It seems to me that a well-trained and efficient librarian might do a very good work by studying the needs, conscious and unconscious, actual and potential, of the various departments and then call to their attention each week, or more or less frequently, the new books, articles, reports, etc., which should interest them. In other words, the library ought, I should say, not only to collect the best material on every phase of the city's problems, but should also proceed with tact and wisdom to tempt hundreds of city employees to use it.

Rebecca Rankin, Municipal Reference Librarian from 1920 to 1952, commented on Williamson's work in an article memorializing him.

> When the City of New York and the New York Public Library made an agreement to provide a Municipal Reference Library for the use of City officials and employees in 1914, Dr. C. C. Williamson was chosen as Librarian. He showed his skill as an organizer and administrator of a new collection and established a model that other municipalities have followed. New York's Municipal Reference Library has grown into the largest and best known of local government libraries.[3]

Paul North Rice, in commenting on this phase of Williamson's career, stated:

> The New York City Board of Estimate in 1914 decided to establish a Municipal Reference Library and authorized the New York Public Library to assume its management. This was the first such library in the United States to serve merely the departments of a city and CCW became its organizer and director.[4]

Keyes Metcalf, former Librarian of Harvard University, stated, "In the following fifteen years when Dr. Williamson was still not widely known, he found time to lay the foundations for the Municipal Reference Branch of the New York Public Library which has been a model ever since."[5]

In an article entitled "Some Aspects of the Work of the New York Municipal Reference Library," which appeared in the October 1915 issue of *Library Journal*, Williamson expressed his views on the functions and responsibilities of a municipal reference library. The article described the work, duties, and functions of the Library as it existed then, as well as his evaluation of its services. He stated that he was pleased with the use of the library, indicating that from "November 1914 to June 1915, the number of volumes circulated increased 200 per cent, while other lines of activity expanded in like proportion."[6] He felt that the "large number of employees and the magnitude and complexity of the city's problems present a large and rich field for library service—a field which in its first year and a half the library has only begun to cultivate."[7] Williamson stated that "New York City has on its payroll about 85,000 regular officials and employees" requiring library service.

He described the purpose of the New York Municipal Reference Library as "primarily a library; it collects and makes available the latest and best materials which are likely to be of use in the manifold activities of any of the city departments. It is not an investigating agency; it is not often called upon to prepare formal reports either for legislative or administrative officials."[8] He felt that the presence of "many trained investigators and specialized investigating bureaus creates a special demand for a well-equipped and efficient library service."[9] He also mentioned the job of preservation which the library must do in attempting to collect and preserve a file of all the publications of all the departments.

Williamson clarified the role of this library as it affected similar institutions in the United States: "A central bureau of information and reference to which officials may turn when need arises is coming to be considered an indispensable adjunct to a city government."[10]

MUNICIPAL REFERENCE LIBRARY NOTES

In the same article he commented on the establishment and purpose of the *Municipal Reference Library Notes*.

> To avoid waste involved in acquiring material which, however valuable, may never be called for, the library in October, 1914, began the publication of a weekly bulletin entitled *Municipal Reference Library Notes*. The principle feature is a classified list of recent additions. In this way new books, reports, periodical articles, etc., are called to the attention of those who can make the information of value in the public service. About 1,600 copies of the *Notes* are distributed directly to employees who desire them. The response to this enterprise has been prompt and enthusiastic.[11]

In the first issue of the new periodical Williamson publicized the new Municipal Reference Library to the officials and employees of the City of New York, asking, "Do you know that there is in the Municipal Building a reference library devoted to municipal problems?"[12] The issue then presented a brief history of the formative period of the library.

> After several years of planning and agitation by various individuals and organizations a library was started in 1913 by Comptroller Prendergast from savings made in the conduct of his department. In a short time it proved to be so great a help in the City's business that when the Finance Department moved into the Municipal Building the new library was consolidated with the old one in the City Hall. At the same time the scope was enlarged and its general administration

put into the hands of the New York Public Library. A commodious room was assigned to it on the fifth floor of the Municipal Building. The collections were moved to the new quarters on April 1st, and in spite of chaotic conditions, the library opened its doors at once. The necessity of acquiring much new material, while at the same time providing the regular service to readers, has caused considerable delay in getting things in order. A part of the equipment, including the book shelves, is still of a temporary character.[13]

In the February 10, 1915, issue of the *Notes*, he included a new feature called the "Monthly List of New York City Publications."

Thus, Williamson developed the Municipal Reference Library of the City of New York. He started work there on October 19, 1914, and left in May 1918, having worked during four formative years to establish the pattern and guidelines which the library would follow. Although today the services and facilities have expanded, the policies and objectives are very similar to those established by Charles C. Williamson in 1914.

Looking back at his work at the Municipal Reference Library Williamson stated, "During my entire service in the Municipal Reference Library I published a simple little weekly bulletin, which we called *Municipal Reference Library Notes*. It served a very useful purpose and has been kept up by my successors."

In 1932 he made another observation concerning his work at the Municipal Reference Library.

> Perhaps by ignoring the contributions of my able associates I could claim that there was something worth mentioning in my service as librarian of the New York Municipal Reference Library from October, 1914 to May, 1918. It had been started a few months before I was put in charge, but I have always had the pleasurable feeling of being its creator. Certainly there was one little by-product of that work which gave me no little satisfaction as long as I was responsible for it. I refer to the Municipal Reference Library *Notes* which I started in October, 1914, and which has been continued without interruption until the present time, for many years now under the capable direction of Miss Rankin. Yes, I think there is

something distinctive about these sixteen volumes of *Notes*, though I was responsible for only the first four.[14]

Williamson also presented his views of municipal reference library service in an article, which appeared in the September 1916 issue of *Special Libraries,* called "The Public Official and the Special Library." In this article he commented that the properly conducted municipal reference library is "in reality a bureau of economy and efficiency; it performs that function principally in saving the time and energy, not only of the high salaried officials, but of the whole body of employees. Personal service is the largest item in a municipal budget."[15]

Later in the article he commented on the active role a municipal reference library should take in city affairs.

> The library should not only economize the time of officials and employees in the routine process of getting together the bare facts of many kinds which are required in the administration of any department, but it should also provide for the officials in executive positions an opportunity to keep abreast of progress, at least in their particular field.[16]

He observed: "The expert in public office will make the fullest use of the library, but he will manage in some way to get the information he needs even without it. The politician in public office needs the library most of all."[17]

In this article Williamson expressed his belief that the "public official who knows, who bases his conclusions upon accurate information, will make few mistakes, and few poor decisions. In the process of acquiring a mastery of the business in hand, whatever it may be, the public official should find the special library his most dependable aid."[18]

He believed the purpose of a municipal reference library was to aid the official in meeting higher standards of efficiency in both public and private business. To this end the special library has developed as an agency for gathering data on every subject in which he may be interested and putting it before him in a form which will give him what he needs with the least effort. The special library, in other words, represents a specialization of function to secure efficiency and economy.

Williamson also believed strongly in a central municipal reference library rather than an endless number of small libraries spread throughout the various departments. He considered a central library particularly essential because all municipal departments covered a wide range of subjects and there was frequent overlapping.

The budget of the Municipal Reference Library increased from a limited amount in 1913-1914 (which came from special revenue bonds) to $13,450 in 1915 and $18,530 in 1918. Library attendance rose from 6,693 in 1915 to a high of 33,137 the following year. There was a decline in 1917 to 27,696 and again in 1918 to 22,350. Book circulation also reflected a high of 11,356 in 1916 and a low of 7,352 in 1918. Except for the drop during World War I, the use of the Municipal Reference Library steadily increased.[19]

Related Activities During This Period

During the time he was working at the Municipal Reference Library, Williamson was active with professional groups and associations and with a few publications pertaining to the field of taxation. He wrote and edited most of the material which went into the 1915 and 1916 editions of the *Municipal Year Book of the City of New York*, although he did not receive personal credit for this work the first year. However, the 1916 foreword did make an acknowledgment:

> The object of the Municipal Year Book is to present in concise and intelligible form the most important facts relating to the city government. The Year Book of 1915 has proved its value and worth not only to the citizens and officials of New York, but also to officials and citizens elsewhere who are interested in governmental administration in this city. The Municipal Year Books of 1915 and 1916 have been compiled by Dr. C. C. Williamson, Librarian of the Municipal Reference Library, in cooperation with the city departments and county offices.

Williamson commented on his work for the *Municipal Year Book* in a letter of March 7, 1921, to Edwin R. Embree, Secretary of the Rockefeller Foundation.

> While I was in charge of the Municipal Reference Library I prepared and published for two years a Municipal Year Book of the City of New York. This is to be sure a very modest affair, but it might be said that I had to do it almost single handed. To get it printed at the expense of the City of New York I had to put it through the Mayor's Office.

Williamson also wrote two articles on taxation: "Shall New York City Untax Buildings?" which appeared in the June 24, 1916, issue of *The Survey*, and "State Budget Reform," which came out in the March 1917 issue of *Case and Comment*, reflecting his continuing interest in the field of economics.

During his association with the Municipal Reference Library he was also associate editor of both the *American Political Science Review* and the *National Municipal Review*.

In 1916 he was a committee member on New Sources of Revenue of the National Municipal League as well as chairman of the National Municipal League's Committee on Municipal Reference Libraries.

In 1917 he became secretary of the Mayor's Committee on Publication of the *Minutes of the Common Council of the City of New York, 1784-1831*. He was deeply involved in this publication, which would fill a gap existing in the published *Minutes*. Williamson also was responsible for all the pertinent orders and correspondence.

Wilson and Tauber commented about Williamson's contribution to the *Minutes of the Common Council*.

> Another publication . . . for which Williamson was responsible was *The Minutes of the Common Council of the City of New York, 1784-1831*. Williamson had noticed that scholars and city officials were constantly going through the bulky and more or less illegible volumes housed in the city clerk's office. He secured appropriations for editing the records, which were issued in 1917 in nineteen volumes, and for a two-volume index, issued in 1930.[20]

Looking back on his work on the *Minutes of the Common Council*, Williamson himself stated in the letter to Edwin Embree:

> While in the City Service I conceived the notion of putting into print the manuscript minutes of the Common Council of the City of New York, 1784-1831, and was able to interest Mayor Mitchel and Comptroller Prendergast in it, with the result that the city appropriated about $45,000 for the purpose. The work required some two years and was carried on by a competent editor under my supervision as Secretary of the Mayor's Committee. The printed set comprises nineteen volumes of 800 pages each.

CONTRIBUTIONS TO THE PUBLIC AFFAIRS
INFORMATION SERVICE

The Public Affairs Information Service was established to serve as a "cooperative organization for collecting, classifying and disseminating information upon all questions relating to government, finance, social welfare, current legislation and other matters of public concern."[21] The broad objective was to keep legislative, municipal, and public affairs reference librarians in touch with materials of interest and to use them in their work.

The bulletin's task was to obtain information about:

1. findings of special legislative committees
2. special reports of state and local government departments
3. important current legislation
4. publications of international, national, and local associations and organizations interested in special subjects
5. programs and proceedings of conventions called by such organizations and associations
6. new books dealing with social and economic problems
7. university bulletins issued on topics of interest to cooperators
8. addresses delivered by public men at important gatherings

9. typewritten bibliographies and digests of legislation.[22]

During the time Williamson was librarian of the Municipal Reference Library he worked on the Advisory Board of the Public Affairs Information Service. According to Wilson and Tauber: "As chief of the advisory board in 1918, he effected certain changes which have remained as permanent features of the service. The usefulness to scholars of this service, dealing with pamphlets, documents, and other ephemeral materials, has long been recognized as of the highest order.[23]

In the March 7, 1921, letter to Edwin Embree he described his role.

> You may be interested in the Public Affairs Information Service, a bibliographical service controlled and supported cooperatively by the more important reference and research libraries. For several years I have been Chairman of the Publication Committee, but the actual management of the service was largely left to the editor and the publisher, the H. W. Wilson Co. Two years ago I discovered that the enterprise has accumulated a deficit of over $3,000. At the request of the Committee I therefore took personal charge, not only of the editorial management, but also of the finances. We have now cleared up the deficit, in spite of an enormous increase in the cost of printing and a considerable increase in the salaries of the staff. The total business this year will amount to about $15,000. I am taking the liberty of enclosing a descriptive circular in the package. You have the service bulletin in your library.

In later years the *Public Affairs Information Service Bulletin* commented on Williamson's contributions during its formative years.

> The early period was an uneasy time for the *Bulletin*, struggling as it was as a cooperative venture, mimeographed, and financially weak.
> . . . It was Dr. Williamson, working in his persuasive and imaginative way with "reasonable" men, who convinced H. W. Wilson, Edwin Anderson and notable librarians that the

Bulletin had a more substantial role to play. He was responsible for its becoming a printed and cumulated publication; he worked out its finances—serving as his own accountant—and he negotiated the transfer of the enterprise to the Economics Division of The New York Public Library, where he was Chief of the Division, and had ready access to the library's vast receipts.

At the library, he examined the publications as they arrived and made selections of items for inclusion in the *Bulletin*, he chose a staff notable for its competence, and he proceeded to see that the *Bulletin* paid full attention to the proceedings of societies and organizations, the documents of the United States and of the separate states, of cities, as well as foreign documents in the English language. He moved to a more substantial coverage of pamphlet material, fugitive publications and the significant periodicals. He wanted to "see progress, to give better service, and to make the *Bulletin* available to more libraries."[24]

Williamson's contributions to the *Bulletin* were the expansion of its coverage and size, increase in its membership, and its establishment as a guide to the literature in the fields it covered. The *Bulletin*, "as published today, is the *Bulletin* he brought about. Its format is similar, its contents—while expanded—derive from the arrangement which he made; the ideas of its coverage are still observed."[25]

The H. W. Wilson Company continued as printer, although editorial work was carried on at the Economics Division of the New York Public Library.

Many librarians acknowledged Williamson's contributions to the *Bulletin*. George S. Godard, State Librarian of Connecticut, wrote him on May 27, 1921:

> Just a word to express to you my appreciation of the splendid work you have done upon the publication of the Public Affairs Information Service not only during the time of your editorship but also as a member of the committee having this work in charge prior to your editorship. I feel that your going will be a real loss not only to the service but also to our circle of friendship in the committee. I certainly hope your going to the Rockefeller Institute does not mean the complete severing of your interests in the service.

Many years later Williamson commented on his work for PAIS.

> There is another long series of bound volumes on my library shelves in which I had a small share. The *Public Affairs Information Service* as a whole seems to be a very real contribution to the special library movement, though I should not claim that my part in it was in any way distinctive. I was not in on it in the beginning, but I think I became a member of its advisory committee during its second year. Some years later, as chairman of the committee, I arranged to have it edited at the New York Public Library, where it could utilize for the benefit of its subscribers the wealth of material pouring into that great institution. Two or three years later the chairmanship and management of the P.A.I.S. passed to Rollin A. Sawyer, in whose hands it has greatly prospered.[26]

Rebecca Rankin made the following observation about Williamson's work for PAIS and its value for special libraries:

> Dr. Williamson was also one of the promoters of a new index, the Public Affairs Information Service, which was established in 1913 under the editorship of Dr. John Lapp. Dr. Williamson made available to the editors of the P.A.I.S., the printed resources of the Economics Division of the NYPL, and they have continued to be the basis of this always successful Index.[27]

Marian C. Manley described the value of PAIS to business librarians.

> One of the steps that was of marked value to all business libraries as well as to any student of economics and sociology took place in 1919, when Dr. Williamson, who had been head of the New York Municipal Reference Library again became head of the Economics Division. Dr. Williamson was also chairman of the Publication Committee of PAIS and from the vantage point of the Economics Division two problems became clear. Comparatively few of the materials that would be indexed in PAIS were flowing naturally into the Wilson Offices for use in such an index. On the other hand, the New York Public Library had an abundant intake of valuable

material from all over the world, both free and purchased. Dr. Williamson's recommendation for the transferance of the Editorial Offices of PAIS from the H. W. Wilson Company to the Economics Divison was approved with benefit to us all.[28]

In the early years John Lapp, as Chairman, was the driving force; he was succeeded by Charles Williamson, who in turn was followed by Rollin A. Sawyer in 1921. Lapp was responsible for founding the *Bulletin*, Williamson developed it as it is known today, and Sawyer made it an economically feasible and continuing publication.

On February 1, 1963, John Fall, then Chairman of the Publications Committee, wrote Williamson, "We cannot but envy you your accomplishment, especially having been the person who made it possible for PAIS to emerge from a transient mimeographed Bulletin to an Index which is a brilliant and permanent record of our society."

In a letter to Louis Round Wilson on January 4, 1943, Williamson reflected on the fact that he considered his contributions to the Public Affairs Information Service "my most important achievement in the bibliographical field."

President of the Special Libraries Association

From 1916 to 1917 Williamson was Vice-President of the Special Libraries Association serving under the presidency of F. N. Morton. In 1916 Morton was unable to continue as president and the Executive Committee of the Special Libraries Association elected Williamson to the presidency to fill the vacancy. Williamson served as President from 1916 to 1918.

He was always interested in the work of this group, since he had helped it in its early years. In 1915 he had established the New York Association of the Special Libraries Association and served as its president for two years.

His term as president began at the end of the association's first decade of existence. He felt "the mere fact that such an association exists may have been of some value."[29] In his presidential address, Williamson mentioned some of the association's accomplishments—successful conferences, establishment of local units, publication of *Special Libraries*, opening of new special libraries, growth in membership, effects of the Special Libraries Association on changes in special libraries, and new publications of interest and value to special librarians—all of which he considered positive contributions.

Williamson was particularly eager for the Special Libraries Association to set about the task of reorganization, which would involve better business and financial record keeping, revision of the constitution, and other changes within the association. He was critical of the rather loose structure which made it difficult for anyone to obtain necessary facts; the association lacked adequate direction and guidance. Thus, he hoped the association membership would consider his suggestions and not misinterpret his criticism, because he "simply felt it to be my duty to point out in a purely impersonal way some conditions which seem to me to call for serious consideration by our entire membership."

Williamson also was a member of the Advisory Board of the Special Libraries Association, serving as district member for New York from 1913 to 1916.

DECISION TO LEAVE THE MUNICIPAL REFERENCE LIBRARY

While he was working at the Municipal Reference Library, Williamson made inquiries about other positions. The good relationship between the city officials and the library during the administration of Mayor Mitchel changed radically when Mayor Hyland came into office. "It was his regime that led Williamson to leave the Municipal Reference Library."[30]

This was part of the reason Williamson wrote to Professor Bourne of Western Reserve University on January 17, 1916. "For some time Mrs. Williamson and I have felt that it would be wise for me to watch for an opportunity for me to get into a university library. My present work is very interesting and very important, but its future depends rather too much upon political conditions. Mrs. Williamson and I have both missed the college atmosphere a great deal." He asked Bourne to plead his cause at Yale University. Professor John C. Schwab, Librarian of Yale, had died; Williamson wondered if he might be considered for this position. He wrote President Arthur T. Hadley, of Yale, on January 14, 1916, indicating his interest. Williamson stated his reasons for desiring to change to university work, which were "based partly on personal grounds, with which I need not trouble you now, and partly on certain political conditions in New York City which seem to threaten the usefulness of my present position."

In a letter of February 22, 1916, Hadley informed Williamson that the Library Committee had studied his letter and references, but "under our present conditions we appear to need a somewhat different type of experience and training from that which you have had." Although Williamson regretted not getting the position, he was "grateful for their consideration."

He received a letter from the War Department on September 7, 1918, which stated, "I have your letter of September 4th, and shall be glad to look out for anything that may present itself here." The letter does not indicate the nature of the request.

On May 1, 1918, Williamson left the Municipal Reference Library to begin work for the Carnegie Corporation of New York on their Study of the Methods of Americanization, thereby leaving his seven-year career in library work to become a statistician.

EVALUATION OF WILLIAMSON'S WORK AS MUNICIPAL REFERENCE LIBRARIAN

Commissioner Eugene Bockman stated in a letter to the author on October 9, 1967, that "there is no doubt in my mind that Dr. Charles C. Williamson really established the sound foundations upon which the library has developed, grown and contributed to government and administration in New York." Bockman felt that the high quality of service to local government officials "can be traced to the philosophy of service established by Dr. Williamson and continued by his most distinguished successor, Rebecca Browning Rankin."

Bockman further commented on Williamson's work as Municipal Reference Librarian:

> It was Dr. Williamson who implemented many of Comptroller Prendergast's guidelines for the operation of this library. Dr. Williamson also was the first editor of the MUNICIPAL REFERENCE LIBRARY NOTES—although he was preceded for seven months by one Robert Campbell. Dr. Williamson also established the Public Health Division of the Municipal Reference Library—(now known as the Haven Emerson Public Health Library—a branch of the Municipal Reference Library). An examination of the early files of the library shows that Dr. Williamson showed great initiative in establishing relationships with high city officials. It was this pattern of relationships, reinforced by the long and skilled tenure of Miss Rankin, that placed the library in the center of administrative and governmental action in New York City.

In the same letter Bockman observed that the Municipal Reference Library works directly with the "highest City officials and is charged with the responsibility of providing information and materials on around the clock basis. This notion of service to city government was established by Dr. Williamson and successive Municipal Reference Librarians have had a solid base upon which to build." In 1977 local law brought about a change in the organization of the Municipal Reference Library, and it was expanded and its duties and functions enlarged. The present structure is that of the New York City Department of Records and Information Services, with Idilio Gracia-Peña as Commissioner. Bockman retired in 1989. This is served by subunits including an Administrative Unit, Municipal Archives, Municipal Reference and Research Center, and the Municipal Records Center. Dr. Williamson would be pleased that the library has continued to grow as part of city government service. This present structure is in keeping with his goal that the library should serve as a "central bureau of information and reference to which officials may turn when need arises [and] is coming to be considered as an indispensable adjunct to city government."

NOTES

1. Sarah K. Vann, "Statement Prepared for the Use of Miss Sarah K. Vann," by Charles C. Williamson, June 27, 1955, p. 9.
2. "The Municipal Reference Library of the City of New York," February 16, 1920, (typewritten) p. 1.
3. Rebecca B. Rankin, "Dr. C. C. Williamson: In Memoriam," *Special Libraries* 56 (February 1965), 120.
4. Paul North Rice, "Editorial Forum: Charles C. Williamson," *Library Journal* 68 (June 15, 1943), 522.
5. Keyes D. Metcalf, "Charles C. Williamson," *Library Service News* 11 (November 1943), 23.
6. Charles C. Williamson, "Some Aspects of the Work of the New York Municipal Reference Library," *Library Journal* 40 (October 1915), 714.
7. *Loc. cit.*
8. *Ibid.*, p. 715.
9. *Loc. cit.*
10. *Loc. cit.*
11. *Loc. cit.*
12. *Municipal Reference Library Notes* 1 (October 28, 1914), 1.
13. *Ibid.*, pp. 1-2.
14. Charles C. Williamson, "My Contribution to the Special Library Movement: A Symposium," *Special Libraries* 23 (May-June 1932), 213.
15. Charles C. Williamson, "The Public Official and the Special Library," *Special Libraries* 7 (September 1916), 114.
16. *Ibid.*, p. 115.
17. *Loc. cit.*
18. *Loc. cit.*
19. Municipal Reference Library of the City of New York, "Budgets," 1914-1918 (typewritten).
20. Louis Round Wilson and Maurice F. Tauber, *The University Library*, 2nd ed., p. 544.
21. Public Affairs Information Service, "Brochure," n.d., p. 1.
22. *Ibid.*, p. 2.
23. Wilson and Tauber, *op. cit.*, p. 544.
24. Charles C. Williamson (biographical sketch). "Charles C. Williamson, 1877-1965," *Public Affairs Information Service Bulletin*, 1965, p. 1.
25. *Loc. cit.*
26. Charles C. Williamson, "My Contribution," p. 213.

27. Rebecca B. Rankin, *op. cit.*, p. 120.
28. Marian C. Manley, "Personalities in the Fifty Years of Business Library Service," n.d. (typewritten), pp. 9-10.
29. "Presidential Address of Dr. C. C. Williamson," *Special Libraries*, 8 (September 1917), 100.
30. Phyllis Dain, "Notes of a Taped Interview with Charles C. Williamson," October 28, 1964, p. 11.

7
THE CARNEGIE CORPORATION OF NEW YORK AND THE AMERICANIZATION STUDY (1918-1919)

WILLIAMSON, THE STATISTICIAN

A BRIEF EPISODE IN Williamson's career involved his work as a statistician for the Carnegie Corporation of New York after he left the Municipal Reference Library.

Williamson discussed some of his activities during World War I in the letter of March 7, 1921, to Edwin Embree.

> I referred today to my Liberty Loan work. That of course was "War work," though I was paid a regular salary as statistician of the Advertising Bureau which was under the direction of Mr. James M. Clarke, now a Vice-President of the National Bank of Commerce. I had no administrative responsibility at all in this connection, my function being mainly to scrutinize every piece of publicity matter and O.K. it from the point of view of accuracy as to fact and impression.
>
> Following this work for the Liberty Loan organization the Guaranty Trust Company through Mr. Harold L. Stanley and Mr. Whitlebey of the Bond Department, offered me a position on the research staff, but I did not care to accept it because it seemed to lead away from administrative work. I believe they said at that time they would make it a standing offer.

Williamson then was tempted away from library work for a few months to become Statistician for the Carnegie Corporation's Americanization Study.

Williamson commented on his activities and work for this study:

Early in 1918 I had left my position as librarian of the Municipal Reference Library to do research work on an ambitious Americanization Study undertaken by the Carnegie Corporation. My title in that set-up was "statistician." The results of the Study were published in a set of ten volumes. This was not as much of a break with my previous work as it may appear on the surface to have been. I had taken my doctorate in economics and sociology and my library work from 1911 to 1918 had been closely related to various kinds of research in public affairs of one sort or another. A little earlier, at the beginning of World War I, I had taken leave of absence from my library work to serve as statistician for the Federal Reserve Bank's Liberty Loan campaign.[1]

THE CARNEGIE AMERICANIZATION STUDY

The Carnegie Corporation's Study of the Methods of Americanization, or Fusion of Native and Foreign Born, developed into a series of monographs written by competent people in various fields. The main purpose of the study was to examine the "existing methods by which Americanization is being fostered."[2]

According to the general statement of purpose,

> our country has suddenly realized the need for uniting all her people in common aims and efforts for the general welfare. Various agencies have arisen in the past twenty-five years, and other and older influences and experiences are potent in fusing the foreign with the native born into national solidarity. Many of these have done useful work; it may be possible that others need to be added. In any case, the present time seems fitted for an examination of these various agencies and processes, their operation, their success and their aims and usefulness for the future.[3]

Allen T. Burns was the director of the study, Adele McKinnie was the assistant to the director; C. C. Williamson was the statistician. The Advisory Council consisted of John Graham Brooks of Cambridge; John M. Glenn, Director of the Russell Sage Foundation; Theodore Roosevelt of New York; and John A. Voll, President of the National Glass Bottle Blower's Association.

The study was divided into ten sections: Schooling of the Immigrant; Press and Theater; Adjustment of Homes and Family Life; Legal Protection and Correction; Health Standards and Care; Naturalization and Political Life; Industrial and Economic Amalgamation; Treatment of Immigrant Heritages; Neighborhood Agencies and Organization; and Rural Developments. Each section was supervised by a chief who was a specialist of national influence in the field. An informational, statistical, and bibliographical division was organized under Williamson's direction to serve as a supplement to the work of the sections.

The Americanization Study was to be a thorough, comparative, and constructive examination. Its purpose was to learn what methods were used in each of the areas under study and to examine typical communities illustrating how these methods worked. The comparisons were intended to yield facts and statistics indicating the effectiveness of the different methods by which Americanization was being fostered. "Americanization" was defined as

> the uniting of new with native born Americans in fuller common understanding and appreciation to secure by means of self-government the highest welfare of all. Such Americanization should perpetuate no unchangeable political, domestic, and economic regime delivered once for all to the fathers, but a growing and broadening national life, inclusive of the best wherever found. With all our rich heritages, Americanism will develop best through a mutual giving and taking of contributions from both newer and older Americans in the interest of the common weal. This study will follow such an understanding of Americanization.[4]

Williamson was involved in much of the research and data gathering for the entire study. He wrote certain sections himself. Although he had a staff to help him, he did most of the checking and verification of facts.

According to Wilson and Tauber:

In the Americanization studies, published under the direction of Allen T. Burns (by Harper, in ten volumes), Williamson recruited a small staff of trained librarians to assist the research workers in carrying out the studies. Although his work was anonymous, he participated in the preparation of the entire work and compiled the greater part of the material for the volume *Americans by Choice*, by John Palmer Gavit.[5]

RETURN TO THE NEW YORK PUBLIC LIBRARY

During this time Williamson still was listed as Chief of the Economics Division of the New York Public Library. Before the Americanization research job at the Carnegie Corporation was completed he was prevailed upon by Mr. Anderson, then Director of the New York Public Library, to go back to the position he had in the Library from 1911 to 1914, its scope and responsibilities to be much enlarged. Toward the completion of the Carnegie study he divided his time between the two jobs, which were only a few blocks apart.

After this one-year hiatus, Williamson returned to the New York Public Library staff by October 1918, and early in 1919 he returned to his former position as Chief of the Economics Division on a full-time basis. The work on the Americanization Study was completed.

On March 21, 1921, Williamson wrote Edwin Embree giving an appraisal of his work with the Americanization Study.

> My experience with Mr. Allen T. Burns of the Americanization Study was pleasant enough but did not satisfy me at all. I did not feel that my division produced the results it should have had. I had only a small staff and most of them had to be trained. By the time the training was finished the survey was completed.

NOTES

1. Sarah K. Vann, letter from Dr. Charles C. Williamson, May 23, 1955, p. 3.

2. Carnegie Corporation of New York, "Study of the Methods of Americanization" (leaflet), p. 1.
3. *Loc. cit.*
4. *Ibid.*, pp. 4-5.
5. Louis Round Wilson and Maurice F. Tauber, *The University Library*, 2nd ed., p. 544.

8
BACK TO THE NEW YORK PUBLIC LIBRARY (1919-1921)

ON OCTOBER 8, 1918, Edwin H. Anderson stated in a memorandum to the library staff of the New York Public Library:

> Dr. C. C. Williamson has been reappointed Chief of the Economics Division, and until he is able to assume his duties Mr. Metcalf will supervise the administration of the Division and Miss Eunice H. Miller will be in charge of the reference work.

Anderson was confronted with a certain personnel crisis to which he felt Williamson's return was the solution. The documents give no indication of the nature of the crisis.

GROWING REPUTATION AS A LIBRARIAN

Karl K. Kitchen wrote of Williamson's accomplishments in the Economics Division under the byline "Clevelander Knows Nearly Everything." In glowing and fanciful prose Kitchen observes:

> Where the stacks of books run high in the New York Public Library a rather young-looking man, with "Harvey Cheaters," hedged in by papers, pamphlets, and volumes, answers queries and directs the gaining of information all day. Seventy thousand books and three times as many pamphlets are on the shelves around him. At any moment any one of these books may be needed for research work. The title will not be called for—someone will ask for a bit of information that one of

107

them contains and the young man at the desk is supposed to do the rest.[1]

Kitchen listed the young man's qualifications.

> When such requests come, Dr. Charles C. Williamson, chief librarian of the economics division of the public library, does not fail. He needs no card catalogs. Through years of sociological research, through reading day and night, through scanning contents pages and hurrying through the text of the thousands of volumes, he has come to have a "speaking acquaintance" with them all.[2]

Although this was an exaggerated account, it did indicate Williamson's reputation as an effective reference librarian. Of particular interest were the comments about contributions Williamson made, not only by reason of his ability as a reference librarian, but also due to the growth and development of the Economics Division.

> When Dr. Williamson took charge of the economics division at the library it occupied one room. Today it occupies the entire north wing, having grown more rapidly than any other library department, due to the widespread interest in economics. In fact, the number of people using its reference books has doubled in the last year.[3]

The article also indicated that Williamson was occupied in various war activities. These activities were not specified, although it can be assumed that they were the Americanization Study and work for the Liberty Loan Campaign.

With regard to Williamson's ability for working in a reference library, Kitchen stated: "Dr. Williamson must know exactly where to find the information desired—and that is why his memory is so keenly developed. . . . Dr. Williamson's responsibility as a walking encyclopedia is not confined to New York. Every day letters come from every part of the country requesting information. Most of them are plausible and can be answered. Many are foolish. But they are all handled by the librarian.[4]

Williamson's work at the New York Public Library included the reorganization of the Economics Division, which was constantly growing and needed more space. On September 29, 1919, he submitted to the director a full and detailed plan for extending the division. His constant concern for proper planning remained strong throughout his life.

Metcalf commented on Williamson's activities during this time.

> In the following fifteen years when Dr. Williamson was still not widely known, he found time to . . . organize, and later reorganize on a broader scale, the Economics Division—including documents, government, and sociology—of the New York Public Library into a unit which, under the direction of the successor whom he trained, stands without a peer in the library world.[5]

Williamson was always pleased about his contributions to library work, and his association with the New York Public Library and the Municipal Reference Library. He felt his activities there had done a great deal for his reputation and his acquaintance in academic circles, which he claimed in the March 7, 1921, letter to Edwin Embree were "pretty extensive, partly because of my relation to both Columbia University and the University of Wisconsin, but mainly because my work in the New York Public Library has constantly brought me in contact with scholars from all parts of the country."

DEVELOPMENT OF INTEREST IN LIBRARY EDUCATION

During this time Williamson became better known in library circles in the United States because of articles on the subject of library education. These articles, presenting his personal point of view and appearing in various issues of *Library Journal,* included "The Need of a Plan for Library Development,"[6] in the September, 1918 issue; "Efficiency in Library Management,"[7] in February 1919; and "Some Present-Day Aspects of Library Training,"[8] in September 1919. These articles were read and widely discussed by many people in the library profession.

Although librarians long had been aware of the problems inherent in library training, Williamson's articles set the library world to thinking again about these problems. The articles widened his reputation; he received many letters of approval, criticism, and praise.

At this stage of his career, Williamson turned to library training and became its outstanding critic. One of the reasons for this development may have been his close relationship and work with the Carnegie Corporation of New York. By 1918 the corporation was decidedly interested in obtaining facts about the status of library training. Williamson was working for the corporation, although in an entirely separate area, yet it is possible that through this connection he became aware of the problem. Since he was a person trained in the scientific method, as well as a librarian, he may have turned his thoughts logically to this area. The corporation, with corresponding logic, considered the possibility of his undertaking the survey. On October 17, 1964, Williamson commented in a letter to the author, "You may care to look at some addresses I made prior to undertaking the study which may have had something to do with the Corporation's decision to ask me to do the job."

Williamson considered some of his ideas to be revolutionary and stated in a letter of February 14, 1919, to Alice S. Tyler, then President of the Association of American Library Schools, that he would like to discuss with the "members of your Association some of the Bolshevist ideas I have about Library Schools." On February 25 he wrote again to Tyler announcing, "It now appears that the Carnegie Corporation may undertake some study of training for library work in the not distant future." Williamson was involved with library problems at a national level; the profession was becoming aware of him.

WILLIAMSON'S IDEAS ON LIBRARY EDUCATION

It is also possible that James Bertram of the Carnegie Corporation suggested to Williamson that he express his views regarding librarianship and library education. The article, "The Need of a Plan for Library Development," might have been generated in this way.

In this article, he proposed the establishment of a purely graduate library school to be conducted as part of a university. "Library school faculties are inadequate to meet the need for trained personnel in the higher ranks. The existing schools are doing good work, though perhaps their courses are not as flexible as they should be in view of the great diversity of requirements in the positions which graduates are called upon to occupy."

The article entitled "Efficiency in Library Management" was an address which Williamson gave to the Indiana Library Trustees' Association and the Indiana Library Association on January 6, 1919, which was reprinted in *Library Journal* in February 1919. In this address he set forth guidelines and principles for the library profession. He concentrated on the concept of library service. "Library development suffers, in my opinion, from a fundamental failure on the part not only of the public but also on the part of librarians and trustees to appreciate the vast difference between a library and a *library service*." He defined the concept of professionalism:

> The genius, perhaps yet unborn, who, with a clear vision of the true significance of library service, sets forth its principles and philosophy, will be concerned less with the tools and technical details of the art, such as cataloging, classification, bibliography, indexing, etc., than with the larger human relations. Library technique is now relatively efficient, but library service has not come into its own because librarians have been bound by tradition to a narrow view of their function and have not grounded their work on the principles of psychology and other sciences.

WILLIAMSON'S ADDRESS AT THE ASBURY PARK CONVENTION

Although these two statements reflected his views of library training and library service, it was his address at the Asbury Park Convention of the American Library Association on

June 26, 1919, which had greater impact. His talk, entitled "Some Present-Day Aspects of Library Training," was delivered at the fifth session and held in the auditorium at 9:30 A.M. The address was published three months later in *Library Journal.*

William Warner Bishop, then President of the American Library Association, had invited Williamson to discuss at this convention his views on library training. In his opening remarks Williamson stated, "The President had invited me to discuss this topic and I had promised to do so before I had any idea that I might have some responsibility for the professional training division by the Committee of Five." He indicated that he had not consulted with his colleagues on the committee "in regard to what I am about to say. In other words, the proposal made in this paper is a personal and not in any sense a Committee affair at the present time." He wanted to make it clear to the audience that his talk would state "my present personal views as clearly and as positively as I can, but not dogmatically, I hope, and only in a general outline." This talk was not the result of any survey or study but merely his own ideas on library training. The talk would contribute greatly to professional reorganization and thinking about library education.

Many years later Louis Round Wilson commented on the events of 1919 and particularly on "Some Present-Day Aspects of Library Training."

> In this paper Williamson proposed a better-organized system of library training agencies under the supervision of a library training board which would adopt standards and regulate the certification of librarians. This was the central idea which he carried into his studies of all types of library training for the Carnegie Corporation from 1919 to 1921, and elaborated in September, 1923, in his famous report on "Training for Library Service."[9]

Williamson's paper presented the seminal idea which evolved into his 1923 report. He pointed out the confused state of the library schools, the lack of conformity to standards, the multiplicity of training agencies, and the indefinite and fluctuating number of training classes, all organized into an asociation (the Association of American Library Schools) "which serves in some respects as a coordinator but seems ineffectual to produce any real co-operation." He recommended that the American Library Association establish a training board to "examine and approve such schools as meet a reasonable standard."

Williamson realized his address at Asbury Park had made a "deep impression on the immediate audience." In a letter of February 25, 1957, to Sarah Vann, he commented that George Utley, the Secretary of the American Library Association who had presided at the meeting, came over to him after the address and said "something about the vast importance of what I had just said . . . I was almost embarrassed by the seriousness with which my proposal was received by that audience."

In this talk, Williamson defined his views of librarianship:

> Let us not delude ourselves into thinking that we already have a system of training for library work. He must be a hopeless optimist indeed who can see in the present training situation anything more than a variety of valuable parts scattered around waiting for vital machinery not yet constructed or even planned. We cherish the delusion that library work is a profession. At best it is only semi-professional. What real profession is recruited largely from wholly untrained persons? Let us face the facts. Every real profession is based on technical training and recognized standards of fitness. That condition is in sight for library work, but it is not here. A system of training adequate to meet the situation, a recognized standard of fitness for different grades of professional work and a system of certificates by which to label those found to be fit, will put library work on a professional basis in the near future. I do not believe anything else will do it in fifty years.

He felt that library schools were inadequate; a survey in 1920-1921 confirmed this hypothesis. Other librarians and library educators may have held similar ideas about the state of library schools, but Williamson stated it publicly, loudly, and emphatically.

On July 11, 1919, Theresa Hitchler of the Brooklyn (New York) Public Library wrote Williamson, stating she had writttten to Everett R. Perry of Los Angeles about the American Library Association Conference and Williamson's address. Perry replied: "I shall certainly read Dr. Williamson's paper. He seems to me to be one of the few librarians of today with large constructive ideas." Williamson was pleased to hear this and in his reply to Hitchler declared, "It is going to be dreadful to have such a reputation."

Everett Perry wrote directly to Williamson on August 15, 1919.

> It was not until last evening that I had an opportunity to read your paper on "Some Present-Day Aspects of Library Training." In this article I think that you go directly to the heart of the trouble with the profession of librarianship today. I said "profession" of librarianship, but I agree with you that librarianship is not yet established as a profession and that we have got to adopt the measures that you propose before it can be. There would be a greater chance of securing general approval of such measures if the majority of us were alive to the need of so doing. The majority is not, and it must be an active minority that will bring about the necessary changes if they are brought about at all. However, there is nothing discouraging in this fact, because I believe that improvements, ninety-nine times out of a hundred, are effected by an active and interested few who impose their ideas upon the rank and file. All I can say is that I wish you great success in your efforts, and promise my most hearty support in any way in which I can be useful. I hope the American Library Association took some favorable action at Asbury Park.

Williamson answered Perry on August 26, 1919, enclosing a copy of Utley's letter of August 14, 1919. He indicated that the majority of people who wrote him favored his plan. "It is very pleasant to read your letter of August 15th, and to find that you in common with everyone else, with the exception of John Cotton Dana, heartily approve of my certification plan."

On July 22, 1919, Williamson wrote to Bishop: "It certainly is a great satisfaction to find that you and other leaders of the library profession think so well of my certification plan. I believe the Executive Board voted approval of the proposal on Friday afternoon and referred it to the committee in charge of the endowment project."

The ALA proceedings of the Asbury Park Conference states: "The Association, having referred to the Executive Board for further consideration the plans for a board on library training as outlined by Dr. C. C. Williamson in his paper, read before the Association . . . the Executive Board took the matter under consideration, Dr. Williamson sitting by invitation with the board to participate in the discussion." On motion from Carl Milam, it was voted "that the plan of Dr C. C. Williamson, set forth in his paper on 'Some present-day aspects of library training,' be approved in general and referred to the Committee on an Enlarged Program for American Library Service for early consideration and report."

Typical of many letters was one from Jessie Welles, who offered her help and concluded: "What you write and say makes me feel there is air to breathe in the library world after all. Usually I stifle."

In these talks and articles Williamson challenged librarians to view their work and service in broader terms—with vision, imagination, and creativity. He deplored the complacency and hopelessness of many librarians who were faced with low salaries, inadequate budgets, poor collections, and woefully inadequate facilities, but he stated that "the responsibility for every advance rests squarely upon the profession and cannot be shifted."

Sarah C. N. Bogle, Assistant Secretary of the American Library Association, was most enthusiastic about Williamson's ideas and felt they deserved earnest and sincere attention. She was certainly one of his staunchest supporters and stated her position emphatically in a letter to him on September 23, 1921.

> I have been convinced for some years that the only solution for the problem is to strengthen existing schools worthy of so doing, eliminate unworthy ones and surround the establish-

ment of new schools with such care and conditions as may result in standards worthy of professional schools.

Some years later Ernest J. Reece observed:

> Important as were Dr. Williamson's activities in the New York Public Library and in the offices of the foundation after coming to New York, they were but one part of the prelude to his major work. The other part was his examination of library schools in the United States, which was authorized by the Carnegie Corporation in 1919 and reported upon in his *Training for Library Service* in 1923. This accomplished, on a scale appropriate to library schools, the kind of thing which the surveys of Flexner, Mann, and Reed had done in the fields of medicine, engineering, and law respectively.[10]

Williamson explained his purpose in undertaking the Carnegie Survey: "It was simply to do a job which the Corporation wanted done, and thought I might be able to do it for them. My contact with the Corporation was mainly through the then Secretary, Mr. James Bertram. So far as I can now recall I had no preconceptions as to what my findings and recommendations might be."[11]

Vann felt that many of the ideas and views formally presented in the report were "in the air," creating a climate favorable for a critical study and evaluation of the conditions of the library schools.

> It was through Williamson's meteoric ascendancy as a proponent for a library training board and his subsequent efforts to foster its establishment within the American Library Association that his name may more properly be regarded as defining the end of an era than in its being affixed to the Corporation report only.[12]

Although Williamson expressed his views about library education in talks and articles, he also was vocal about his ideas in corresponence with friends and colleagues.

In a letter of February 27, 1919, to John B. Kaiser, Williamson explained his position that the public library had no teaching function and should not be involved in the business of running a library school.

Perhaps I am following a false scent, but I have gotten the notion that library service as a branch of the public service can be dignified and magnified in importance and utility by breaking away from its present vague and uncertain status as a branch of the education department and assuming an independent status as one of the essential public services in every civilized community where people work with their heads as well as their hands, and play with their imaginations and their emotions as well as their physical senses, and have a system of education for children and adults that stimulates the use of books and print outside of text-books and throughout life.

He felt that his opinion regarding libraries and education was a topic "on which I anticipate a good deal of dissent, partly because I did not develop the idea sufficiently and partly because it is novel and may perhaps be debatable." He continued:

However, I do not intend to drop it until I have at least become convinced that it will not help in putting the library business on a more secure foundation. If there are other points from which you dissent in any particular, you will do me a very real favor by stating your own view as fully as you care to. I am after straight thinking that will help the profession and the public.

Williamson was open-minded about his own plans and concludes, "I may wish to restate or modify my ideas when I get the advantage of the comments and points of view of thoughtful and progressive librarians." He was aware of the comments and criticism of librarians and library educators, and openly sought their ideas, advice, comments, and criticism.

Williamson received a letter from George F. Bowerman, Librarian of the Public Library of the District of Columbia. He responded with a five-page letter on March 28, 1919, answering Bowerman's criticism. Again he reaffirmed: "I am not at all interested in getting a blank endorsement of my ideas and interpretations. I should have been disappointed if nobody at all questioned anything I said."

Williamson told Bowerman of his grave concern over the continuation of library education as a branch of the public library. Previously he had told Kaiser of his feeling that the public library is not an educational institution; this point, "as I anticipated, has created a good deal of interest." In his article in the *Cyclopedia of Education* John Dewey defines education, a definition with which Williamson agreed.

> From whatever side education be defined, whether from that of the community carrying it on or that of the individuals educated, it will be found to involve three factors, which may be distinguished but not separated. These are (a) the specific institutions which are differentiated for the special work of education, (b) the subject matter, (Curriculum), and (c) the typical methods of discipline and instruction employed to realize the end in view.

Williamson thought Dewey had put the case very well indeed. He added in the letter to Bowerman:

> Even if we admit that the public library is one of the specific institutions differentiated from the special work of education (which, by the way, I do not admit), it does not involve the two other inseparable factors to which he refers. . . . I fail to find in educational literature anything that applies to the public library's function and distinctive mission as a specialized agency of organized society. I don't want to seem to be dogmatic about this. I am just explaining briefly how I have come to the conclusion that we are on the wrong track in trying to attach ourselves to an agency and a branch of applied science that does not recognize us and has nothing to offer us.

Williamson felt strongly on this point; it was one of the major recommendations in his report of 1923. It was also one of the recommendations which was followed, so that eventually all the library schools affiliated with public libraries became part of universities or became defunct.

On July 19, 1921, Williamson received a letter from a librarian in a New England public library who was greatly concerned at the announcement that Williamson was leaving library work to go to the Rockefeller Foundation.

Your letter stating that your change of work may interfere with efforts for raising the standards of librarians has been the most discouraging thing received in many a day. Just as you were getting us accustomed to lean upon you for a solution of our present grave difficulties, you knock out the prop! Please don't,—if ever the profession needed clear thinking it is just now when we are in the throes of creating a profession. You have won the confidence of thinking librarians who would urge you not to let go at this critical moment, but to "put over" this plan for creating professional standards.

We hear that the library profession in general is choked up with poor help taken on during the war, many of whom are being overpaid for qualifications offered.

In some instances library courses have been put in at State Normal Schools where it is a question whether they will attract students of sufficient background. Is the library to open up its doors to candidates who will not be of the type desired? We ask you to help us solve these difficulties.

By now Williamson enjoyed the high regard of many librarians; he had achieved national recognition. This letter also indicates that librarians were well aware of conditions of library training and recognized the problems which beset librarianship and library educators. Librarians had become accustomed to look to him to assist and lead them to a solution of their problems.

THE ROLE OF THE AMERICAN LIBRARY ASSOCIATION IN LIBRARY EDUCATION

The American Library Association was interested in the problems of library training, even though it did not take an active role or assume its responsibility in this area until after the Williamson report. At its early meetings, starting in 1876, the association was concerned with the training of library assistants, in 1883 it became involved with Melvil Dewey's proposal to establish a School of Library Economy. Throughout the years the American Library Association had appointed many committees to deal with problems concerning the training of librarians. In 1901 the association appointed the Committee on Library Training. After publication of the Williamson report of 1923, the association established a Temporary Library Training Board, which in 1924 became the Board of Education for Librarianship. Churchwell comments on these developments:

> The Temporary Library Training Board, whose activities led to the creation of the Board of Education for Librarianship, was the result of a group of related and sometimes interacting postwar discussions and proposals on the shortage of trained librarians and the weaknesses of library education. The postwar expansion and the fragmenting forces of specialization revealed an acute shortage of suitably trained librarians and some basic inadequacies of the library training agencies. Interest aroused, individuals and groups began to identify the weaknesses of the training agencies and to describe the kind of training that was needed by school, college, university, and special librarians, but was unavailable to them. The proposals that were submitted by Charles C. Williamson and Emma Baldwin for improving the quality and variety of library training caused the Special Committee of Certification to be created, and its activities caused the Committee on Library Training, the Association of American Library Schools, the Professional Training Section, and the Library Workers' Association to become deeply concerned about the problems of library education. The accumulation and interaction of their activities culminated in the recommendation from the Committee on Library Training to the American Library Association that a temporary training board be established to investigate the field of library education and to make recommendations for its improvement.
>
> By appointing the Temporary Library Training Board, and by acting upon its recommendation to establish the Board of Education for Librarianship, the American Library Association abandoned its irresolute role in the field of library education and established itself as a powerful force for shaping the course of development of education for librarianship.[13]

Florrinell Morton commented on the role of the American Library Association after the Williamson report:

Not until the Williamson report in 1923 had called attention to the chaotic condition of library education and made certain clear and definite recommendations for its improvement, did the ALA undertake to formulate and adopt standards, and to apply these standards in the evaluation and accreditation of library education programs. The establishment of the Board of Education for Librarianship in 1924 and the formulation of its first set of standards in 1926 and their revision in 1933 resulted in the assumption of responsibility on a profession-wide basis for the nature and quality of professional education through accreditation. Since that time, with the exception of the brief period of the moratorium on accrediting in the fifties, the library profession, through its national membership organization, has exercised some degree of control over the education of its practitioners.[14]

The Board of Education for Librarianship became, in 1956, the Committee on Accreditation. Since 1924 the board and its successor, the committee, formulated standards for the use and guidance of library schools and also established and applied accrediting procedures. Various sets of standards were developed from 1925 to 1972. In 1966 the American Library Association established the Office of Library Education to work with the Committee on Accreditation in developing standards for library education. This office was later discontinued.

During this time Williamson was most active serving on numerous committees of the American Library Association which were concerned with various phases of the problem of library training. This work focused his attention increasingly on the problems of training.

On February 26, 1919, President Bishop of the American Library Association, appointed a Committee of Five on Library Service to "give an honest, fair, unbiased statement of facts, based on actual conditions in library work in America, concerning every phase of library maintenance, administration, and service." The committee consisted of Arthur E. Bostwick, Chairman, with Linda Eastman, Carl Milam, Azariah Root, and C. C. Williamson as members. This committee was "to make a general survey of American library service, particularly in view of the post-war conditions of readjustment." Bishop wanted this committee to "survey the whole field of American library service and to present a preliminary report at the Asbury Park Conference in June, 1919." The work of the committee went slowly until 1924, when a grant from the Carnegie Corporation "enabled it to go forward more rapidly." The size of the committee was enlarged to six and the name was changed to Committee on Library Survey. The survey was published in 1926, appearing in four volumes. At the time of publication only Bostwick, Milam, and Root were still on the committee, and C. Seymour Thompson was director. This landmark publication was entitled *A Survey of Libraries in the United States.* In the 1919 discussion of this survey, Williamson was given the task of undertaking the study of the section dealing with formation, education and training, library staff, etc.

Williamson also served on the Committee of Five on Standardization, Certification, and Library Training, established in 1920 after the termination of the ill-fated Committee on an Enlarged Program for American Library Service, which had opposed his views on library education. The new Committee of Five on Standardization, Certification, and Library Training consisted of Frank K. Walter, Chairman, Azariah S. Root, Alice Tyler, Adeline B. Zechert, and C. C. Williamson. The committee offered to the council a plan containing ideas similar to those proposed in Williamson's articles; the council approved all but one. It did not approve the establishment of a National Board of Certification for Librarians within the American Library Association. One of the approved recommendations called for a Committee of Nine on National Certification and Training, which was established on November 30, 1920, with C. C. Williamson as Chairman. However, in 1921 he resigned as chairman and a second Committee of Nine on National Certification and Training was established with Frank K. Walter as Chairman.

The next step in this complicated series of events was the establishment on April 24, 1923, of a Temporary Library Training Board, "to investigate the field of library training, to formulate tentative standards for all forms of library training agencies, to devise a plan for accrediting such agencies and to report to the Council."

Vann has commented on these events.

> Thus four years after Williamson had advanced his original proposal in his address, "Some Present-Day Aspects of Library Training," a library training board was established, at first temporarily but in the following year on a more enduring basis as the Board of Education for Librarianship. It was that original proposal of Williamson's which the Committee had supported throughout the period, even while the American Library Association evaded the responsibilities inherent in the establishment of such a board.
>
> Four months after the establishment of the Temporary Library Training Board, Williamson's study on *Training for Library Service* appeared. But it was Williamson's contributions, before its publication, which more properly identify the era of library training prior to 1923 as the "Dewey to Williamson" period. Dewey had organized the first School of Library Economy, but it was Williamson who initiated the concept that the Association had a bounden duty to create an agency for accrediting its professional training agencies. Upon the implementation of that concept by the establishment of the Temporary Library Training Board, the pioneer period in the history of training for librarianship had come to an end.[15]

Vann concluded that Williamson's work on the report was the final phase of the period from 1887 to 1923. She also considered this a period marked by conflict, experimentation, confusion, divisiveness, and uncertainty. This confusion was reflected in the professional organizations. For many years the American Library Association was unable to assume any responsibility for unifying the many different concepts of library training, and the Association of American Library Schools was ineffective, contributing little toward the raising of standards. Williamson's accomplishment was to unite many librarians behind his plans.

From 1887 to 1923 the American Library Association did not acknowledge its responsibility in the accrediting of training agencies.[16] Williamson pointed out to the association its responsibility to formulate standards and to accredit library training agencies as well as to assume an active role in the future development of library education.

According to Vann,

> Not only, then, as a time of conflict and experimentation but as a precursor of ideas may the "Dewey to Williamson" period be characterized. It was neither dormant nor quiescent, but, prior to this study, little attention had been given to the activities of the period. In marking the end of the epoch, the report on *Training for Library Service* has loomed large, not only because of the prestige of Williamson and the Carnegie Corporation, which undoubtedly enhanced it, but because it came at a time ripe for its recognition by the profession. The major ideas were not original, but for that very reason they had a better chance to make an impact than if they had been completely new. The "Dewey to Williamson" period may seem to have accomplished little within its own time, but, in reality, the post-1923 achievements may be viewed as the culmination of the forces at work in the 1876-1923 era.[17]

One of Williamson's major contributions was his insistence that the American Library Association assume its long overdue leadership in the field of library education. He identified the association's responsibilities as being the formulation of standards and the accrediting of training agencies, and upheld the view that the improvement of standards lay in the creation of an authoritative body controlled not by the schools but by the profession.

Williamson in his addresses and published articles had alerted librarians, library educators, and the profession to the problems they faced and to the poor job being done by the training agencies. He was critical of the American Library Association for failing to provide leadership. His views were backed by many, including Adam Strohm, Librarian of the Detroit Public Library, who served from 1923 to 1924 as Chairman of the Temporary Library Training Board of the American Library Association. Strohm observed: "Someone has said that Dr. Williamson tell us nothing new. Maybe not. Who does? But he has done this. He has vitalized the silent thoughts, the deep concerns, the earnest hopes of a good many of us. He has made the dormant fact alive. We are aroused."[18]

Many developments were occurring in library education at this time and this ferment eventually led to the report which Williamson was about to start and which would have a profound effect on librarianship and library education.

Wilson also agreed that this period and the events within the American Library Association from 1920 to 1923 "in fact . . . largely prepared the way for the discussion and acceptance of [the Williamson] Report."[19]

According to Norman Horrocks:

> Prior to the publication of the Williamson *Report*, ALA had established a Temporary Library Training Board drawn from all sections of the membership to look into library training, standards, and an accrediting plan. In 1924 ALA replaced that temporary body with the Board of Education for Librarianship (BEL), later the Committee on Accreditation (COA). Williamson's proposal for a National Examining Body was not accepted but accreditation of schools was. To carry out the accreditation process, *Standards* were developed by BEL, and later the COA, and adopted by ALA Council in 1925, 1933, 1951, and 1972.[20]

The preliminary work had been done; the profession was aware of the problem and looked to Williamson for guidance and leadership. The stage was set for the Williamson report.

NOTES

1. Karl K. Kitchen, "Just Ask Dr. Williamson" (unidentified newspaper clipping), December 30, 1920.
2. *Loc. cit.*
3. *Loc. cit.*
4. *Loc. cit.*
5. Keyes D. Metcalf, "Charles C. Williamson," *Library Service News* 11 (November 1943), 23.
6. Charles C. Williamson, "Need of a Plan for Library Development," *Library Journal* 43 (September 1918), 649-655.
7. Charles C. Williamson, "Efficiency in Library Management," *Library Journal* 44 (February 1919), 67-77; and *Library Occurent* 5 (1919), 148-154.

8. Charles C. Williamson, "Some Present-Day Aspects of Library Training," *Library Journal* 44 (September 1919), 563-568; and *American Library Association Bulletin* 13 (July 1919), 120-126.
9. Louis Round Wilson, "Historical Development of Education for Librarianship in the United States," in Bernard Berelson, ed., *Education for Librarianship*, p. 47.
10. Ernest J. Reece, "C. C. Williamson: A Record of Service to American Librarianship," *College and Research Libraries* 4 (September 1943), 306.
11. Sarah K. Vann, "Letter from Charles C. Williamson," May 23, 1955, p. 1.
12. Sarah K. Vann, *Training for Librarianship Before 1923*, p. 3.
13. Charles D. Churchwell, *The Shaping of American Library Education*, pp. 24-25
14. Florrinell Morton, "Education for Librarians," p. 11.
15. Sarah K. Vann, *Training for Librarianship Before 1923*, p. 178.
16. The American Library Association was established in 1876 while the year 1887 marks the founding of the School of Library Economy at Columbia by Dr. Melvil Dewey. This was the first formal training school for librarians.
17. *Ibid.*, p. 193.
18. Adam J. Strohm, "The Library Training Board," *American Library Association Bulletin* 18 (January 1924), 4.
19. Louis Round Wilson, "Historical Development," p. 47.
20. Norman Horrocks, "Library Education: History," in *ALA World Encyclopedia of Library and Information Services*, 2nd ed., p. 492.

9
LIBRARIANSHIP AND LIBRARY EDUCATION

THE HISTORY OF library education in the United States can be divided into five major periods:

Before 1887: The period of apprenticeship and in-service library training classes, which were in existence before and for some time after 1887, when the School of Library Economy was established by Melvil Dewey at Columbia College.

1887-1919: The so-called "Dewey to Williamson" period, which extended from the founding of the first formal training schools for librarians to the survey of library education that resulted in the Williamson report.

1920-1939: The period between the two World Wars, which saw the implementation of some of the recommendations of the Williamson report and the affiliation of library schools with institutions of higher education, and the accreditation of these schools by the American Library Association.

1940-1960: The period after World War II, which saw experimental changes in the curriculum and degree structure of the library schools, resulting in the professionalization of library education. It also was the period of change from accrediting schools to accrediting programs.

1961 to the present: The period that marks the new emphasis on information science and documentation and their integration into traditional library school curricula.

Prior to 1887 libraries were small, and librarianship was mainly a custodial function with relatively simple procedures of administration and maintenance. The users of libraries were few; those few were highly literate. The increase in the number of libraries—and especially with the building of Carnegie libraries starting in 1881—brought about the need for a change in their structure and administration. With this, the growing use of libraries by the public also contributed in changing the concept of the librarian from a custodial job to a position involving library service. Although the emphasis remained on the preservation of collections and the techniques needed for such work, these duties were passed on to various apprentices and library workers. Library experience and scholarly attainments were usually considered sufficient professional background for executive library positions. "In general librarians and governing boards in that periods saw little need for formal library training."[1] During this time, training for library work grew directly out of actual practice, since "the early librarians learned by doing."[2] When there were sufficient numbers to warrant it, training classes were established within the libraries to give instruction related to the actual work performed in that particular library.

According to C. Edward Carroll:

> The fact is that librarianship was not considered a separate and distinct calling in the early colleges, and until the passage of legislation establishing free public libraries there was little need for full time library personnel. These factors account for the fact that librarianship, unlike older trades and occupations of the 18th and 19th centuries, did not develop an apprenticeship in the historic sense of the word. Training there was, but it was the product of obtaining paid employment and working one's way up.[3]

During this period "there was in the United States, [and] in the English speaking world, for that matter, no school or organized agency for the training of librarians."[4] The usual suggestion to individuals who were interested in becoming librarians was "to read available printed material on library economy, simulate the example of successful librarians, and seek employment in a well run library for on-the-job training. It was generally conceded that there was no substitute for actual experience in library work."[5]

Librarianship and Library Education 129

In the early days of library education in North America, librarians were trained on the job as apprentices. The nineteenth century saw the rise of schools replacing apprenticeship as the most effective method of educating people for trades or professions. The so-called technical education in trade schools and technical schools gained in popularity.[6]

The early method of learning library science, and the most popular one in this early period, was seeking guidance through apprenticeship. Experience was the major qualification for library positions. The American Library Association, established in 1876, was formed to arrange for formal meetings of librarians and the exchange of ideas. The purpose of such a step was to establish an organization "for . . . promoting the library interests of the country and of increasing reciprocity of intelligence and good will among librarians and all interested in library economy and bibliographical studies.[7]

The history of library education in all periods has followed an evolutionary process based primarily on utilitarian practice. Modern library education began in 1887 with the establishment by Melvil Dewey of the Columbia College School of Library Economy. Dewey opened his school in the face of opposition from the faculty and trustees at Columbia. He left after two years, to establish and head the library school at Albany, New York, when he became Librarian of the New York State Library. In commenting on Dewey's work, Elmer Johnson stated:

> This instruction in library science was slow in coming, however. A few universities did begin to offer courses in "reference and bibliography" or "books and reading," but it was not until 1887 that the first school of librarianship was opened. Melvil Dewey had proposed a formal library school at the Buffalo meeting of the American Library Association in 1883, and in the fall of 1887 he opened such a school at Columbia University in New York City. This location was not satisfactory, so in 1889, Dewey moved his school to Albany when he became librarian of the New York State Library there. He gradually built up a competent faculty and soon had a student body of 30 to 50 each year. His curriculum was a practical one, in line with the general educational tendency

toward technical training that was then in vogue. He taught the actual processes of selecting, acquiring, processing, arranging, and circulating library books. His courses included phases of library work now considered clerical rather than professional, such as typewriting, library handwriting, book lettering and book repairing.[8]

After 1887 training agencies spread throughout the United States. "When library education . . . moved into formal institutions of education, much the same content and method moved with it that had been prevalent before that time. There followed the establishment of library institutes and round tables (where librarians discussed mutual problems), schools conducted by public libraries, summer schools, state library agencies, and some schools located in institutions of higher education. This growth met the immediate demand for trained library personnel caused by the extensive building program of the Carnegie libraries. There was also the "need for schools and colleges to meet the library standards of State educational authorities and regional accrediting associations."[9] In addition, many of these library training agencies were involved in training personnel to fill vacancies in local libraries. These training programs "reflected the philosophy and methods of the vocational schools of that time."[10]

By the end of the nineteenth century, library schools had been established at Pratt Institute in Brooklyn (1890), Drexel Institute in Philadelphia (1892), and the Armour Institute of Chicago (1893). The Armour Institute was transferred to the University of Illinois in 1897. Other training schools included Carnegie Library Schools at Pittsburgh (1901) and Atlanta (1905), Simmons College (1902), Western Reserve University (1904), and the University of Wisconsin (1906). There also were a few short-lived attempts at offering library training courses at Amherst Summer School (1891-1905), Maine State College of Agriculture and Mechanical Art (1893-1896), and Columbian University in Washington, D.C. (1897-1904). In addition, several public libraries established schools, including the Los Angeles Public Library Training Class, which was established in 1891 and continued until 1914 when it became a one-year professional school, and the New York Public Library School, as well as training courses at the Denver Public Library, the Cleveland Public Library, the Atlanta Public Library, the St. Louis Public Library, the Pittsburgh Public Library, and the Riverside (California) Library Service School. The purpose of the training programs in public libraries was mainly to train people to work in each particular library, a practice Williamson disliked. These schools and training programs were modeled on the curriculum of the New York State Library School, which at that time was considered the official school of the American Library Association.

Williamson faced this proliferation of library training programs in 1920 when he undertook a survey of library schools for the Carnegie Corporation. "Wherever it was taught, library training in the early years of the century emphasized the practical aspects of librarianship, and the highest prerequisite for library courses was usually the junior year of college."[11] It is significant, however, that during this period the profession decided to "educate" librarians rather than continue the apprenticeship method. Not all librarians agreed, but the trend was decidedly in that direction. In his 1923 report Williamson stated, "Professional training calls for a broad, general education, represented at its minimum by a thorough college course of four years, plus at least one year of graduate study in a properly organized library school."[12]

Sarah K. Vann thoroughly covered the period from 1887 to 1923 in *Training for Librarianship Before 1923*. She stated that this was a "period of cautious but positive progress in the direction of professionalism."[13]

> During the period, divisive and conflicting ideas emerged which, while delaying progress, readied the library field for Williamson's report. The conflict flourished because of the suspicion as to the value of and the instructional methods in formal training which was encountered both by graduates of the programs as well as by certain strong-willed individuals who fostered new concepts.[14]

During this period, various committees were established to deal with the problems of library training. In 1909 Julia

Elliott, of the Pratt Institute Library School, described the situation as chaotic,[15] and said that librarianship was a "divided house with an ill-coordinated set of institutions resulting from different views on how to train librarians."[16] The need was beginning to be felt for "an organized channel through which to assert the profession's interests."[17]

Carl M. White outlined the developments in this confusing period.

> The formation of the ALA Committee on the Library School in 1889 was the first step toward such machinery [of national planning for library training]. The Committee's responsibilities grew as it became the Committee on the Library School and Training Classes (1895), then the Committee on Library Schools (1896). Proceedings of the Chautauqua Conference (1898) show that the profession was awakening to the significance of personnel development in all its aspects and was drifting toward impartial encouragement of any and every style of training that improved performance on the part of library workers. After the Dana report of 1900, this mood hardened into ALA policy and the Committee on Library Schools was reconstituted as the Committee on Library Training."[18]

Donald G. Davis, Jr., in his history of the Association of American Library Schools stated:

> The new group, the Round Table of Library School Instructors, met in Chicago on January 5, 1911, with sixteen persons representing nine schools. Only Syracuse University Library School and the Carnegie Library Training School for Children's Librarians were not represented. The discussion on Windsor's [Phineas L. Windsor of The University of Illinois] suggested topics was valuable enough to move the participants to decide on meeting again the following year. Similar meetings were therefore called for the mid-winter conferences of 1912 to 1915. . . .
>
> During the meeting of January 1, 1915, the group considered "the advisability of forming a more permanent organization than the Round Table." Those present voted to form the Association of American Library Schools and appointed the first president and secretary. Eligibility for membership included administrators and faculty members of "regular library schools!"[19]

Librarianship and Library Education

Norman Horrocks provided a summary of the events of the various committees on library training during the 1883 to 1915 period.

> The first committee (in 1883) was intended to serve as a liaison with Columbia but it was followed by Committees on Library Examinations and Credentials (1900), on Professional Instruction and Bibliography (1901), on Library Training (1903), on Professional Training for Librarianship (1909), and a Round Table of Library School Instructors (1911). Four years later that Round Table separated from ALA to become the Association of American Library Schools (AALS), renamed in 1983 the Association for Library and Information Science Education (ALISE).[20]

The Association of American Library Schools, then comprising ten schools, helped increase the awareness of librarians to library education and established certain standards schools must meet to be "approved" or "accredited." However, the effectiveness of this group always has been limited. The function of establishing standards and certifying library schools eventually was absorbed by the American Library Association and its various committees. According to Robert B. Downs, "that organization [AALS] has never lived up to its potentials in influencing the course of American library education."[21]

Many of the ideas which emerged during this period became part of the Williamson report and its recommendations. Williamson's ideas about library training were not entirely his own. Actually, the report recommended little that was new or had not been discussed in the pre-Williamson period. This fact is revealed in the work of Melvil Dewey and especially in his plan of 1888 to broaden the program of library education.[22] The various reports of committees of the American Library Association were increasingly critical in their evaluations of library schools. Aksel G. S. Josephson recommended in 1896[23] and again in 1900[24] that library schools be truly professional and not merely technical, urging that the schools be affiliated with universities. Josephson also developed programs of training for specific types of positions, recommending a second-year program leading to the

A.M. and Ph.D. degrees. There were others who were very much concerned with library education during the period from 1887 to 1923.

Among these critics were Katherine L. Sharp, founder and head of the Armour Institute at Chicago, who agreed with Josephson. In 1898 William H. Brett[25] suggested the adoption of an examining board similar to that which examines lawyers. Brett was Director of the Cleveland (Ohio) Public Library, and for many years Dean of the Library School at Western Reserve University. Salome Cutler Fairchild predicted in 1901 that the future library school would be part of a university. Fairchild was one of the original members of the regular staff of instructors at the Columbia College of Library Economy with Melvil Dewey. Mary Eileen Ahern, in the strategic position of Editor of *Public Libraries,* also was a severe critic of the existing library schools. Mary Wright Plummer, who was the Director of the Pratt Institute Library School, played an important part as Chairman of the Committee on Library Training. Another person who was vitally concerned with library education at that time was Azariah Smith Root, Librarian of Oberlin College, who was Chairman when the committee made its plans for another examination of the library schools. Emma V. Baldwin, who was active in library matters for over four decades, held a variety of positions, including Assistant to the Director of the Brooklyn (New York) Public Library. She also was Director of the Roanoke (Virginia) Public Library, and later Director of the District of Columbia Training Center for Professional Librarians. Later in her career she served as Acting Head of the Public and School Library Services Bureau of the New Jersey State Education Department. Marian C. Manley stated that "few library leaders can match the range of Emma Baldwin's experience."[26] Baldwin was also a strong advocate of change in library training, and in her article, "The Training of Professional Librarians," she added yet another voice to the criticism of the existing program of library education.

The picture of library training during this period reflects the general status of higher education in the United States at the time. At the end of the nineteenth century and the beginning of the twentieth, higher education was, in the opinion of William K. Selden,

> ... a variegated hodgepodge of uncoordinated practices—in school and college alike—which had never undergone any screening from anybody, and many which were shoddy, futile, and absurd beyond anything we now conceive of; and the Age of Standards—as the period from 1890 to 1915 may come to be called—brought order out of chaos.[27]

Library training had grown and was developing in the same uncontrolled pattern. During this period members of the field began to inquire, probe, question, and examine themselves and their standards, thus establishing the direction library training would take, eventually culminating in Williamson's survey and his findings and recommendations. The need to establish standards was felt in all aspects of higher education as well as in education for the professions of medicine, law, engineering—and librarianship.

In 1920, sponsored by the Carnegie Corporation of New York, Williamson undertook a survey of library schools, which was published in 1923 under the title *Training for Library Service*.

NOTES

1. Willard O. Mishoff, "Education for Library Service," in Lloyd E. Blauch, ed., *Education for the Professions*, p. 123.
2. Lowell A. Martin, "Research in Education for Librarianship," *Library Trends* 6 (October 1957), 207.
3. C. Edward Carroll, "History of Library Education," in Mary B. Cassata and Herman Totten, eds., *The Administrative Aspects of Education for Librarianship: A Symposium*, p. 3.
4. *Loc. cit.*
5. *Ibid.*, p. 4.
6. Miriam H. Tees, "Accreditation and Certification," in Richard K. Gardner, ed., *Education of Library and Information Professionals: Present and Future Prospects*, p. 111.
7. "Conference of Librarians, 1876" (proceedings), *Library*

Journal 1 (November 1876), 140, as quoted in William Z. Nasri, "Education in Library and Information Science," in the *Encyclopedia of Library and Information Science*, vol. 7, p. 417.
8. Elmer D. Johnson, *Communications*, p. 269.
9. Willard O. Mishoff, *op. cit.*, p. 123.
10. *Loc. cit.*
11. Elmer D. Johnson, *op. cit.*, p. 269.
12. Charles C. Williamson, *Training for Library Service* (1923), p. 136.
13. Sarah K. Vann, *Training for Librarianship Before 1923*, p. 191.
14. *Loc. cit.*
15. Julia E. Elliott, "Library Conditions Which Confront Library Schools," *American Library Association Bulletin* 3 (September 1909), 427-436, as quoted in Carl M. White, *A Historical Introduction to Library Education: Problems and Progress to 1951*, p. 115.
16. Carl M. White, *A Historical Introduction*, p. 113.
17. *Loc. cit.*
18. *Loc. cit.*
19. Donald G. Davis, Jr., *The Association of American Library Schools, 1915-1968: An Analytical History*, pp. 22-23. The literature is often misleading and confusing on the sequence of events leading to the founding of AALS. Davis provides the factual data and settles the matter.
20. Norman Horrocks, "Library Education: History," in *ALA World Encyclopedia of Library and Information Services*, 2nd ed., p. 492.
21. Robert B. Downs, "Education for Librarianship in the U.S. and Canada," in Larry Earl Bone, ed., *Library Education: An International Survey*, p. 4.
22. Melvil Dewey, "Library Instruction: Summary of Plans Proposed to Aid in Educating Librarians," *Library Notes* 2 (March 1888), 286-306.
23. Aksel G. S. Josephson, "Is Librarianship a Learned Profession?" *Public Libraries* 1 (September 1896), 195.
24. Aksel G. S. Josephson, "Preparation for Librarianship," *Library Journal* 25 (May 1900), 226-228.
25. American Library Association, "Proceedings," *Library Annual* 23 (August 1898), 123.
26. Marian C. Manley, "Emma Baldwin," *Library Journal* 77 (March 15, 1952), 487.
27. William K. Selden, *Accreditation*, p. 28.

10
THE CARNEGIE CORPORATION OF NEW YORK AND THE WILLIAMSON REPORT

INTEREST OF THE CARNEGIE CORPORATION OF NEW YORK IN LIBRARIES AND LIBRARY EDUCATION

In 1881 Andrew Carnegie began to donate money for building libraries. The corporation continued this activity after his death. From that time through 1916, the corporation made grants of millions of dollars to build 2,509 public libraries, mainly in the United States, as well as in other parts of the English-speaking world. In 1917 the grants for the building of public libraries were discontinued, although a few gifts were made in the 1920s. The major portion of these grants was made prior to 1917. Some funds were donated to library development between 1917 and 1925, but it was a time "devoted primarily to appraisal and planning."[1]

On November 18, 1915, Alvin S. Johnson, an economist, was commissioned by the Carnegie Corporation of New York to undertake a survey of selected Carnegie libraries. He did the study and in 1916 submitted his private report, "A Report to Carnegie Corporation of New York on the Policy of Donations to Free Public Libraries." Johnson's findings indicated that the Carnegie libraries were providing inadequate service because of the lack of trained librarians. He specifically recommended that "the Corporation, before giving more money for buildings, do something about the preparation of librarians."[2] Johnson drew a dismal picture of library personnel and advised the corporation to develop a broader concept of library training. He focused on the need to be "more concerned with the low quality of many of those staffing these libraries." He was also critical of the "low standards of the library schools."[3] The Johnson report provided a background for a second inquiry dealing with the problems of library education.

In George Bobinski's study of Carnegie libraries he stated:

> During the Corporation's first fifty years of operation, from 1911 to 1961, it spent $33,457,142 to improve library service. Although this expenditure represents only about 11 percent of the total of all its grants during the first fifty years, the Corporation has been associated with every major development in library service in the United States. A brief review of these library involvements will show their importance and also demonstrate that the Carnegie Corporation did follow through on many of Alvin Johnson's recommendations. The Corporation has given support to all types of libraries. . . .
>
> Following World War I, Corporation trustees did not resume gifts of money for buildings. Instead, during the period 1917-25, they organized a series of conferences to determine the manner and means by which the Corporation might be of assistance in improving library services and training.
>
> In 1918 the Corporation asked Charles C. Williamson to make a study of library training. His report recommended that librarians should receive their education in a university rather than in a training school sponsored by a public library. Williamson also recommended the establishment of a graduate library school for advanced study, a national accrediting and certification for library schools, and numerous fellowships. His study was a monumental work which resulted in a complete revision of the curriculum in library schools.[4]

THE NEED FOR WILLIAMSON'S SURVEY

The Trustees of the Carnegie Corporation discontinued the library building program after World War I and decided to "look into librarians' training." The corporation, acting on Johnson's recommendations, "commissioned C. C. Williamson, a social scientist turned librarian to make a field survey of training for library service."[5]

Williamson criticized the Johnson report, stating that it

contained "nothing particularly new to the library profession. . . . Many of his observations as to conditions and needs are pertinent and valuable, but his suggestions for methods for improvement and extension of training facilities were either very general or of questionable practicality."[6]

In a letter of October 17, 1964, to the author, Williamson identifies the events which he believed led to the decision of the corporation to make this survey and to select him:

> At the time the study was undertaken I was employed by the Corporation on a research project of a very different nature. Because of my previous interest in libraries the officers of the Corporation, notably the then secretary, Mr. James Bertram, often discussed with me the problems the Corporation was facing in regard to its library buildings and its limited support of certain library schools. I believe the decision to ask me to make the study was based largely on these discussions no part of which was reduced to writing so as to find a place in my files.

Vann also commented on Williamson's role in the Carnegie Corporation survey:

> Confronted with the assignment of March, 1918, James Bertram, secretary of the Carnegie Corporation, obtained the aid and advice of Charles Clarence Williamson, who had been appointed to serve as statistician for the Study of Methods of Americanization, a project being sponsored by the Carnegie Corporation. He was, in addition, librarian of the Municipal Reference Library in New York City and president of the Special Libraries Association. Bertram requested Williamson to perform two preliminary tasks before the study of library training was undertaken officially: (1) to confer with representative librarians concerning the study, and (2) to offer some suggestions for the education of the unprofessional librarian. Both tasks Williamson performed promptly, the first by attending the Saratoga Conference of the American Library Association; the second, by his contribution, "The Need of a Plan for Library Development."[7]

According to Florence Anderson, the influence of the Williamson report on the work of the Carnegie Corporation was substantial.

The resulting document by Charles C. Williamson has been called one of the most influential studies of professional education ever made; it is still referred to frequently in current literature. Certainly it had a great influence in the subsequent program of the Corporation. One of Mr. Williamson's major recommendations was that librarians be educated in a university context rather than in a training school sponsored by a public library. He also recommended the establishment of a graduate library school for advanced training, a national accrediting and certification system for schools, and liberal fellowships.[8]

Williamson attended the Saratoga Springs Conference of 1918 and spoke to many individuals about training for library work. Part of his work at the conference was to obtain names of people who might serve on an advisory committee to the corporation. According to Vann:

> Williamson made a prompt report to Bertram on the results of his Saratoga mission, summarizing his encounters with individuals who might participate in the investigation. Of the possible results of his consultation, two may be cited: (1) the opportunity provided Williamson for acquainting himself further with the problems and personalities in the field; (2) the informal indication given to the library profession of the interest of the Carnegie Corporation in the problem of training. His thoughtful reporting on possible members of a committee to investigate the training programs was invalidated when on March 28, 1919, the Trustees of the Corporation appointed him director of the study. He had, however, during the interim, published his views on training in the *Library Journal*.[9]

On the basis of the Williamson report and a complementary study published by William S. Learned,[10] in 1924, the Carnegie Corporation "embarked upon a large-scale expansion of its library program."[11] In March 1926, the trustees approved a Ten-Year Program of Library Service, which resulted in the expenditure of "approximately five million dollars much of which was for the support of various aspects of education for librarianship."[12] This program was intended to strengthen the library profession by supporting the activities of the American Library Association. The work of the corporation and the American Library Association continued with both organizations working "together to identify the needs in library service and to develop programs to meet them."[13]

The Carnegie Corporation has always relied heavily on the suggestions and recommendations of the American Library Association's Board of Education for Librarianship "in distributing funds for the development of library schools. The board, which was itself partly supported by the corporation, played a significant role in establishing standards for library training and in accrediting schools."[14]

According to George S. Bobinski, the Carnegie Corporation gave "$549,500 for the general support of the Association [ALA] from 1924 to 1926; in 1926 it added $2,000,000 in endowment funds. . . . Gifts for the endowment and support of library schools and the establishment of the first graduate library school at the University of Chicago totaled $3,359,550. . . . Following World War II, the Corporation provided $212,170 to the Social Science Research Council for the Public Library Inquiry. . . . Again, financial assistance from the Carnegie Corporation helped the ALA in 1956 to formulate and publish what popularly became known as the Public Library Standards."[15] The corporation also provided funds for many fellowships to men and women interested in library education. Since World War II "training grants, instead of providing general support for library schools, as in the past, were made for special purposes."[16]

Because of its activities in the field of librarianship, the Carnegie Corporation of New York has "been associated with every major development in library service in the United States and in most parts of the (British) Commonwealth. Dollars are of course not the only measure of its contribution but the total of $33,457,142 spent by the Corporation to improve library service is impressive."[17]

When the Carnegie Corporation shifted its emphasis from the building of libraries to an investigation into the training of librarians, it wanted to employ a person who would be able to examine the status quo and make specific recommendations to guide future corporation policies and programs. The Williamson report was not intended to be a public document. The survey was requested, financed, commissioned, and prepared for the use of the Carnegie Corporation of New York. Eventually this report generated such interest that parts of it were printed and made public. It must be remembered, however, that this document was primarily a report for the corporation, and secondarily a statement for the library world.

INITIATING THE SURVEY

On March 28, 1919, the Board of Trustees of the Carnegie Corporation of New York passed a resolution which formally authorized an inquiry into library training and invited Williamson to undertake the project "in cooperation with an advisory committee consisting of Dr. Herbert Putnam, Librarian of Congress, Dr. James H. Kirkland, Chancellor of Vanderbilt University, and Mr. Wilson Farrand, Principal, Newark Academy." The survey was entitled "Study of Training for Library Work." Williamson was in charge.

Henry S. Pritchett, Acting President of the Carnegie Corporation, indicated the scope of the study in the foreword to the published report.

> The subject of training for library service, while possessing an intrinsic importance that is as yet but little appreciated in this country, is of such dimensions as to lend itself well to the unitary and comprehensive treatment which follows. All of the library schools in the United States were visited and carefully examined; the most expert opinions on the problem were analyzed and compared; and, finally, the use made of the product of these schools, together with the need and demand for more and better training, was subjected to as thorough a statistical study as the available material permitted.

Dr. Pritchett then addressed himself to the value of the survey.

> As a whole, therefore, the problem is one which a single, inclusive study of this character may do much to illuminate; and it is believed that Dr. Williamson's report will prove to be of decisive value in clarifying a situation which was not so difficult as it was neglected.

Carnegie Corp. of N.Y. and Williamson Report

During the summer of 1920, certain preliminary studies were made and a complete outline was prepared of the topics on which the corporation sought to obtain data and opinions from library school officials and teachers. During December 1920 and January 1921, Williamson visited all the library schools except two, which were inspected later—in April and May. He personally inspected the schools and conferred with the principals and directors.

Williamson's purpose was

> to present the library situation in this country with reference to the training problem so that the educator and the layman interested in educational problems may be able to form a correct judgment as to what the present situation demands. The possibility has also been kept in mind that if the report in some form could come to the attention of library school authorities, they may find in it some suggestions or constructive criticism that will bear fruit.

No criticism of individual schools was undertaken, because the survey was to examine the total picture of library education rather than concentrate on the strengths and weaknesses of individual cases. The following schools were included in the study and visited; all of them claimed to give at least one academic year of instruction:

New York State Library School, Albany, New York
Pratt Institute School of Library Science, Brooklyn, New York
University of Illinois Library School, Urbana, Illinois
Carnegie Library School, Pittsburgh, Pennsylvania
Simmons College School of Library Science, Boston, Massachusetts
Library School of Western Reserve University, Cleveland, Ohio
Library School, Carnegie Library of Atlanta, Atlanta, Georgia
Library School of the University of Wisconsin, Madison, Wisconsin
Syracuse University Library School, Syracuse, New York

Library School of the New York Public Library, New York, New York
Library School, University of Washington, Seattle, Washington
Riverside Library Service School, Riverside, California
Library School of the Los Angeles Public Library, Los Angeles, California
St. Louis Library School, St. Louis, Missouri
University of California, Courses in Library Science, Berkeley, California

In a letter to Sarah Vann on February 25, 1957, Williamson explained the procedure he followed in gathering the data for this report. "All the library schools knew exactly how I got my materials together. They filled out questionnaires, gave me files of their catalogues, reports, and other publications, and subjected themselves to long interviews, group and individual. The facts collected in this orthodox and obvious way were all set forth in the report."

Although the fieldwork was complete in 1921, there was a delay in preparing the report for publication, which was not until 1923. Many reasons were given for the delay, all legitimate and acceptable. In his 1921 typewritten report, Williamson commented, "Unexpected delay in the final preparation of the report has been due to a number of causes but principally to the necessity which the writer has been under of devoting the major portion of his time to other duties which could not well be put aside for an extended period." At the time this delay gave rise to speculation as to why the report had not been published. All sorts of questions were circulated about the survey and its conclusions, giving it an air of mystery.

Williamson had to work through the Carnegie Corporation and its Secretary, James Bertram, as well as through the Advisory Committee. In addition, he conducted the survey during a time when he also held a full-time position, so that the writing and compilation of the survey had to be done in his spare time. Williamson always regarded this survey as a part of his professional activities. He confessed in a letter of June 29, 1955, to Sarah Vann, "The library training business was a side issue most of the time, never a part of my full-time job."

The main difficulty in getting the report published was that he was then changing jobs from the New York Public Library to the Rockefeller Foundation; this interfered more with his work on the report than he thought it would. He was advancing with the report, but progress was not as rapid as he would have liked.

On September 24, 1921, he reported his progress to James Bertram, wishing he had more time to devote to the report.

> If I could get three or four weeks to devote exclusively to the report, I could get it in shape to submit to the advisory committee. As that is impossible, I am working along slowly, some weeks getting very little done. I had to be in Ithaca all of last week, for example, to attend the annual meeting of the New York Library Association, of which I was President. As a matter of fact, the general interest which has seemed to develop from some of my preliminary studies and inquiries has involved me more deeply in library discussions than I like—yet I do not feel that it is desirable to turn a deaf ear to opportunities to discuss problems of library service which are involved in this school study. The opportunities enlarge my conception of the problem and pave the way for the acceptance of my report by the librarians of the country.
>
> A considerable part of the first draft is now in type. Some of the necessary statistics are not yet in hand but are promised and I now expect to have it in tentative form in two or three months.

Williamson maintained an open mind about his report and was willing to listen to members of the library world discuss matters relating to the study. He found these communications of value, and learned a great deal from their comments and observations. The quality of a good listener was another of his traits.

He also wanted the reaction of others to his report. On October 8, 1921, he sent a copy of the chapter relating to the library school situation in New York City to Dr. John J. Coss, Director of the Summer Session at Columbia University, "to get your reaction toward it." In this letter Williamson also commented on the delay. "The completion of my report to the Carnegie Corporation on library schools has been delayed far beyond my expectations; however it is now being put in final shape for submission."

Williamson discussed his work on the survey in a letter to F.W.K. Drury, of Brown University Library. Drury was Chairman of the American Library Association Recruiting Committee and wanted information about the establishment of schools so that the members of his committee could be prepared to make suggestions or recommendations, if asked. He wrote Williamson on December 8, 1922, inquiring about a "survey for the Carnegie Foundation of library conditions," and indicated that he felt Williamson was the best person to write to for advice "from data well in hand as to the necessity of further library schools in the United States."

Williamson replied:

> On December 1, 1921 I submitted to the Carnegie Corporation an elaborate report on training for library work which was the result of considerable study of existing facilities, including a visit to all the schools which belong to the Association of American Library Schools. That report is to be published, I understand, but until it is I am not in a position to give out the findings in any detail.

He repeated his constant plea, "I might say that I believe the great need is now, and will for some time be, for better rather than more library schools." In the same letter he commented further on present conditions: "The schools, practically without exception, have pitifully inadequate incomes. The total budget in many cases about equals a fair salary for one first class librarian. I should regret to see more schools started on the present budget standards."

He felt librarians should press for action, especially regarding salaries and adequate budgets for the library schools, rather than be continually concerned with setting up more inadequate library schools.

> Instead of encouraging and stimulating the establishment of new schools, it would, in my judgment be a much greater

service to do something to bring to the attention of library and educational authorities the fact that a worthy professional library school cannot be run on next to nothing. If some A.L.A. committee would work out a standard budget for a self-respecting library school, providing the salaries necessary to get and keep first class instructors, and adequate funds for equipment and other essentials, it might at least cause some people to think twice before bringing into existence another poor struggling school. . . . I know that my views on this subject are not likely to be at all popular. However, you asked for my opinion and now you have it.

The Williamson report would reveal that the conditions of the existing schools in 1920 and 1921 were generally deplorable. His letter to Drury contained practical suggestions for bringing about change not by radical developments but by merely improving the situation in the existing schools. In fact, he deplored the tendency to continue establishing schools here and there, without study, investigation, or knowledge of the facts or examination of the need.

SUBMISSION OF THE REPORT

On December 1, 1921, Williamson had the report in completed form and in the hands of the Advisory Committee. The committee met on February 3, 1922, to discuss it. They met again on March 30, 1922, and submitted their recommendations regarding the report to the Carnegie Corporation. Dr. Herbert Putnam, Librarian of Congress and Chairman of the Advisory Committee, signed the memorandum to the corporation, "*In Re*: Survey by Dr. C. C. Williamson of Training for Library Work," dated March 23, 1922.[18]

The report to the Carnegie Corporation indicated that the Advisory Committee was in complete agreement regarding the following points of Williamson's survey:

1. That the Survey had been both appropriate and thorough;

2. That the Report embodies useful information, much of it novel, and a discerning analysis of the strength and the weakness in the existing systems of training which make the Report in itself a valuable contribution. The publication of the general portions of it (that is to say, all except those dealing with particular library schools) would, in the judgment of the Committee, be highly desirable;

3. As to both the conclusions and recommendations regarding particular library schools, the Committee assumes that it is concerned only with the general questions involved.

4. With the general conclusions the Committee finds itself in hearty agreement. It especially commends and supports these two general conclusions:

   a. That, as to the schools, the present need is not the further multiplication of library schools or diffusion of grants in aid of them, but the concentration of aid in grants to a few selected schools;

   b. That even in the interest of the service in the smaller libraries, the most effective grants (apart from the creation of demonstration units) may prove to be those tending to raise the general standards of the Library profession and render definite the qualifications.

5. With the general recommendations underscored in the Summary accompanying the Report, the Committee also unanimously agrees: and this will include all through page 11 of that Summary, leaving only (as outside of the responsibility of the Committee) the recommendations touching particular schools, beginning with that at New York City.

The memorandum also indicated that the Advisory Committee made no estimates regarding grants, since it felt this matter could be taken care of if and when the corporation was concerned.

The original report to the Corporation was a typewritten document entitled "Training for Library Work: A Report Prepared for the Carnegie Corporation of New York," by Charles C. Williamson, Ph.D., and prepared in 1921. The original report consisted of several chapters containing confidential matter which was omitted from the printed report of 1923, including the chapters "The Library School Situation in New York City"; "The Proposed Library School in the Portland (Oregon) Public Library"; "Library Service for Small Towns and Rural Districts"; "The Riverside Library Service School"; "The Library School of the Carnegie Library of Atlanta"; and "Other Library Schools." Other confidential material also was omitted from the published report. Much of these confidential data related to specific schools and individuals and were intended only for the use of the Carnegie Coporation. The identities of the schools were not revealed in the published report. Although Williamson received a number of requests for the key, this "was never divulged." In addition, the typewritten report contained reprints of his articles entitled "Some Present-Day Aspects of Library Training," "Report of the Special A.L.A. Committee on Certification, Standardization, and Library Training," and the "Report of A.L.A. Committee on National Certification."

At the end of May 1922, Williamson wrote Thwing that the Carnegie Corporation had made no decision regarding the report. "The report on library schools and training conditions in general has not yet been acted upon by the Carnegie Corporation. The various recent conferences I have had with officers of the Corporation indicate that they are deeply interested in the whole subject. As you know, such bodies move slowly."

The next step was to edit and revise the original report, which had been accepted by the Advisory Committee, and prepare it for publication. On August 3, 1922, Williamson wrote William S. Learned, Assistant to the President of the Carnegie Corporation, saying: "Dr. Putnam's copy I have edited, eliminating the confidential matter, and have sent it to Mr. Milam, the Secretary of the American Library Association in Chicago. He has promised to read it critically and to have it read also by Miss Bogle, the Assistant Secretary, formerly Principal of the Pittsburgh Library School. As soon as I hear from Mr. Milam, I shall be able to send you a copy for printing."

The copy was sent to Milam on August 18, 1922, and by the end of the month Milam had returned it to Williamson with a seven-page memorandum of "Notes on Dr. Williamson's Training for Library Work." This memorandum of August 29, 1922, containing Milam's comments, suggestions, and general observations, revealed his deep interest in the "splendid piece of work which ought to be published in its present form practically without change. Some of the statements you make are rather critical but if they are true, and I think they are, I believe they will do more good than harm."

Sarah Bogle wrote Williamson on September 5, 1922, expressing her appreciation of the work he had done on the survey "in bringing together and presenting it in the form which came to our attention. I went over the report several times considering it from different viewpoints. I realize that its publication may result in some controversy but I believe that the ultimate result would be one which would be eminently desirable and which could be brought about in no other way." She suggested a few people as readers of the preliminary report, including Ernest J. Reece, Arthur Bostwick, and Josephine Adams Rathbone. Apparently Williamson and the corporation were open about the report and did not consider it a secret document.

After the preliminary work came the time-consuming tasks of preparing the manuscript, printing, and proofreading. Another delay was caused by lack of funds in the current budget of the corporation to print this report. Milam wrote Williamson on November 15, 1922:

> I did have time and did make an opportunity to inquire about your report when I saw Mr. Bertram and to express an interest and a belief in its recommendations. Mr. Bertram's reply was to the effect that there had been no appropriation in

the budget for this publication but that there was such an item in the budget now and that there would probably be no considerable delay in the issuing of the book.

Work continued slowly as there were many details in preparing the report for publication. Questions had to be answered regarding what tables to include, how to label the charts, and an endless number of technical points. At the end of 1922 the actual text was in the printer's hand. On February 16, 1923, Williamson received a letter from Learned: "We have at last received from the printer complete copies of the proof of your library report."

Williamson sent copies of the proof to Andrew Keogh of Yale and Ernest J. Reece of the Library School of the New York Public Library for comments. Keogh stated in a letter of February 21, 1923, that he was "impressed with its thoroughness and sanity."

In April 1923, Williamson took advantage of the Easter holiday to complete his "Summary of Findings and Recommendations." He also indicates in a letter to Learned on April 1, 1923: "I am sorry it has taken me so long to get this stuff back to you. An evening hour now and then is all I have been able to give to it until yesterday."

Phineas L. Windsor, Librarian of the University of Illinois and Director of the Library School, wrote to Williamson on March 19, 1923, asking, Is there a "chance for us to see that report you made for the Carnegie Corporation on library schools?" Williamson answered him on April 15, 1923: "I honestly believe that you will sometime have a chance to see the Carnegie report on library schools. I have read the galley proofs and I presume it will move on its leisurely way so that copies ought to be distributed by June."

In this letter Williamson elaborates on the report and its limitations. "I didn't plan to report specifically on any schools except the half dozen or so that were applying to the Corporation for funds. The other schools, yours among them, were visited, more for the purpose of conferring with their directors about library school problems in general than to examine and report on them." The aim of the report was directly related to the activities of the Carnegie Corporation.

In this same letter Williamson attempted to predict reaction to the report.

> In general I think the library school people will not like the report. It will have to speak for itself; I shall not undertake any defense. It is two years old now. I'm stale on it—had literally to drive myself to go back to it for proofreading. However, I did find myself getting interested in it again and if I had the time, I would like nothing better than to thresh out with the critics the questions that I suppose it is bound to raise.

Williamson was hopeful that the report would stir up the library profession, provoking discussion and action.

H. L. Koopman, Librarian of Brown University, who had seen the proofs, was pleased.

> From the uniformity of my admiration for your analysis of the situation, and the judgments that you pass I feel curiously at a loss to say anything more than what my feelings prompt me to say in the way of praise and gratitude, especially in view of my sense of the importance of your report.

On March 31, 1923, Williamson answered Koopman.

> Some of the library school people who have seen the proof seem to be a bit upset about it. Many of my judgments will doubtless be challenged. I shall not be sorry if it does provoke some discussion for if everybody concurs in all my findings and straightway forgets them, the report will not have the healthful influence I hope it may have.

Williamson referred to the concern that the report was a secret document in a letter to William F. Yust, Librarian of the Rochester (New York) Public Library. Yust wrote on May 12, 1923, "There seems to be something mysterious about this report." Three days later Williamson answered, "There is absolutely nothing mysterious about the Carnegie Corporation's library school report." He indicated that it had been in the process of publication for a long time, but this was unavoidable: "The Corporation has a very small staff and this report had to wait until other publications were out of the way." Williamson also commented on the report itself, "They won't like it when they get it, but that has nothing to do with the length of time it has taken to get it published."

Yust was pleased to learn that it was to be published and made available. He was concerned that only some people would see it. The few who had seen it were the people whom Williamson wanted to provide him with advice and criticism. Yust commented: "You say the schools won't like it when they get it. That may be just the reason why the report is desirable if it is worth anything."

The report originally was entitled "Training for Library Work." This was the title Williamson used on his typewritten report of 1921, and it was changed by officials at the Carnegie Corporation, not by Williamson. On May 19, 1923, Helen Mulvaney, assistant to Dr. Learned, wrote Williamson to ask: "How does the title 'Training for Library Service' appeal to you for your book? Dr. Learned and I think it is a little more dignified than 'Training for Library Work.' " Williamson agreed, and Mulvaney wrote back, "We shall call the book 'Training for Library Service,' since that title is agreeable to you."

Many years later, Williamson reminisced about his relationship with the corporation during the time of the publication of the report. He stated in a letter to Sarah Vann on February 25, 1957:

> I might say that the bulk of what I might call, routine correspondence was with a Miss Helen Mulvaney, Assistant to Dr. Learned. She was a very intelligent go between for Dr. Learned, myself, and the Updike Press . . . In any matter of substance the letters were between Dr. Learned and myself. . . .
>
> Mr. Bertram, I might also explain, fell out of the picture as soon as it was decided to publish. That was out of his realm. The presidency of the Corporation was vacant, and Dr. Pritchett, the President of the Carnegie Foundation, was Acting President. Dr. Learned was Dr. Pritchett's assistant. About the time the report was published Dr. Keppel came in as President of the Corporation. This interregnum may have had something to do with the long delay in getting the report into print.

The Carnegie Corporation spent a total of $8,248 for Williamson's study of library schools.[19]

PUBLICATION OF THE WILLIAMSON REPORT

In the summer of 1923, *Training for Library Service* finally was published in a printing of 1,500 copies done by Daniel Berkeley Updike at the Merrymount Press in Boston, Massachusetts. It includes Williamson's "Summary of Findings and Recommendations," which gives his major recommendations to the Carnegie Corporation for the improvement of library education. In eleven categories, Williamson presented what he hoped would bring about the needed change in practices and solutions to problems inherent in library training. These included the following points and his recommendations:

Types of Library Work and Training: Williamson indicated that library work contains both "professional" and "clerical," duties and that each of these requires distinct and separate demands and each should require appropriate training. He also felt that the difference between these two types of library work had not been kept clearly in mind in library organization and administration; therefore, they tended to be confused in the work of the library schools. He advocated that professional training should require a broad, general education, represented at its minimum by a thorough college course of four years, plus at least one year of graduate study in a properly organized library school.

The Library School Curriculum: Williamson advocated a certain degree of standardization in the first year of profesional library school study; he felt that with the adoption of certification systems and the development of various agencies for training in service, it would be necessary to formulate minimum standards for scope and content of courses. He always advocated the dynamic approach and felt that the standards should be based on firsthand acquaintance with the most progressive library service rather than tradition and imitation.

Entrance Requirements: Williamson was concerned

about the problem of library school admission. He stated in the survey that he felt the methods then used were crude and unscientific.

> One of the most fundamental conclusions of this report is that professional library training should be based on a college education or its full equivalent. Joint courses, in which the student completes a library school course and earns a bachelor's degree in four years, represent a higher standard than that maintained in most library schools at present, but should nevertheless be looked upon merely as a step toward placing library schools on a strictly graduate basis.

The Teaching Staff and Methods of Instruction: The survey revealed that the majority of instructors in library schools were not equipped to give instruction of high professional character to graduate students. Williamson strongly urged that efforts be made "to raise the quality of instruction in library schools by increasing salaries and making teaching positions more attractive in various ways to trained and experienced librarians of the highest ability." He also urged the production of acceptable professional literature in the form of suitable textbooks and handbooks. He was extremely critical of so-called fieldwork, usually known as "practical work." He felt that it was emphasized excessively and that it should be considered as merely "one important method of instruction." He considered fieldwork generally unsatisfactory and of doubtful value to the student.

Library School Finances and Salaries: The survey revealed a dismal picture, which Williamson believed was one of the "fundamental causes of many of the deficiencies," of the library schools. Inadequate financial support of the school was revealed in meager budgets and low salaries, indicating that the library schools "are not keeping pace with the needs of the libraries for trained service."

The Need for More Library Schools and More Students in Training: Williamson hit at the heart of the problem in this section; he stated that the "recruiting problem can be solved only by making library service as attractive and desirable a career for well-educated men and women as other learned professions." He emphasized the need for a better grade of student and higher standards of instruction in the existing library schools rather than a need for many new library schools. His suggestion was to fill "existing schools rather than to establish new ones with the same meagre financial support and small enrollment." The responsibility of the library schools for recruitment can best be met by

1. Maintaining the highest standards of professional education;
2. Taking a leading part in the movement to put library service on a satisfactory economic and professional basis; and
3. Cooperating with professional organizations and college and university authorities in presenting to college men and women the rich opportunities for service in the library field.

Williamson felt that the "schools should be strengthened in every way, enrollment multiplied, standards of fitness for library work raised, and salaries increased to a point that will lead college men and women to look upon library work as a desirable career." He strongly advocated increased fellowships and scholarships to stimulate the interest of desirable candidates for admission and to enable the university library schools to compete with other graduate departments for the best students.

The Library School and the University: One of the most controversial aspects of the report was Williamson's insistence that the "professional library school should be organized as a department of a university, along with other professional schools, rather than in public libraries, state or municipal. Schools now conducted by public libraries should either take the definite status of training classes or be transferred to university auspices in fact as well as in name." He felt that the library schools lacked the prestige enjoyed by professional schools because (1) the library schools were small; (2) existing courses were too brief; (3) women predominated on the faculty and in the student body; (4) the preponderance of teachers had only the rank of instructor;

and (5) there was a total lack of anything recognized as productive scholarship.

Specialized Study: Williamson recommended that the first year of professional study continue to be general and basic but that the work of the second and following years be definitely and even minutely specialized.

Training in Service: Williamson abhorred the lack of opportunity and incentive on the part of library workers to seek continued professional growth and improvement. In order to rectify this situation, he recommended "well-developed schemes of service, with proper efficiency ratings, and a comprehensive certification system." Here he favored the development of correspondence courses for the continuing education of librarians. This is one part of the report which did not make an impact on library education. Williamson tried this while he was Dean of the School of Library Service at Columbia University but after a few years discontinued the effort.

Certification of Librarians and Standardization of Library Schools: Williamson was concerned that "no generally recognized standards of fitness of library workers have been formulated." He recommended that the profession itself formulate standards through voluntary action. He advocated a voluntary system of national certification to be worked out by the American Library Association, which he felt could be inaugurated at once. Here he proposed that the national certification board also serve as "a standardizing agency for library schools, having authority to enforce its decisions through its power of certifying without examination the graduates of approved schools. Besides its functions in the certification of librarians and accrediting of library schools, the board would naturally become an effective central agency for the promotion of all types of library training."

The Problem of the Small Library: Williamson felt that general improvements in standards of service, through "certification of librarians, strengthening of professional library schools, and the training of leaders, will accomplish more in the long run for the small public library than the multiplication of library courses and training schools of the usual type." Williamson also advocated that the small, isolated, independent libraries change from this "fundamentally unsound system" to one "in which the administrative unit is large enough to make it economically possible to command the services of an educated, professionally trained and skilled librarian. In most states this means the so-called county library system." Today throughout the United States this practice has gained in importance and is accepted in the many states that have developed county library systems, particularly California and New York.

Williamson Challenges the Library Schools: In commenting on the overall problems of library schools and library educators, he challenged them to strive for greater things.

> It would be ungracious to criticize the schools for not doing more to put library service on a higher plane. Within the limits of their pitifully small resources they have probably done all that can fairly be asked of them. Not, therefore, as a criticism but an encouragement to push on to better things, it should be pointed out to the library schools that an opportunity is theirs to wield a potent influence in bringing about a new library movement. Some of the epoch-making advances just ahead in the library world are discussed elsewhere in this report. Standards of service are to be worked out; a certification system inaugurated; methods of training in service for library workers devised; including an effective system of correspondence instruction; and county libraries and library extension promoted to the point where "books for everybody" will be a reality. In university, research, and other types of library, equally rich opportunities await the advent of leaders with vision and enthusiasm to set new standards of service. It is to the library schools that we should be able to turn for inspiration and guidance; but it must be confessed that trained leadership of the quality now demanded is not likely to be produced by the present curriculum and personnel of the professional schools.

He observed: "No school has ever attempted or is now preparing to disregard what has been done in the past and make a thorough, scientific analysis of what training for professional library work should be and build its curriculum upon its findings, instead of following tradition and imitating others. A more aggressive leadership is needed."

AFTERMATH OF THE WILLIAMSON REPORT

With the publication of the 1923 report, Williamson had completed his work for the Carnegie Corporation of New York, and his findings and recommendations were now available for all librarians and educators to read, study, and discuss. Some of his recommendations have remained the foundation of library programs to the present day. The report will remain a tribute to his zeal, energy, and ability. Robert D. Leigh felt that "the report was weighted with factual evidence, forthright in its criticism of the existing schools, and specific in its recommendations for an improved program of library school education."[20]

Frank K. Walter, commenting on Williamson's qualifications for undertaking this survey, stated, "No one who has the pleasure of knowing Dr. Williamson or who has discussed with him the matters treated in this report can doubt his ability, his interest, his intellectual honesty or his accuracy, so far as the facts on which his conclusions are based are concerned."[21] Walter acknowledged that the report was extremely critical of library training but the "attack is not vicious muckraking. The *facts* discussed are mostly matters of open record or common knowledge."[22]

Williamson came on the scene and presented his report at a time when librarians were deeply concerned about library training. Although not everyone agreed with all his findings or supported all his recommendations, whatever the attitude toward Williamson and his report, library education would never be the same again.

Williamson described his reaction to criticism of his ideas on library training and the report in a letter of April 3, 1923, to William Warner Bishop, who—as usual—disagreed with Williamson on certain aspects of the report. He was concerned that Williamson might take the criticism personally. Williamson reassured him.

> I have not the slightest personal feeling in a matter of this kind. I long ago learned to differ radically and even violently with folks I like personally. I expect to see plenty of criticism, both fair and unfair, heaped upon the Report. And of course I know also that it will be cordially approved by many people whose opinions carry equal weight. This means that the problems discussed will be threshed out and some progress made, I hope. It does not greatly matter whether all my judgments are sound or not, if the report starts people to thinking.

The impact of the report on library education was immediate and lasting. According to Elmer Johnson:

> Williamson's report was completed and most of it published in 1923 (the complete version—*The Williamson Reports* of 1921 and 1923—was issued in 1971 by Scarecrow Press). In many respects it marked a turning point in the modern era of library training. Williamson surveyed the library school curriculum, entrance requirements, teaching staffs, methods of instruction, and textbooks. He found confusion between professional and clerical training and recommended that library schools teach professional courses only, while training classes conducted by libraries could be used for teaching library techniques to clerical workers. He recommended more standardization in the library school curricula, particularly in the first year. Finding only two schools that required a college degree for admission, he recommended that all should have this requirement. Concerning the teaching staffs in the library schools, Williamson noted that only 52 per cent were college graduates themselves, only 7 per cent of them had ever had any training in teaching and nearly a third had had little or no practical experience in library work. He particularly noted the lack of adequate textbooks and the reliance on the lecture method of teaching. He recommended better qualified teachers, more class discussion, more and better supervised field work, and improved textbooks. The need for more library schools and more students was pointed out, as well as the need for certification of professionally trained librarians. Finally, the need for postgraduate library courses in specialized and advanced fields was recognized and considerable emphasis on cultural rather than technical courses

THE WILLIAMSON FAMILY around 1886. Clarence and Lizzie Williamson with Alfred and Mary; Charles is at the far right. *Courtesy of Alfred Williamson and Charles S. Watson*

The Class of 1897, Salem High School. Williamson is standing in the back row, second from the right. Only ten of the twelve graduating students were photographed. *Courtesy of Robert J. Dixon, Salem (Ohio) High School Alumni Association*

CHARLES C. WILLIAMSON, 1898, when he was a teacher in District 6, Goshen Township, Mahoning County, Ohio. *Courtesy of Grace Richards*

CHARLES C. WILLIAMSON, early 1900s, probably when he was a student and secretary at Western Reserve University. *Courtesy of Genevieve H. Williamson and Charles S. Watson*

CHARLES C. WILLIAMSON. *Far left*, at his desk at the Municipal Reference Library in the City of New York, where he worked from 1914 to 1918. *Courtesy of Kenneth R. Cobb, Municipal Archives, Department of Records and Information Services, City of New York.*

THE MOUNTAINEERS, October 15, 1937. *Left to right:* Charles C. Williamson, Charles S. McCoombs, Frank Waite, Paul North Rice, Keyes Metcalf, and Harry Miller Lydenberg, at the cabin in the Catskills. *Courtesy of Genevieve H. Williamson and Charles S. Watson*

CHARLES C. WILLIAMSON, 1940, at his home at Hastings-on-Hudson, New York. *Courtesy of Genevieve H. Williamson and Charles S. Watson*

CHARLES C. WILLIAMSON, November 1954, in retirement. *Courtesy of Genevieve H. Williamson and Charles S. Watson*

CHARLES C. AND GENEVIEVE H. WILLIAMSON, August 1964, at their home in Greenwich, Connecticut. Probably one of the last photographs of C.C.W. *Courtesy of Genevieve H. Williamson and Charles S. Watson*

was encouraged. On the whole, Williamson's findings concerning library training were not flattering to the profession but his recommendations were sound and they were adopted in considerable degree, if gradually, over the next decade.[23]

Today most of Williamson's ideas about library education have become part of the curriculum and program of study in library schools throughout the United States. According to Leigh, "The Williamson recommendations became the major program for discussion and action regarding library education for the next quarter century. Much that he proposed was translated into practice during that period."[24]

As training schools closed or merged with teaching institutions, library schools affiliated themselves with universities and began to grant degrees in the field of library science. At first the Bachelor of Library Science (B.L.S.) was awarded as a fifth-year degree after the undergraduate baccalaureate. By 1950 most library schools offered regular graduate programs with a master's degree as the fifth-year degree beyond the baccalaureate. The baccalaureate now is a prerequisite for entrance to a graduate library school.

According to Elmer Johnson, "Along with the funds for the Williamson study, the Carnegie Corporation provided support, over a ten-year period, for the promotion and extension of library training."[25] The corporation also aided "in the establishment of the graduate school of library science at the University of Chicago. . . . With the beginning of advanced library study leading to M.A. and Ph.D. degrees, the training of librarians entered a new phase."[26] [In 1926 Williamson proposed a doctoral program at Columbia University, but while he was there not one doctorate was granted.]

CRITICAL REACTION TO THE REPORT

On October 8, 1923, Ernest J. Reece wrote Williamson, "Mr. Bowker is preparing for the *Library Journal* a number of symposia on your report, including one by heads of library schools, one by non library school people, and one by graduates of library schools who are now in positions of some prominence." Williamson had not heard about this and told Reece: "I did not know that Mr. Bowker is planning such an extensive symposium on my report. Bowerman wrote me he had urged Bowker to publish reviews by different people, but I did not know that he had acted on the recommendations. It goes without saying that I shall be much interested in seeing the various comments."

The November 1,[27] and December 1, 1923,[28] issues of *Library Journal* published these comments. The two-part presentation of the views and reactions of the library world revealed a wide range of opinion and criticism of the report, ranging from praise to annoyance.

The reactions of library school faculties and directors were much more antagonistic than those of librarians working in the field. This was to be expected since the report focused directly on the library schools, and offered criticisms and recommendations for change in matters pertaining to programs, budgets, faculties, students, and curricula.

The members of the New York State Library School faculty were annoyed because they felt that the report showed a "pervading note of disparagement" so strong and insistent that the general public would have the impression "that there is nothing good to be said of library schools." Many library schools agreed that the broad lines and principles of Williamson's survey were justified, but they disagreed with him strongly about many of the immediate problems. One note of criticism was that the survey was taken in 1920-1921 when "all of the schools, due to post-war conditions, were below normal especially in attendance."

Josephine Adams Rathbone, Vice-Director of the Pratt Institute Library School, strongly criticized the report and incorporated a note of sarcasm: "It is kind of Dr. Williamson not to reproach the schools for the high percentage of marriages." The fact that Williamson had no formal library training was also considered a weakness. "His lack of experience with actual working conditions in the smaller libraries is shown by Dr. Williamson's criticism of the retention in the school curriculum of minor record work and certain mechanical processes. He does not realize that high school librarians, heads of departments in the smaller

Carnegie Corp. of N.Y. and Williamson Report 163

libraries, and many librarians of public libraries have to do themselves or teach others how to do many simple and 'unprofessional' tasks."

Williamson had commented on his lack of professional library training in a letter of December 31, 1919, to William F. Yust, then Librarian of the Rochester (New York) Public Library.

> I came in to library work from the teaching profession without the advantage of library school training. For some years I was inclined to question the necessity of value of such training for the particular kind of specialist work in which I had been interested, but experience . . . has thoroughly changed my attitude towards library school training.

Reece thought that there was really nothing new in the Williamson report and that people in the area of library training long had recognized the problems. He expected that the faculties of the schools "will be found anxious to do their share in remedying existing weaknesses."

Some of the commentators also challenged Williamson's findings, especially his statistical charts and tables.

In general, the comments were praiseworthy; all agreed that the study would help bring about changes. This view was well expressed by Elisabeth G. Thorne, Director of the Syracuse (New York) University Library School.

> With such thorough agreements concerning the fundamentals of Dr. Williamson's timely, able and comprehensive report the singling out of minor points upon which we think practice is at variance or further adjustment desirable seems captious. Considered not as a criticism but as an encouragement to push on to better things it bears all the marks of patient investigation, thorough study of conditions and startlingly accurate conclusions. Dr. Williamson's findings are not flattering but they certainly are illuminating. The instinctive reaction of the library schools is defensive but a close study of the reports shows only the kindly knife of the surgeon wielding it in the interest of separating dead from living tissue.

Tommie Dora Barker, Director of the Carnegie School of Atlanta, stated:

Whether or not one sees eye to eye with the writer in his conclusions, none would underestimate the importance of the report in setting forth an ideal to be attained and its value in bringing together so complete a body of fact relating to library schools. Apparently library schools are sailing an uncharted course.

William E. Henry, Director of the University of Washington Library School, felt Williamson, even without formal library training, was the best man for the task of surveying the library schools. In fact, Henry considered this a decided advantage since Williamson was "not a product of any library school, and therefore clear of the prejudices for or against any one or all." He thought it "would have been difficult to select a better equipped person for the rather difficult task."

> Dr. Williamson impressed me as a good academic scholar, one who had seen much of the inside of library service. . . . His report shows a searching investigation of the institutions, and what seems to me a remarkable ability to place his finger upon both the centers of strength and of weakness of the schools as a group.

Many observers felt the library schools had been lenient with themselves and had failed to be critical of their own work. Part of the problem was identified by Elisabeth G. Thorne, who stated that most of the schools were bound by "the limitations of poverty."

Williamson also appeared able to speak for the librarians who had remained modest and inarticulate too long, expecting their work to speak for them.

Librarians generally were favorable toward the report and did not tend to be as hypercritical as the schools and faculties.

Clarence E. Sherman, Assistant Librarian of the Providence (Rhode Island) Public Library, declared:

> Many of Dr. Williamson's conclusions I have found to be eminently satisfactory, and to me the spirit of the survey is sympathetic even though decidedly incisive and at times jolting. Perhaps it is because I agree with so much that he has

written, that I applaud so loudly, and not on account of any particular merit in the report itself.

C. B. Roden, Librarian of the Chicago (Illinois) Public Library, stated:

> Dr. Williamson has rendered a valuable and timely service in collecting and putting in order the facts as he found them, and, being a trained investigator with many qualifications for the task, he has performed it to the evident satisfaction of a much larger circle of readers than the organization that retained him to make this survey. That he had no axe to grind seems clear enough.

George Bowerman, Librarian of the District of Columbia Public Library, felt that the real value of the report was not necessarily to influence librarianship or members of the profession but "also and perhaps more especially . . . those outside the profession."

Dr. Milton J. Ferguson, Librarian of the California State Library, was pleased Williamson was doing the "gentle prodding" which the library schools needed. Ferguson thought the library schools had done well, all things considered, and he held high hopes for the effects of the report.

> Particularly I am in sympathy with Dr. Williamson's recommendations that schools be placed on a firmer financial basis, that schools become departments of universities thereby putting themselves in touch with student supply and also ranging library instruction on a plane with other professions, and that instructors be required to be better trained for their jobs and very much better paid. Experience will dictate changes in the curriculum. Certification will come; and with it a better understanding of requirements and higher standards of service. Without question organization or reorganization of the library, outside of large cities, on a county unit will have a far reaching and beneficial effect upon personnel and services alike.

Williamson's Reaction to the Critics

Williamson maintained in a letter of June 29, 1955, to Sarah Vann:

> As to the reception of the published report by the library profession I was quite indifferent. Of course I knew [what] I said in the published part of the report would be unwelcome in many quarters, but I never doubted the validity of my conclusions. . . . I prefer not to attempt any evaluation of the permanent contributions of the report. That will be left to the historians.

He again commented on the report and the reasons for undertaking it in his letter to Sarah Vann on February 25, 1957:

> I do not think a more objective study of professional training in any field has ever been made. I was asked to get the facts and report them with recommendations as to how the existing situation could be improved. The Corporation was being importuned all the time to put funds into training for library service, and with the hundreds of small Carnegie libraries in the country it naturally felt some degree of responsibility for the service they were giving. It needed to have the facts and be able to formulate some kind of policy to guide it in its relations with its existing and would be beneficiaries.

In addition to the published comments regarding the report, Williamson also received letters expressing the feelings of friends and colleagues.

Thomas J. Jones, of the Phelps-Stokes Fund, wrote to Williamson on October 8, 1923: "On my return to the office, I have found your very important book on TRAINING FOR LIBRARY SERVICE. The comprehensive and accurate statement which you have prepared will undoubtedly not only enlarge the facilities for library service, but become the guide of all those who are concerned in the effective training of librarians."

A letter on October 30, 1923, was received from Ernest C. Richardson, Honorary Director of the Princeton (New

Jersey) University Libraries and Research Professor of Bibliography who stated: "I have not before congratulated you on your remarkably lucid and well organized report on library training . . . It gives precisely what any of us need to orient ourselves on the situation."

Frederick N. Keppel, President of the Carnegie Corporation of New York, also was aware of the growing controversy caused by the publication of the report, and it pleased him. He wrote Williamson on November 9, 1923, "Nothing will do more to keep your report in the minds of the profession than a bright little controversy."

Judson T. Jennings, President of the American Library Association (1923-1924), addressed a memorandum "To the A.L.A. Council Members," on December 10, 1923, indicating some of the items to be included on the program of the association's midwinter meeting at Chicago. One item concerned library education; Jennings recommended that the members read Williamson's *Training for Library Service* as background for discussion. Mr. C. L. Cannons, Chief of the Acquisition Division of the New York Public Library wrote to Williamson on January 7, 1924, that Jennings at the Chicago midwinter meeting characterized the report on library training agencies as "the most stimulating document concerning library methods which has appeared in many years."

A letter of March 28, 1924, from Corinne Bacon, former Director of the Drexel Library School, clearly expressed the feelings of librarians who disagreed with Williamson but could not ignore him.

> Has your "Training for library service" brought you, I wonder, more thanks or bricks? I am not going to throw bricks, tho' of course I don't agree with you on all points, but I've been meaning for some time to write and thank you for saying, in a voice that cannot be disregarded, some things that I have had much at heart for years. You should have the gratitude not only of the schools, but of the library profession at large. . . . I just want you to know how deeply interested I am in the re-making of library schools and how keenly I appreciate your valuable report.

In an undated holograph manuscript Williamson's sense of humor, as well as his farm background, is revealed in his comment on the criticism that his certification plan would make all librarians similar.

> Because I came out 10 years ago in favor of certification of librarians I was accused of wanting to make librarians as alike as peas in a pod. I have never really thought it worthwhile to take any notice of such an absurd deduction. I have merely wished to be sure that there are good peas in the library pod. There is necessarily a good deal of resemblance between peas whether they grow in the same pod or not, yet I suppose the biologist would say that no two peas are precisely alike, but if you want peas you don't want beans or corn or any other vegetable. We are growing peas—we want them all to be of uniformly high quality.

EFFECTS OF THE REPORT

In a letter to the author on October 17, 1964, Williamson observed that the corporation was greatly increasing its financial support for ALA activities "that could be interpreted as an outgrowth of my report. One thing, for example, was my insistence on some system of accreditation for library schools. I think you may find that the ALA, with Corporation support, had much to do with implementing many of my recommendations."

Florrinell Morton described the effects of the Williamson report in the area of accreditation.

> In seeking to provide, in a realistic way, the standards for which Mr. Williamson called, the Board of Education for Librarianship found necessary to provide for eleven different types of programs in 1926 . . . but the mere process of surveying the types of library education offered, and of fitting the programs into the descriptive categories to which they belonged had a beneficial effect upon library education. This first halting step toward accreditation sought to establish structure out of the formless mass that was library education, and to begin progress toward a system of library education into which all parts would fit. That by 1933 it was possible to

reduce the number of types of programs to three may indicate that the hard look at library education which the Williamson report had caused librarians to take, and this first effort at standards and accreditation under standards, had had more than a little effect in bringing order out of chaos. The structure which evolved as a result of the impact of the Williamson report was that of academic affiliation.[29]

In 1954 the report still was considered an important document on library education. According to Dr. Robert Leigh:

> Thirty years have passed since the Williamson Report struck the library world with the impact of a thunderbolt. This seems ample time for recovery from the shock. It is now time to reexamine the Williamson recommendations as stated in 1923 and reemphasized by Leigh in the Public Library Inquiry in 1952. In our search for some general framework for the education of librarians, it appears that with modifications the Williamson proposals are still the best starting point. Williamson criticized the methods [existing at the time of the survey] for giving a background in the basic principles of librarianship *and* a knowledge of practical skills. He also recognized the inadequacy of unsupervised work in a library as a means of education. The ideal curriculum according to the Williamson recommendations would include a first year of general instruction in the basic subjects and a second year of specialized training. Between the first and second years students should have a full year of library experience. Other recommendations emphasized the need for a system of accreditation for library schools, for voluntary certification of librarians, for preparation of better textboks and manuals, and for summer schools and institutes to provide for in-service training of professional librarians.[30]

Dorothy Bevis stated:

> The now famous report of Dr. C. C. Williamson in 1923, *Training for Library Service*, studied in detail and evaluated formal education for librarianship in the United States. It is true that the Williamson report was limited to the fifteen schools which at that time required a bachelor's degree for admission, but it held implications for all library education as

it urged that "professional library training should be based on a college education or its full equivalent" and that library schools should be placed on a "strictly graduate basis."[31]

According to Leigh, "the Williamson report had established a distinctly different pattern of thinking for library school education."[32]

Dr. Lester Asheim, former Director of the Office of Library Education of the American Library Association and formerly Dean of the Graduate Library School of the University of Chicago, stated, "In my own work, the Williamson Report was the most important contribution he made, and it continues to be of value because it raised basic questions that we still are raising."

Dr. Leon Carnovsky, Professor at the Graduate Library School of the University of Chicago, observed in 1967: "By all odds, his Training for Library Service is his major contribution to graduate library education. . . . This book repays reading even today. It stands as a sort of watershed between library preparation through training classes and the attempt to achieve true professionalism through affiliation with universities. Its impact may be seen in numerous ways." Carnovsky summed up Williamson's significance in the field of librarianship as "probably his contribution to establishing library education as a reasonably respectable element on a university campus."

Dr. J. Periam Danton, Professor of Library Service, University of California at Berkeley, stated that unquestionably Williamson's outstanding contribution was the report, "which influenced every library education program for twenty-five years. A very important work. Without it—or its parallel—we'd still be in the nineteenth century."

Dr. Robert B. Downs, Dean, University of Illinois Library School at Urbana, considered Williamson's major contribution "his study of library education for the Carnegie Corporation and subsequent application of these findings to Columbia School of Library Service." Downs evaluated the effect of Williamson's work: "The impact was tremendous. After his Carnegie Report, library education was never the same again. His ideas made important contributions to [the] improving of professional librarians' status."

Dr. Lowell A. Martin, former Professor at the School of Library Service, Columbia University, and former Dean, School of Library and Information Science, Rutgers University, observed that

> the one report that is acknowledged as having decisive influence on library education is based on research. The Williamson report set the path for university schools with instruction by means of professional principles, a path which has taken over twenty-five years to follow to the point where they can discern where it leads. He also pressed for full-time faculty members of distinction, in place of part-time practitioners, and urged that the first year of graduate instruction should be general and basic. His tenets have increasingly prevailed in the years since. Williamson's conclusions were rooted in extensive research, including data on faculty, students, and methods. He visited all the recognized library schools of his time.[33]

Martin also felt that "from a certain view the many articles on education for librarianship which appeared in the following years were addenda to the Williamson thesis, with intermittent spicing in the form of contrary views which often took on an aggravated, shrill tone."[34]

WILLIAMSON'S EVALUATION OF HIS CONTRIBUTION

A letter of May 24, 1937, to Herbert Putnam, then Librarian of Congress, indicated Williamson's own opinion of his contribution. He asked if Putnam recalled that in the "dim and distant past you were a member of the Advisory Committee which supervised the preparation and publication of a report on training for library service, sponsored by the Carnegie Corporation? That was in 1921." He asked Putnam to read Louis Round Wilson's article entitled "The American Library School Today,"

> hoping that you may find time to glance at it and that you may be impressed, as I have been, with the rather remarkable degree to which the recommendations of that report have

been carried out. The explanation probably is that, consciously or unconsciously, I was able to incorporate in my recommendations the actual trend in library training. I do not assume that the report has been solely responsible for what has taken place.

Williamson's own approach to his report was casual. In a letter to the author on October 17, 1964, he observed:

For a good many years after publication I was much interested in following events which seemed to have been influenced by my findings and recommendations. Now after so many years have gone by and my interests having long ago shifted to other fields I will have to confess that my memory is a bit hazy as to the content of the report. I believe I have never read it through since I finished with the proof sheets.

Louis Round Wilson commented on the place of the Williamson report and its effect on librarianship.

The Williamson Report was the first to make itself felt. Williamson spent considerable time visiting the existing library schools and carefully studying all aspects of education for librarianship. Trained in the field of political science, and experienced as a municipal reference librarian and director of the information service of the Rockefeller Foundation, he was able to view the schools objectively and critically. His analysis of the status of library school faculties, budgets, curricula, and students revealed a situation wholly unflattering. His prescription for the improvement of the condition of the schools included recommendations that they become integral parts of universities; that their staffs contain a high percentage of full-time instructors chosen for distinction in ability and training; that the first year of study be general and basic; that there be a sharp differentiation between professional and clerical studies, with the latter largely eliminated; that specialization be reserved for the second and third years; that financial support be substantially increased; and that a national examining board be created to formulate requirements concerning library training in general and to pass upon the credentials of library school graduates. Here was a bold, penetrating analysis that defined the professional field, described the serious limitations within it, pointed out the possibilities of improvement through advanced study and investigation, and, in a very real sense, charted the possible course for a sound development within the field. The report was widely discussed and, as a result in part of the preceding studies and discussions by the American Library Association of certification and training, many of the recommendations were carried out later at Columbia, under Dr. Williamson's direction, and at many other library schools.[35]

On January 4, 1943, Williamson wrote Louis Round Wilson discussing the Williamson report and observing that "in the library world I suppose the survey of the library schools which I undertook in 1920-1921 at the request of the Carnegie Corporation has had and may continue to have the most far-reaching results of anything I have ever done."

Norman Horrocks stated that the "Williamson *Report* is generally regarded as the most important document to have appeared in the history of library education."[36] As a result of the report "background and understanding were urged as the basis for library education, rather than practice. Library schools moved to the centers of background and understanding, the universities, and away from the centers of applied instruction, the training classes and the institutes."[37] Since 1923 the majority of accredited library schools have been established in connection with programs of higher education and "have achieved a recognized status in professional education."[38]

Dr. Frederick E. Keppel, President of the Carnegie Corporation, summed up the aftermath of the Williamson report in a letter to Williamson on April 9, 1924, when he observed, "Apparently the Williamson Report has started something that won't stop in a hurry."

NOTES

1. Florence Anderson, *Library Program, 1911-1961*, p. 5.
2. *Ibid.*, p. 6.
3. Norman Horrocks, "Library Education: History," in *ALA World Encyclopedia of Library and Information Services*, 2nd ed., p. 492.

4. George S. Bobinski, *Carnegie Libraries: Their History and Impact on American Public Library Development*, p. 197.
5. Robert D. Leigh, "The Education of Librarians," in Alice I. Bryan, ed., *The Public Librarian*, p. 307.
6. Sarah K. Vann, *Training for Librarianship Before 1923*, pp. 170-171.
7. *Ibid.*, p. 171.
8. Florence Anderson, *op. cit.*, p. 6.
9. Sarah K. Vann, *Training for Librarianship Before 1923*, p. 173.
10. William S. Learned, *The American Public Library and the Diffusion of Knowledge*.
11. Florence Anderson, *op. cit.*, p. 6.
12. Louis Round Wilson, "Historical Development of Education for Librarianship in the United States," in Bernard Berelson, ed., *Education for Librarianship*, p. 47.
13. Florence Anderson, *op. cit.*, p. 7.
14. *Ibid.*, p. 11.
15. George S. Bobinski, "Carnegie, Andrew (1835-1919)," in *ALA World Encyclopedia of Library and Information Services*, 2nd ed., p. 167.
16. Florence Anderson, *op. cit.*, p. 20.
17. *Ibid.*, p. 24.
18. Carnegie Corporation of New York, "Report of the Advisory Committee *In Re*: Survey by Dr. C. C. Williamson on Training for Library Work," to the Carnegie Corporation, March 23, 1922 (with permission of Florence Anderson, former secretary of the Carnegie Corporation).
19. Florence Anderson, *op. cit.*, p. 93.
20. Robert D. Leigh, "The Education of Librarians," p. 307.
21. Frank K. Walter, "A Dynamic Report," *Library Journal* 48 (September 1, 1923), 709.
22. *Loc. cit.*
23. Elmer D. Johnson, *Communications*, pp. 270-271.
24. Robert D. Leigh, "The Education of Librarians," p. 308.
25. Elmer D. Johnson, *op. cit.*, p. 271.
26. *Loc. cit.*
27. "Williamson Report: Comment from the Library Schools," *Library Journal* 48 (November 1, 1923), 899-910.
28. "Williamson Report: Comment from Librarians," *Library Journal* 48 (December 1, 1923), 999-1006.
29. Florrinell Morton, "Education for Librarians" (conference held April 22-23, 1960, Kansas State Teachers College of Emporia), *Bulletin of Information* 41 (January 1961), 12-13.

Carnegie Corp. of N.Y. and Williamson Report

30. Robert D. Leigh, *Major Problems in the Education of Librarians*, p. 16.
31. Dorothy Bevis, "Windows—Not Mirrors," *American Library Association Bulletin* 57 (January 1963), 47-48.
32. Robert D. Leigh, "The Education of Librarians," p. 310.
33. Lowell A. Martin, "Research in Education for Librarianship," *Library Trends* 6 (October 1957), 210-211.
34. *Ibid.*, p. 211.
35. Louis Round Wilson, *op. cit.*, p. 48.
36. Norman Horrocks, *op. cit.*, p. 492.
37. Lowell A. Martin, *op. cit.*, p. 207.
38. Willard O. Mishoff, "Education for Library Service," p. 123.

11
THE ROCKEFELLER FOUNDATION 1921-1926

DURING THE PERIOD FROM 1920 to 1923, when Williamson was involved with the publication of his report, he still maintained full-time positions. Until 1921, he remained at the New York Public Library in his position as Chief of the Economics Division, leaving in 1921 to assume the duties of Director of Information Service of the Rockefeller Foundation.

DEPARTURE FROM THE NEW YORK PUBLIC LIBRARY

In his letter of resignation of May 3, 1921, addressed to Edwin H. Anderson, Williamson stated, "I hereby tender my resignation as Chief of the Economics Division to take effect June 1, in order to accept a position with the Rockefeller Foundation." He expressed his regret at leaving the New York Public Library, where he had worked since 1911. "I cannot make this formal statement without adding informally that I take this step with very great reluctance and a deep sense of regret; regret not only in leaving work which I have always found most congenial and thoroughly worthwhile, but also in interrupting the personal relationships with yourself and other members of the staff, which have come to mean more than I can find words to express."

Anderson replied on May 7, 1921: "I have your formal resignation dated May 3. I reported your resignation to the Executive Committee on May 6, and it was accepted with regret by them as well as by myself." He continued: "I can only repeat here what I have said to you face to face, that personally and officially I very much regret the severance of

The Rockefeller Foundation

your relations with this institution. I know I voice the general opinion of all our associates here when I say that we are sorry to have you leave, and that you will be greatly missed."

Return to Earlier Interests

On March 3, 1921, Williamson had received a letter from Edwin M. Embree, Secretary of the Rockefeller Foundation at 61 Broadway, New York City, confirming his conversation of the same day with Embree and George E. Vincent, President of the foundation. The purpose of the interview was mainly to discuss a proposed position at the Rockefeller Foundation.

In this letter, Embree outlined the functions of the new service and the duties of the new director. He asked Williamson to examine the outline, stating that if he was interested in the work, "we should be very glad to talk with you again at your convenience." In this letter he identified the duties Williamson would assume as Director of the Information Service:

1. Surveys of various situations and problems undertaken by a staff of investigators.
2. The gathering of information with respect to medical education throughout the world.
3. The gathering of similar information about public health administration and activities on a worldwide basis.
4. A register of international fellows and scholars in the field of medical education and public health.
5. Free information service for medical educators and public health officers.
6. The publishing of an International Medical and Public Health Yearbook. (This has not yet been decided. I am enclosing a tentative prospectus of such a publication and would appreciate your comments upon it.)
7. Other proposals not definitely decided upon, which may be undertaken from time to time, including the

preparation of various aids to medical libraries in this country and abroad, preparation of lists of books and possibly a bibliographical service which would list the total resources of medical literature in a given country.

In this same letter Embree further informed Williamson that the Information Service "would comprise the work at present carried on by three separate departments of the Foundation: the Department of Research and Surveys, the Department of Statistics and Records, and the Library." The staffs of these departments totaled about twenty-five persons, all of whom worked under the leadership of the director.

In his answer Williamson gave an account of his work up to that time, emphasizing his interest and activities in the field of sociology and public health. The major concern of the Rockefeller Foundation was to find a person who would be involved with their publications; the Library was of secondary importance. For Williamson the change really represented a return to his former interests.

Williamson indicated to Embree:

> My interest in matters of public health was originally based in part at least in my college study of social problems combined with special courses in biology. At Bryn Mawr I had a course on Municipal Problems, confined largely to health problems, somewhat along the lines of Godfrey's "Health of the City." As I told you today, during my Administration of the Municipal Reference Library I found that the Health Department needed a far better and more intimate service than we could give it from the Municipal Building. I therefore proposed to Dr. Haven Emerson, Commissioner of Health, and Dr. J. S. Billings, Deputy Commissioner, that they turn over their so-called library to us and let us run a library and information service for them in their own building. They were delighted at the proposal and finally by patient persistence we got the money for it. . . . So far as I know no other city in the country has a similar library service.

Williamson stated the reasons for his resignation from the New York Public Library and his decision to work at the

Rockefeller Foundation in a letter of March 7, 1921, to Embree.

> My interest in library work has developed of late principally along administrative lines and as there is a very limited opportunity in that direction in my present position I shall feel free to make a change when something more important presents itself. Recently I was asked to go to Peru for five years to organize a national system of libraries, but felt obliged to decline to consider it.

Williamson felt that the Rockefeller Foundation position would be an advance; he had reached an administrative dead end at the New York Public Library.

By April 20, 1921, the decision was made. Williamson received a letter informing him that at a meeting of the Executive Committee of the Rockefeller Foundation, held on Friday afternoon, April 29, the following resolution was adopted:

> RESOLVED that Dr. CHARLES CLARENCE WILLIAMSON be appointed DIRECTOR OF INFORMATION SERVICE for the period June 1-December 21, 1921, with salary at the rate of Eight thousand dollars ($8000) per year.

The Rockefeller Foundation was pleased to have a man of Williamson's caliber to head the new department. In fact, at the meeting of the Executive Board, Dr. Albert Shaw and Mr. Raymond B. Fosdick, both of whom knew of Williamson's work, "spoke in high terms of it and in appreciation of the fact that the Foundation seems likely to be able to avail itself of your service." Embree expressed the fact that the officers of the "Rockefeller Foundation look forward with anticipation to the prospect of your association with us in this important department of the Foundation's work."

Williamson was reluctant to start work at the Rockefeller Foundation until he could "close up promptly the little piece of work I have in hand for the Carnegie Corporation. Though I have been at it for several months and have the field work done and report well underway, it still has to be threshed out with the Advisory Committee after it is written. By working intensively on it perhaps I could get it pretty well out of the way by June 1st. This would of course end my outside work for the Carnegie Corporation." The "little piece of work" was *Training for Library Service*. This arrangement was accepted by the Rockefeller Foundation.

Williamson also told Embree that he did not regret giving up some of the numerous activities which occupied him. He wrote: "Perhaps you will recall that when I called at your office three or four weeks ago I said that the opportunity appeals to me especially because, among other things, it would give me a chance to concentrate all my time and energy on a single one of the many interesting fields among which I am now forced to divide myself, with constant danger of overworking."

On May 3, 1921, Williamson accepted the appointment "on the terms stated in your letter of April 30." He admitted that he still knew little about the work of the foundation, "which I hope to take up with results which will not fall greatly short of your expectations." Although the work of the foundation was closely related to some of Williamson's earlier interests, Williamson was taking a bold step and he knew it.

THE MOVE TO THE ROCKEFELLER FOUNDATION

Whatever his misgivings, Williamson began work on June 1, 1921, as Head of the Information Service of the Rockefeller Foundation. He received a letter on May 9, 1921, from President Vincent: "Welcome to our staff! We are looking forward with pleasure to working with you."

Williamson's friends and acquaintances showed mixed reactions to his new position and particularly to his leaving library work.

Andrew Keogh, Librarian at Yale University, submitted Williamson's name to Embree and called Williamson in a letter of May 13, 1924, "in my judgment the best equipped person in the field." Keogh felt it would be difficult to replace Williamson at the New York Public Library.

However, Everett R. Perry, Librarian of the Los Angeles Public Library, wrote him on May 17, 1921, that he was shocked to learn that "you were intending to leave library work." Perry found it hard to reconcile himself to this change. "Is your decision irrevocable? I think the profession can ill afford to spare you." Williamson replied six days later, "Yes, the decision to leave the New York Public Library and go to the Rockefeller Foundation is irrevocable." He then described his deliberations about making this change: "I considered the subject long and prayerfully and could reach no other decision. . . . It is quite possible that I shall be able to do a more important work, even for libraries, at the Foundation than I can do here. Some very interesting possibilities are opening up."

Before his association with the Rockefeller Foundation, Williamson had become interested in the development and improvement of some of the bibliographical tools dealing with the fields of medicine and public health. This interest continued throughout his entire life. He was not just a working librarian, but one who was always vitally interested in the compilation and publication of material that eventually would go into libraries.

In a letter to Vincent on May 21, 1921, Williamson set forth the idea that "one of the first concerns is the organization of the bibliography of medicine and public health. . . . I believe a very important contribution can be made to research and education in medicine and public health by organizing and extending the bibliographical work now being done."

A "Memorandum in Re: Publication of 1922 Reports," dated December 20, 1923, showed the extent of Williamson's activities at the foundation. He was kept busy preparing the annual reports of the foundation, the report of the International Health Bureau, and a pamphlet for the Retirement System. In the memorandum, Williamson discussed the problems of getting the reports out on time and offered recommendations to improve the publications schedule.

Williamson was a hard and meticulous worker. This characteristic sometimes annoyed people, while at other times it earned him high praise. He certainly was extremely careful to check and recheck his material and make sure that all aspects were examined. He based his investigations on the principles of fact-finding.

While working at the foundation he earned the praise of F. R. Strong, Sales Manager of the Rumford Press, which handled printing for the foundation:

> I want to express my gratification at the way the work on the Reports has been handled this year by Dr. Williamson. In all our experience in handling the various reports, none have ever been handled so well as has been the case this year. . . . It is my great pleasure to deal with Dr. Williamson and I trust that we have the opportunity of keeping on as official printer for the Foundation. . . . I trust that you may convey our compliments to Dr. Williamson in this matter, although I have said much the same thing to him in talking with him. But I want you all to know, who are connected with him in the work there, how much we appreciate his uniform courtesy and efficient handling of the work.

BEGINNINGS OF DISSATISFACTION

Although Williamson enjoyed his work at the Rockefeller Foundation, it was not without its problems. One problem dealt with his title as Director of Information Service, which some members of the staff wanted changed. For a time, Williamson held the title of Editor because the title of Librarian already was held by another staff member, although Williamson's administrative authority included that of Head of the Library.

From June 1, 1921, until December 21, 1923, Williamson held the title of Director of Information Service. However, after he submitted his resignation on July 19, 1923, which was not accepted, this was changed to Chief, Information Service, effective January 1, 1924.

Organizational and personnel problems were present during Williamson's tenure at the Rockefeller Foundation.

The Rockefeller Foundation

Part of the problem appeared to be in the area of administrative responsibilities and authority where there seemed some confusion and overlapping of duties. Various staff members suggested making the library independent, a plan with which Williamson did not agree.

Another indication of problems at the Rockefeller Foundation was revealed in a letter of July 19, 1923, from Williamson to Vincent, recommending the reorganization of the Information Service. Williamson felt that some features of this report were "designed to constitute a hint that my services were no longer desired." However, he talked with several people at the foundation and decided he might be mistaken. Williamson continued, "Since that time, however, several things have occurred which seem clearly to mean that my resignation would not be unwelcome."

In this letter Williamson tendered his resignation to take effect December 31, 1923. He wanted the time to help train his successor and also to have an "opportunity to renew some of the contacts and interests I dropped, as requested two years ago, in order to devote myself fully to my duties here at the Foundation. In this way I hope to find without great delay some work that will be as interesting and worthwhile as what I have been doing for the Foundation." No reasons were given, nor were those "several things which have occurred" identified. Williamson did not leave at that time. In 1924 his title was changed to Chief, Information Service.

By March 1926, Williamson had decided to leave the Rockefeller Foundation and accept a position offered him by Columbia University in the City of New York. On March 6, 1926, he informed Vincent of the offer and submitted his resignation: "Columbia University has offered me a position I have felt I cannot decline. Will you therefore please accept my resignation as Chief of the Foundation's Information Service, to take effect, if agreeable to you, on June 1st." Williamson was leaving the position he had held for five years to embark upon the final, most important phase of his career—that of Director of Libraries and the School of Library Service at Columbia University.

EVALUATION OF THE EXPERIENCE AT THE ROCKEFELLER FOUNDATION

Williamson's work with the Rockefeller Foundation and the Carnegie Corporation certainly "added to his usefulness as a librarian, as did his tremendous energy, his efficiency as an administrator, and his interest in new library developments ranging from gadgets and building plans to library school curriculum and duplicate pay collections."[1]

Wilson and Tauber evaluated his work at the Rockefeller Foundation.

> From 1921 to 1926 he occupied the newly created post of director of Information Service at the Rockefeller Foundation. The extensive library of the Foundation was placed in his department, and he was charged with the foundation's publicity and the compilation, editing, and publication of its reports. . . . The relationship of these activities to the later service of Williamson, both as librarian and as dean, are apparent.[2]

Williamson commented on his work at the Rockefeller Foundation in a letter of January 4, 1943, to Louis Round Wilson:

> President Vincent had the idea that my library experience would be useful to them and it was. The Foundation had a rather extensive library devoted to the subjects in which it was especially interested, certain aspects of public health, for example, and medical education. The Library was put in my department which helped me to keep my library contacts. I also had charge of the Foundation's publicity which had previously been in the hands of the famous Ivy Lee Associates. I compiled, edited and published the Foundation's reports and other publications until I came to Columbia on May 1, 1926.

He considered his experience at the Rockefeller Foundation most valuable to him at Columbia. "These years at the Rockefeller Foundation may seem like an interlude in my library work but I never regarded them as such."

Williamson's career was a varied one. His approach to problems was that of a man trained and knowledgeable in the methods of scientific investigation. He had achieved national stature as a critic of library education. He was a man with vision and a broad understanding of the problems of the many people who would make use of the libraries at Columbia University. His approach to professional library training now would be tested in the newly formed School of Library Service.

He was about to begin the most important work of his career and to relate his concept of professional librarianship, embodied in the report of 1923, to a graduate library school, and to the work of professional librarians at Columbia University.

According to Keyes Metcalf, "The Economics Division, the Municipal Reference Branch, and the Carnegie Corporation report were only stepping stones to Dr. Williamson's work at Columbia which began in 1926."[3]

NOTES

1. Keyes D. Metcalf, "Charles C. Williamson," *Library Service News* 11 (November 1943), 23-24.
2. Louis Round Wilson and Maurice F. Tauber, *The University Library*, 2nd ed., p. 544.
3. Metcalf, *op. cit.*, p. 23.

12
COLUMBIA UNIVERSITY IN THE CITY OF NEW YORK
(1926-1943)

APPOINTMENT TO COLUMBIA UNIVERSITY

NEGOTIATIONS WITH WILLIAMSON started early in March of 1926 for the position of Director of Libraries and of the Library School at Columbia University. On March 7, 1926, Williamson wrote Trustee Frederick Coykendall that he had decided to accept the offer.

> Perhaps it may be in order for me to confirm in writing the assurance I gave you yesterday that I am happy to accept the position you offered me, of Director of Libraries and Director of the Library School in Columbia University, at a salary of $10,000 a year, the duties and functions of the positions to be essentially as outlined in my letter of February 12 to Mr. Fackenthal.
>
> To this normal statement may I add some expression of the feeling of pleasure with which I look forward to being associated with you and the other officers of administration and instruction in this most interesting and important branch of the University service.

Williamson was not the first choice for this position. President Nicholas Murray Butler of Columbia University, and Secretary Frank D. Fackenthal had originally sought William Warner Bishop, then librarian of the University of Michigan who

> had tentatively accepted Columbia's offer pending the outcome of a meeting of the Board of Regents of his University, but was induced to remain at Michigan by a series of flattering

concessions, including a substantial increase in salary and the deanship of a new library school to be established there. Dr. Bishop was then asked to suggest the names of other librarians for the position. He mentioned several candidates but recommended Dr. C. C. Williamson as the "right person" for Columbia.[1]

The original plan was for Williamson to start work at Columbia on July 1, 1926. However, the University officials were eager for him to start at an earlier date, since so much organization and preparation was necessary if the Library School was to open in the fall of that year. It was imperative for Williamson to spend a good deal of time in organizing the program, developing the curriculum, working with faculty, students, and staff, working on the material for the Library School collection, and taking care of the transfer of material from the library schools of New York State and the New York Public Library, now newly merged with Columbia University. Williamson informed Butler that he had made arrangements with the Rockefeller Foundation to spend some time at Columbia during April and start full time on May 1, 1926.

Williamson's official appointment was dated May 7, 1926. The resolution adopted by the trustees at their meeting on May 3 stated:

> RESOLVED, that Charles C. Williamson (A.B. Western Reserve, 1903; Ph.D., Columbia, 1907) be appointed to be Director of the University Libraries and Head of the School of Library Service if and when established, from May 1, 1926 during the pleasure of the Trustees, at a salary at the rate of $10,000 per annum.

In addition he was also appointed "from July 1, 1926, during the pleasure of the Trustees . . . to be Professor of Library Administration, without salary."

Williamson was to work with President Butler for the next seventeen years, and their relationship always was cordial and friendly. During times of stress Butler backed Williamson completely; through various major and minor crises he offered him constant support.

Nicholas Murray Butler was born in Elizabethtown, New Jersey, in 1862 and was educated in the public schools, entering Columbia College in New York City at the age of sixteen. He graduated in 1882 and the next year received the A.M. degree and in the following year his Ph.D. He also studied in Berlin and Paris. From 1887 to 1889 he was an assistant tutor at Columbia University, after which he was promoted to the position of adjunct professor of philosophy, which he held for one year. From 1890 to 1901 Butler was a full professor of philosophy, ethics, and psychology, and elected as dean of the faculty of philosophy at that time. In 1901 he was appointed President of Columbia University, a post he held until his retirement in 1945.

As President he did a great deal in "expanding the university's effectiveness and prestige."[2] He was a world traveler and was awarded honors and degrees from many universities. In 1931 he won the Nobel Peace Prize, which he shared with Jane Addams. He received honorary degrees from so many United States and foreign institutions that he was called the champion international visitor and retriever of foreign orders and degrees.

Butler was a friend of most of the notables of his day, active in education, political, and public affairs. In 1912 he was the Republican vice-presidential nominee. He was always extremely active in educational affairs, and with professional and scholarly organizations. He instituted many changes at Columbia University during his forty-four years as president. He died on December 7, 1947.

Butler was pleased with Williamson's appointment; throughout Williamson's service at Columbia, a major concern of Butler was the fear of losing him. "The one thing which I do not wish to have confront me is your own separation from the direction of the Library under any circumstances whatsoever."

Prior to Williamson's appointment as Director of Libraries, a number of acting librarians had served Columbia since 1913; these were various members of the administration or faculty.

Roger Howson, Assistant Librarian at Columbia, commented in his *Annual Report* for the year ending June 30, 1926, that this was a "year of anticipation":

> To the library, as to the University as a whole, the appointment of Dr. C. C. Williamson as Director of Libraries, and the advent of the School of Library Service are reasons for great hopefulness as to the future. The school does not come to us as a stranger, with a need for introduction and for time to find itself in new surroundings. It is a return, rather, after 38 years of absence, and words of welcome are not necessary. Dr. Williamson brings to us wide experience in administration and in library questions, and a wise and reasoned plan of development is assured by his appointment.

IMPLEMENTATION OF THE 1923 REPORT

In his position as Director of Libraries, and especially as Head of the School of Library Service, Williamson now could implement the plans and recommendations of his 1923 report. In *Training for Library Service* Williamson advised what should be done; now at Columbia he had the opportunity to show what could be done.

Many people felt that Williamson's appointment as Director of the Library School at Columbia put him in a position that would be a proving ground for his theories about library education. As a strong exponent of changes in library education, Williamson was in a strategic position to bring about change. Charles McCoombs wrote to him on April 6, 1926, that he considered Williamson's appointment to Columbia as "nothing less than poetic justice."

On March 31, 1926, William Warner Bishop wrote Williamson:

> I have but recently learned that you are to take the vacant post at Columbia. I am delighted to hear it, and I offer you my hearty congratulations on a great professional opportunity. And I am sure you will find the new work interesting and profitable. My best wishes go with you in your transfer to new duties.

Williamson answered Bishop on April 16, 1926, in a letter which expressed his concern that he lacked experience in university library work. The letter revealed this shortcoming and expressed his feelings about the situation.

> The opportunity at Columbia is almost limitless, or, rather, it will be limited only by my own capacity to rise to meet it. It is too bad that they were unable to get a man with a long and rich experience in university library work. When it was finally passed down the line to me I felt that I ought to accept it and do the best I could. I shall have to draw heavily on the wisdom and good will of my friends, among whom I am happy to count the distinguished librarian of the University of Michigan.

James Thayer Gerould, Librarian at Princeton, was pleased with Williamson's appointment to "what is probably the most difficult job of its kind in the country and the most interesting."

Grace L. Cook, former employee at Columbia, was "delighted to hear that you are to be at the helm" and observed that it was a "great pity that Columbia has been so long without a real librarian."

Williamson received many other congratulatory letters when his appointment at Columbia University was announced. A reading of these letters shows the high esteem in which he was held by library educators and librarians; the congratulations of his colleagues often expressed a warm, personal touch.

Harry E. Koopman, Librarian at Brown University, wrote him on April 23, 1926: "Congratulations to Columbia, and incidentally all round! You have the cordial good wishes of our entire profession."

Isadore G. Mudge, of Columbia, wrote on April 6, 1926: "The announcement that you are to be Director of Libraries here is of the happiest augury for Columbia, and I want to express to you my very hearty pleasure and satisfaction over the news. I look forward with much pleasure to working under your direction."

Elbert Benton, of Western Reserve University, considered this a great opportunity "for a large future you would like and for which you are admirably prepared. I trust you will find great happiness and the fullest success in the new field."

A note from Roger Howson, of Columbia, stated:

> I can say now, and could not say then, what was in my mind when we met . . . the other day. Which is how much I expect of pleasure in working with you. You hardly need a welcome to Columbia, where you have so many friends and associates—I do think you will find good spirit of willingness in the library, and for myself I am sure I can promise it.

DIFFICULTIES OF THE DUAL RESPONSIBILITY

It is impossible to separate Williamson's dual responsibilities as Director both of the Libraries and of the School of Library Service at Columbia University. The increasing complexities of these two positions became ever more burdensome to him. At first the idea seemed right—to have the person who was in charge of the libraries and concerned with the work of professional librarians also carry the responsibility for training professional librarians. In theory it was ideal; but in practice it proved impossible even though he believed the University Libraries and the Library School should be under a unified directorship.

The Carnegie Corporation on March 20, 1926, assured Columbia of its "intention to contribute $25,000 per year for ten years for the Library School, beginning with the school year 1926-27."[3] President Butler felt "that a moral obligation existed with the Carnegie Corporation to maintain the same organization which was established in 1926 when the School of Library Service was opened on the Columbia campus."[4] However, a later examination of the correspondence between the Carnegie Corporation and the Columbia administration disclosed "that no such agreement existed or was implied."[5] Several times the suggestion of separating the two positons was made but each time Butler refused. Not until 1953 did Columbia separate the two positions and appoint two officials, one to assume the duties of Director of

Libraries and the other as Dean of the School of Library Service.

The dual role which Williamson held for seventeen years was most taxing. In his memorandum of June 4, 1953, to the alumni of the School of Library Service, President Grayson Kirk certainly was referring to Williamson and his work when he wrote:

> It has been true too frequently that Columbia has attempted to meet new responsibilities without commensurate increase in administrative personnel at the top level. Men of marked abilities, men who are leaders in their fields, have been permitted to assume greatly increased duties and responsibilities. This they have done unselfishly, unstintingly, at real sacrifice to themselves in many instances. Great though their ability, their energies, and their loyalty, there comes a time when in their own interests and in the interests of the larger programs, such men must not continue to spread their activities so widely.

President Kirk commented specifically on the dual posts. "Each, of course, is a job to tax the abilities of the best trained and most energetic individual."

In 1926 Williamson knew full well that he was to assume both posts, but prior to that time the title of Director of Libraries did not exist and the duties of the position were nebulous. The designation of Head of the School of Library Service was merely a title; there were no students, faculty, or program. The fact that it grew so rapidly into one of the largest library schools at that time certainly can be credited to the work of Williamson and his faculty, but in 1926 these were in the future. As the years passed, all aspects of both positions grew in size, complexity, and responsibility, including personnel, budgets, services, facilities, and resources. Williamson was to be occupied with these problems for the next seventeen years; it was no wonder he worked fifteen to eighteen hours a day.

Melvil Dewey was interested in Williamson's work and concerned about him. Dewey wrote on January 25, 1930, from Lake Placid (Highlands County, Florida), in his reformed spelling, that he was worried about Williamson's overworking, "a hazard so comon in N.Y., for never, since creation has eni place been burning out so meni of its ablest men by overstrain." Mrs. Williamson was troubled about her husband's health and had written confidentially to Dewey, hoping he would convince Williamson to take a vacation. Dewey also commented on Williamson's work: "I lyk yu personali & shd keenli regret seeing yu cripld but my great interest is in librarianship & yu ar the captain of the flag ship in our fleet." Dewey also reminisced about his own contribution to library work and his hopes. "My mynd went bak to my librari skool babi of over 40 years ago & and my growing hopes of its wonderful usefulness to the world." Dewey had high praise for Williamson and wrote to Butler on September 18, 1929, referring to Williamson as "a myti good man."

Dewey urged Williamson to get away from the job and take a vacation at Lake Placid, Florida. "Cum down to our perpetual June for a fu weeks wher we now hav the best golf in the south, the fynest clymat on erth & evri temptation to spend most of the day in our perpetual sunshyn." Williamson heeded Dewey's advice and went in March of that year for two weeks. The pressures of his work at Columbia had brought him to the point where he sorely needed the vacation.

Williamson mentioned these pressures in his correspondence with Fackenthal and Butler, discussing the problems of the dual positions and searching for a solution. By 1930 the pressures were increasing steadily; he observed in a letter to Fackenthal on March 3, 1930:

> It seems to be physically impossible for me to continue much longer with my present program of work. . . . For two years it has been obvious to me that I must lighten up if I expect to keep fit until I am sixty, but instead of that I appear to be getting in deeper all the time.

He analyzed the difficulty:

> There seems to be three elements in the work load, which can perhaps be thought of separately even though in practice they are inseparable: (1) The Library, (2) the School and (3) the indirect responsibilities that both positions involve. There is

no item in the whole range that I do not enjoy, or would not enjoy if the pressures of the total were not so heavy and continuous.

He examined all the possible ways to ease the work load and pondered "every way out." He suggested resigning the directorship of the School and devoting himself "entirely to the interests of the Library." He confessed that he was "now neglecting shamefully many of my responsibilities to the libraries of the University." He preferred to remain as Director of Libraries, feeling "better fitted for the library job than for the School." His reasons for this preference were his feelings that the School was inadequately housed and that he might succumb to depression over the situation, the fact that the School lacked the resources to develop a second year and advanced work, and because it was a twelve-month job as long as there was a summer session.

Williamson believed that there was "a great advantage in a unified administration of the School and the Library, but the advantages are outweighed by the burden of routine and detail." This revealing document was written to obtain Fackenthal's advice and help "in finding a way out."

Williamson wrote to Butler on April 24, 1930, more or less repeating the points he had discussed previously with Fackenthal.

> The pressures of duties which require my personal attention, either because they cannot be delegated or because there is no one to whom they can be delegated, has become so great that I have gradually come to the conclusion that I must either give up the directorship of the School of Library Service or have an assistant who can relieve me of responsibility for a great many details that I have hitherto taken care of myself.

Williamson's threat to resign was not carried out. The problem was solved by hiring additional office staff and a general assistant. Throughout his entire career at Columbia, Williamson held the dual positions and the responsibilities of both.

Williamson's Contributions as Director of Libraries

Williamson wrote his own evaluation of his contribution to the field of academic librarianship in a letter to a former student on May 25, 1957. "I really do not think I ever made any notable contribution directly in that field except perhaps in the training of librarians."

This was not completely true, but it reveals his modest appraisal of his contributions. In his seventeen years at Columbia University he was able to expand the library, placing it among the five largest university libraries in the United States. His energy and zeal, even in the face of formidable internal problems, made Columbia University into a major research library.

Williamson maintained high standards for the conduct of the University Libraries. He met with department heads frequently and gave advice and guidance based on all the facts. He was constantly concerned about new developments which could make the Library more useful to the academic community. He began a rental collection and photo reproduction services; he was involved in the work and services of the Reference and Cataloging Departments. Williamson never lost his interest in experimentation.

Williamson's primary contributions at Columbia were the reorganization of the Libraries, the development of the collections, and the building of South Hall or, as it is called today, Butler Library. His contribution to university librarianship was internal, within his own organization at Columbia. His contributions to other libraries are more likely to be evident as imitations of his procedures, plans, and ideas, rather than as a direct influence on university librarianship.

He did express some of his views of academic librarianship in an article "Essentials in the Training of University Librarians—III," which appeared in the December 1939 issue of *College and Research Libraries*. Although his views were briefly presented, they revealed his feelings on the education of academic librarians. He felt that it was difficult for the library schools to train for top positions in university libraries as it would be to turn out university presidents. He advised training on the job for those who show a capacity for administrative work. He was concerned with the mediocre applicant who sort of got involved in library work as a student and although not suited for other professions was encouraged by others that he would make a good librarian, often rated as average or below, but exceptional for library work, assuming that less is required for libarianship than for other professions. He felt that college and university libraries have a special responsibility to send good students to the library schools, to provide them with practical training on the job, after the library school has done "the best we can for them in one or at most two years of professional training."

Williamson was responsible for "developing a well-coordinated library system for Columbia University." Robert B. Downs has described Williamson's contributions as: "Emphasis on development of scholarly research collections; creator of bibliographical tools (e.g., his aid in completing Bibliothèque Nationale *Catalogue*); library cooperation; and his development of the Columbia University Library and its physical facilities under his direction."

Williamson's strength as a university librarian was his ability as an organizer and administrator. Yet this was in contrast to one of his major weaknesses: his inability to avoid becoming buried in detail. Several people who worked with him mentioned this trait. Although he could plan ahead and his administrative ability was tremendous, he tended to become involved in details which could have been left to others.

Paul North Rice commented on the challenge facing Williamson at Columbia:

> In 1926, the Columbia University Libraries presented a challenge that might have overwhelmed an administrator with less energy and ability. Alone among the great universities, Columbia had been without a library head for some years, the Provost serving as Acting Librarian. It was apparent that much reorganization was necessary in spite of the fact that individual members of the library staff had attained national recognition. As Director of the University Libraries, Dr. Williamson was given oversight of the entire library adminis-

tration, and it required rare courage to solve some of his difficulties with personnel.[6]

Rice thought that Williamson's major task was to bring all the varied Libraries at Columbia for the first time under one director. In addition, he also planned one of the world's great library buildings.

In an interview with the author on July 14, 1966, David H. Clift said that Williamson's work as a university librarian, although important, will always be overshadowed by his contribution to library education. Clift attributed this likelihood to the fact that the report of 1923 "had a more far-reaching effect on the profession than his work in university library work." Clift considered Williamson's career "highly successful" because of four major accomplishments: (1) strengthening of the library; (2) development of its service; (3) training of the professional and nonprofessional staff; and (4) the resulting ability of the library to meet better the needs of its users.

Williamson worked well with top administrators and was able to obtain cooperation by working closely with them. He was able to present the library's needs to the provost and the president, with whom he had excellent relations. He did not enjoy the same rapport with the university faculty, other than his own faculty in the School of Library Service. In an interview on July 11, 1966, Carl White said that Williamson was unable to "reach" the university faculty, observing that Williamson worked from the top down, rather than obtaining a consensus on which to base policy and administrative decisions.

Williamson had a strong sense of responsibility in seeing that the library provided the very best service possible. His actions were strongly guided by this objective.

Ernest J. Reece also commented on Williamson's university library work.

> The other undertaking before Dr.Williamson in 1926 was even larger and more intricate, if less pressing. The university libraries had functioned for years with varying degrees of effectiveness but without full coordination as regards the

building of collections, the systematizing of service, and the administering of personnel. The physical facilities also were a handicap at some points. The applying of remedies here was a long-term task. Gradually and over a period of years procedures have been reorganized; a personnel scheme has been introduced; staff appointments have been made with a view to strengthening weak spots and stepping up efficiency; and a new building has been erected which typifies the workshop principle and assures adequate quarters both for a large section of the library activities and stock and for the School of Library Service. All of these, and especially the problems of staff and building, entailed major efforts and tested anew the director's powers of organization and administration.[7]

Williamson's successor, Dr. Carl M. White, summarized Williamson's contributions in a letter to the author on July 20, 1966:

1. setting up the School of Library Service;
2. making progress in the development of centralized administration of the University library system;
3. planning of Butler Library;
4. fostering of acceptance by the university of library school graduation as a basis of appointment to professional positions on the library staff; and
5. taking the Libraries and the School of Library Service forward without allowing the combined responsibility to wreck his health or his reputation.

In the early years, the Columbia administration was not convinced that a library school belonged in a university. Others in the field also were concerned about having a library school curriculum operate in a university environment. Williamson had

> an immediate, insistent job on his hands. It was to take the faculty resources and the experiences of two schools and build a new one. He streamlined the two-year Albany program, helped establish a workable pattern of work for a fifth-year Bachelor's program, and evolved a Master's program which if not well related to doctoral work at Columbia, nevertheless

proved workable and produced some of our leading librarians.

Library schools did not develop programs which related more closely to their universities until during and after World War II.

Prior to Williamson's appointment, the control of the Columbia University Library was mainly in the hands of the faculty; for years the various units operated without central leadership. Williamson's notable achievement was his attempt to consolidate and establish a more centralized university library administration.

Williamson also had to deal with the job of fostering acceptance of library school graduation as a basis for appointment to professional positions. Gaining recognition for professionally educated librarians in some of the universities was a major undertaking and at no other American university was "the struggle . . . so dramatic as at Columbia." White maintained that Williamson was mainly responsible for "effecting the change." However, the change was not achieved without years of hard work or without a struggle. The concept of professional librarianship now is generally accepted in the United States, yet few realize the part which Williamson played in this achievement. He was eager "to see the Libraries put into practice the ideals which the School was established to serve." The challenges and problems at Columbia were enough to test the limits of one man's "creative and administrative powers, and . . . absorb as much energy as he has to give."

White also commented on whether the Libraries or the Library School at Columbia were neglected by Williamson during his administration.

> During Dr. Williamson's time, the Columbia Libraries and the School faced extraordinary problems and the demands on him were likewise extraordinary. It is easy to say that the Libraries were neglected or that the School was neglected; both charges were made. It would be more accurate to say the conditions he inherited made it difficult to give either one the amount or the order of attention they needed. President Butler believed till his death that the Trustees had a moral

obligation to the Carnegie Corporation to have these two units of the University under one head. The point was not cleared up until 1953, the year the two positions were separated. In the language of the track meet, it was not given to Dr. Williamson to concentrate separately on the hurdles and the hundred-yard dash; both races had to be run at once. Any appraisal of his work should take the nature and the local weight of the total responsibility he bore into account.

During his years at Columbia, Williamson could devote only part of his time to either position, each of which had developed into more than a full-time job.

These comments, coming from the man who succceeded Williamson in 1943, help to place the problems which both men faced at Columbia in perspective and permit a deeper understanding of the difficulties, the successes, and the failures which have been attributed to Williamson's years at Columbia.

Louis Round Wilson commented in a statement to the author on July 13, 1966, on Williamson's contributions to university librarianship.

> At the same time he solved a number of problems in the administration of the Columbia library which was complicated by the inadequacy of the building, poor organization, and lack of guidelines for personnel selection. He likewise carried out an extensive building program that required planning for six or more floors, a stack that was completely enclosed, and depended upon air-conditioning and electric lighting. All this required ability and constant attention.

Wilson thought Williamson "rather quiet and conservative, not particularly interested in causes or movements, not inclined to seek prominence in professional organizations, and less demanding for greater freedom and recognition of his library and school in the administrative organization of the University than he might have been."

Expansion of Library Facilities—Beginning of South Hall

On September 3, 1932, President Butler laid the cornerstone of South Hall for Columbia University's new library building. South Hall was the name used for the building during Williamson's tenure at Columbia; today it is called Butler Library.

Williamson spoke briefly at the ceremony observing that the building should be ready for occupancy not later than May 1, 1934. He pointed out this was the third library building Columbia had erected in the past fifty years.

> Has ample provision been made for the growth of the University, the expanding stream of important printed matter which a great university library must have, and for the growing importance which books and an abundance of printed matter play in programs of instruction and research in a university? Frankly, we do not know. The history of every university library building in this country is evidence that it is next to impossible to plan a library building that will satisfactorily serve its purpose for much more than a single generation. Perhaps it will turn out that we are wiser than our predecessors, but I doubt it.

In speaking of South Hall he observed: "This splendid building, which we owe to the generosity of Mr. Edward S. Harkness, has not been designed to be a complete modern university library building. Many important collections and activities were left entirely out of consideration in its planning because they were to be provided for in the Low Library." He concluded:

> It is customary on occasions of this sort to speak in terms of centuries. On laying the cornerstone of the Low Library thirty-five years ago President Low said, "I hope this stone will remain where it is for centuries." Grateful as we are for

this much needed building, I must express the hope—in which I am confident the gracious donor would join—that this stone will remain in place only so long as the building serves to promote the highest and noblest service which the University seeks to render to mankind.

In an article by Trusten W. Russell in the *New York Times* on July 8, 1934, South Hall was hailed as "a fine piece of architecture, a new interpretation of modern education."[8] It was also "one of the largest library structures in the world."[9] The building was erected in two years at a cost of $4 million. Adequate library space was urgently needed to replace the crowded conditions in Low Memorial Library and to

> make the great reservoir of books on all conceivable subjects available to all the varying needs of a huge university with the least possible delay and difficulty. The collection of books already numbers 1,300,000, and the library is built to house ultimately 4,000,000.[10]

OBJECTIVES IN PLANNING SOUTH HALL

In this article, Williamson discussed the problems he faced in planning South Hall and some of the guidelines which were used in plans for the new building.

> We hope, and we really feel, that we have gone a step ahead in solving the problem of convenient book storage. In affording facilities for scholars who gravitate toward such large collections of books and manuscripts as are available in New York City, we must provide for advanced work on an exceptional scale. By supplying 200 private studies and 700 private desks, all with direct access to the central stacks, we believe that we have met this problem squarely. On the side of library technique and in the evolution of stack planning and equipment we feel sure that we have taken a big step forward, and we are confident that we have contributed something that future libraries will take advantage of and, I suppose, improve on.[11]

In this same article, he commented on the development in the facilities of academic libraries.

> The interior decorations represent the same attitude implicit in the structure, that of tempting the student to use the facilities for wide reading. The exterior, a notable example of Italian Renaissance design in brick and stone, in harmony with the other neighboring university buildings, is, when compared with the stately Low Memorial Library across 116th Street, striking evidence of the phenomenal improvement in facilities for advanced teaching and research that have come to American universities in the last half century.[12]

President Butler thought highly of the building, as he indicated in his statement to the *New York Times* on October 7, 1934:

> The new library building, to which the trustees of the university have given the name of South Hall, is believed to be as finely planned and as well constructed an academic building as is to be found on either side of the Atlantic.
>
> It is distinctly a laboratory library—that is, a library building designed not merely for the storage and distribution of books but for constant working with books, by teachers and students themselves, under circumstances and surroundings of the greatest ease and convenience.[13]

With the official opening of South Hall in the summer of 1934 Columbia had, "for the first time since it became a great university, an adequate physical plant for its library." Williamson planned South Hall primarily for graduate and advanced work and for the central service of the University's library service. "The professional libraries, including those of science, law, architecture, journalism, and fine arts, will remain in the various professional schools."[14]

The actual plan for the library building included fifteen tiers of book stacks in the central part of the building; these were air-conditioned to provide the proper atmospheric conditions for book storage. In this way the books were protected from dust and light with carefully regulated humidity and temperature.

Whatever problems developed in later years in the use of South Hall, in 1934 this building was considered an important landmark in the development of library architecture. According to Carl White, "given the circumstance, Butler Library was an important achievement,"[15] especially since "Dr. Williamson did not have the freedom he desired in planning this building, and he would of course alter the plan if he were developing it a third of a century later."[16]

Keyes D. Metcalf, former Librarian of Harvard, has commented that the new library was planned and built "in spite of the fact that during the construction period Dr. Williamson was desperately ill. The building naturally suffered from his enforced absence, but it is one of our university library buildings, and in most ways a successful and noteworthy one."[17]

Paul North Rice felt the building of South Hall was one of Williamson's major contributions as Director of Libraries, in spite of later criticism of the building.

> Columbia had far outgrown the inadequate quarters of Low Memorial Library. Through the generosity of Mr. Harkness, Dr. Williamson was able to plan the present South Hall. Although he was stricken with a long and dangerous illness while the building was being erected, it none the less shows in its general plan and in innumerable details the thought and inspiration of a rare craftsman.[18]

A letter of December 27, 1934, from Nell A. Ungar of the Reed College Library to Williamson declared: "Your friends rejoice with you in the completion of the new library building. . . . This building is the greatest tribute to you and vivid evidence of what you have accomplished at Columbia."

With all its strengths and weaknesses, Butler Library still stands today as a tribute to Williamson's work.

Development of the Library's Collections

During his years as Director of Libraries, Williamson was vitally concerned with and encouraged the growth of the library's collections. He fostered and promoted acquisition of books and other materials and especially donations of rare book material and special collections. Throughout his term of office at Columbia he constantly maintained this interest, which is revealed time and time again in his correspondence with potential donors and his desire to obtain material to enrich the Columbia Libraries. He commented on June 20, 1964, on this interest in a letter to Charles W. Mixer of the Friends of the Columbia University Libraries, "We used to be proud of our intake of rather rare materials."

From the beginning of his administration Williamson was deeply aware of the need to build up the library's collections and to pursue an active policy of purchase and donations. On February 1, 1926, he wrote a letter to Professor David Eugene Smith expressing his views on obtaining gifts to the University Libraries.

> I was much interested in the question which you (or was it Professor Trent?) asked me how the Columbia Library could make sure of becoming the ultimate repository of the many fine collections that are to be found in New York City. My reply was, I think, the best way would seem to be to keep in touch with them and show a real interest in them.

Williamson realized that this was only a partial answer to the question. He believed there were

> many ways of convincing the owners that valuable private collections should be left to the University Library. The condition of first importance is ample and worthy housing facilities. Then a continuous campaign of appropriate publicity seems to me to be necessary—publicity relating to the special collections which the library already has and their value in the educational and research work of the University. This can be accomplished not only through articles of various kinds, but by means of frequent exhibits. This would seem to be sound psychology. I am sure that if I had a valuable collection I would prefer to leave it to an institution that gives evidence of appreciating it and endeavoring to make it widely useful.

He continued in the letter to Smith: "Columbia should lose no time in adopting a policy which both Harvard and

Yale are following of stimulating the interest of undergraduates in rare and fine books. In the years to come the best friends of the University Library are likely to be men of wealth and culture whose interest in books was aroused in their students days." He indicated a practical way to accomplish this aim through the Library School, which "should have a professor of bibliography who could give in the undergraduate college the kind of course that would appeal to undergraduates and instill in them a deep interest in books that would mean much to them in after life as well as to Alma Mater."

The quantitative growth of the Columbia University Libraries during Williamson's tenure can be seen in the statistics for the period between 1926 and 1943. In this period there was a low of 30,777 accessions during the 1925-1926 year, a high of 91,072 added to the collection in 1930-1931; the average number of accessions was about 45,000 items per year. The recorded use of the libraries fluctuated a great deal, with the lowest attendance in 1929-1930 of 1,628,095, and the highest count in 1928-1929 of 2,381,428. The records reveal that there is a constant and continuous growth of the total number of volumes added to the University Libraries. When Williamson became Director of Libraries the collection totaled 1,055,198; on his retirement it was recorded as being 1,935,425. In his seventeen years at Columbia 880,227 items were added to the collection. This shows a record of steady progress, an ever-growing collection, and constant use revealing a picture of healthy growth.

These statistics reveal numbers, not the quality of resources or of services. The *Annual Report*s list the materials which were added, presenting in detail the major items purchased or donated. The policy was to obtain material which would aid in research and extend the scope of materials needed in Columbia's constantly growing graduate programs. These acquisitions included special collections, primary source materials, rare books, and bibliographical and reference items. The constant needs of undergraduate and graduate programs were reflected in the growth of the collections, although the needs of scholars were not neglected. A positive policy of acquisitions did much to encourage and foster this development. During Williamson's years at Columbia he always encouraged the program of acquisitions; he was assisted in this work by Roger Howson. Both men deserve credit for building the resources of the Columbia University Libraries during these years.

From 1926 to 1943 major collections were added to the Libraries, including the Henry Smith Munroe Collection of Mining, in 1926; a major purchase of Greek papyri, in 1927; the Paterno collection of material on Italian history and literature, which was acquired in 1928, as well as the Edward Seligman collection of economics; in 1931 the David Eugene Smith collection of the history of mathematics was added; in 1933 a large collection of Hebrew manuscripts and the Park Benjamin collection of American literature (1835-1860) were added. In 1936, a most active year, the George A. Plimpton collection was added containing 13,000 items in the history of education, mathematics, and the development of the English language, and a major collection of over 16,000 items from the American Type Founders Library of Printing and the Graphic Arts; the Salem Hyde collection of Ralph Waldo Emerson was obtained in 1938; and in the following year the addition of the Gottheil collection of Arabic and Syriac books; in 1940 the Coykendall collection of nineteenth and twentieth century poetry, and the Stedman collection of about 10,000 manuscripts and letters on American literary activities. This list reflects some of the major acquisitions, and the range and extent of these acquisitions, during Williamson's period as Director of Libraries. This list does not include many other gifts of books and money which were contributed to the Columbia University Libraries by administration, faculty, and friends. Williamson and his library staff were most active in promoting a dynamic program of purchases and donations which did much to develop Columbia as a major research library.

WILLIAMSON'S WORKING RELATIONS WITH HIS STAFF

In the course of research for this biography, correspondence with students, staff, and faculty revealed that Williamson used a good deal of discretion, tact, insight, common sense, compassion, and understanding of human nature in dealing with people. He was forthright, but just; honest, but fair; and always insisted on learning the facts before arriving at conclusions.

Many of the letters revealing this aspect of his work were marked "confidential" or "personal." The anonymity of the individual is respected, since the present concern is the handling of various situations and not the people involved.

Typical is Williamson's comment on February 20, 1942, to a letter from a librarian: "I am sure you will realize, if you reflect upon it, that whatever I have said in a critical way has been designed to correct what seems to be a mistaken emphasis. . . . I can't see any useful purpose in even trying to convince you that many of your interpretations are mistaken."

Another letter from a staff member showed the reaction to Williamson's handling of a difficult situation. "There's no way of telling you, Dr. Williamson, because I lack words, how much I appreciated your kindness last week when I threw myself on your sympathy."

Williamson was devoted to his staff. His correspondence with administrators at Columbia included requests for staff and faculty needs, for salary increases, problems of resignations, pleas for transfers and leaves. Williamson's answers consistently revealed his concern for the welfare of his staff. He was extremely proud of their work and stated their case frankly and emphatically to President Butler and other members of the administration.

David Clift, who worked as Williamson's assistant in the Columbia University Libraries maintained, "These five years I worked under him and for him were the most useful and important ones of my career." Clift felt he learned a great deal from Williamson because "he was so wise—and so patient with a young man who had so much to learn. He could be a fine teacher for he knew there was only one way to do things and that was the right way."[19]

BACKGROUND OF THE HOWSON CONTROVERSY

On February 1, 1915, Roger Howson, who had been in charge of the Kent Hall reading rooms, became Bibliographer and Assistant to the Acting Librarian, Dean P. Lockwood, who was an Assistant Professor of Classical Philology. Howson worked mainly in the Order and Accession Divisions. When Lockwood resigned in 1916, the Library Council voted to recommend Roger Howson as Acting Librarian for one year. Instead, "the Trustees appointed Howson, Assistant Librarian and empowered the president to ask Provost William H. Carpenter to accept the designation of Acting Librarian beginning July 1, 1916."[20] Carpenter was to be in charge and guide library policy, while Howson was to deal with the faculty and the general public and "with those large questions of policy which would test his administrative capacity and his largeness of view."[21]

Roger Howson was born at Overton, Flint, Wales, on May 8, 1892. He received his B.A. and his M.A. from Trinity College, Cambridge University, England, in 1904 and 1913 respectively. He married Julie Benjamin; they had three children. Howson came to the United States in 1908 and was naturalized in 1919. He worked in the Columbia University Library from 1913; serving as Assistant Librarian from 1916 to 1926, and as Librarian from 1926 to 1939, when he was transferred from the Library to become an Associate in History. He served with the United States Army from 1917 to 1918. He was author of several works, including *His Excellency a Trustee and Some Other Columbia Pieces* (1945); he was editor of the *Autobiography of John Stuart Mill* (1924) and *Book Shelf of Brander Matthews* (1931). He retired in 1948 and died on April 22, 1962, in Newton, Connecticut.[22]

From 1916 to 1926 Carpenter served as Acting Librarian until his retirement on June 20, 1926; during this time Roger Howson was Assistant Librarian. Carpenter's last *Annual Report* to President Nicholas Murray Butler stated that resentment toward supervision by the Assistant Librarian had disappeared and the various parts of the organization were working in harmony. Carpenter also commented on the efficiency of the Assistant Librarian, especially in building up the library collection.

Carpenter was granted a leave of absence in 1925-1926, during which time Howson was in charge of the University Libraries. The president's office instructed Howson to refer to that office "all matters that would ordinarily have required the Acting Librarian's attention."[23] This action was indicative of the fact that Butler was not inclined to turn over the complete administration of the library to him.

In the 1926 *Annual Report* Howson asked all library departments to indicate conditions in 1913 and to compare them to 1926. It is difficult to say whether "this action represents a defensive attitude or a natural desire to give a faithful description of the library situation at the time of a major administrative change."[24] Howson's report of the progress revealed "no evidence to show any decrease in effectiveness, any uncertainty of objective, any lessening in morale of the staff. There is indeed much to prove that these last dozen years have been the most useful years of the existence of the library." Butler did not seem to agree completely with Howson's glowing report of the administration of the Libraries. In his *Presidential Report of 1926* he stated that Columbia had not maintained the necessary professional contacts, which he hoped would be resolved with the establishment of the Library School and the appointment of Williamson.[25] For many years Columbia had had a succession of Assistant Librarians.

CHANGES IN ADMINISTRATION

During the year when Carpenter was on leave, the University undertook a search for a new librarian and head of the proposed library school. In 1926 the New York State Library School and the Library School of the New York Public Library were transferred to Columbia University. This transfer included a grant from the Carnegie Corporation of New York of $25,000 if and when a suitable person was appointed to direct both the Libraries and the Library School. When Williamson was appointed to be Director of the University Libraries and Head of the School of Library Service the trustees gave Howson the title of Librarian. Howson thought the opening of the Library School might necesssitate two separate administrative positions, but he "could see no valid reason for having two officers for the administration of the libraries as such"—an indication he considered himself head of the Library. The Columbia administration did not agree. Secretary Fackenthal wrote Carpenter on April 23, 1926, that, under Williamson's regime, "Howson, as you can easily surmise, will devote all of his time to the actual administration of our collections and reading rooms, work for which he seems to be admirably adapted."

At the time, it was hoped that Williamson's administration would be able to resolve these problems.

> It seems clear that by 1926 all concerned had concluded that it was time to end one era and to begin another which would insure not only that a responsible administrator with a knowledge of professional librarianship should have full time to devote to the Columbia situation but that the Columbia library should once again establish more active contacts and through them and through its support of library training make its own special contributions to the development of the library profession.[26]

Howson was to work under Williamson, but the exact range of the authority and responsibilities of each position was never made clear. This confusion was intensified by the fact that immediately prior to Williamson's arrival, Howson assumed the actual duties and function of the person in charge of the library. Another strange situation was that from 1926 through 1936 the annual report of the libraries was prepared by the Librarian, Roger Howson, under his title as Librarian of the University. It was not until 1937 that Williamson prepared the annual report as Director of Libraries. The fact that Howson prepared and signed these annual reports indicates that he held a position of authority within the university. During these years Williamson only prepared the report as Director of the School of Library Service. Also not made clear was the difference between the position of Librarian of the University and Director of Libraries. Under such conditions it almost was inevitable that confusion and controversy would result.

In the early reports Howson mentioned that "the first year of the Library School has gone by in close contact without friction and in cooperation without discord." In the 1928-1929 report he called for the close linking of the Library School and the University Library if "the work of the Library School is to progress without impediment." He continued in the same report: "There has been nothing to interfere as to mental and moral harmony between the members of the School of Library and Service and the Staff of the Library. Physically, however, there have been problems, and these have been met with mutual adjustment."

Although Howson often was highly critical of Williamson, he was pleased with the plans for the new University Library and praised Williamson in the *Report of the Library for 1929* for solving the problem of lack of space in an "answer that is complete and entirely satisfying," as revealed in the "plans that Dr. Williamson has in process of formation for the welding of the Library and of University Hall into a single building. . . . The plans under discussion have the security that belongs to all things that are well and firmly founded."

Early Signs of Difficulty

Part of the problem which developed in later years can be seen in Howson's views of librarianship. In his 1930-1931 *Annual Report* he maintained that "no clear line can be drawn between clerical labor and professional skill in the day's work in a library." This concept was diametrically opposed to Williamson's ideas about the profession of librarianship. Williamson commented in an undated holograph manuscript that Howson was "anti nearly everything I stand for."

There were always problems between the Library

School and the Library, even though Howson in his report of 1934-1935 notes that the misunderstandings and discontent of both sides were a "thing of the past now." This situation was aggravated by Williamson's enforced and prolonged absence due to his illness, during which time Howson temporarily assumed the duties as head of the libraries. When Williamson returned, the situation worsened. The controversy accelerated by 1937, reaching its zenith in the following year.

The situation was reflected in one minor problem after another, one remark after another, unpleasant incidents, disregard for Williamson's authority as Director of Libraries, resulting in a slow but steady erosion in their relationship. Each matter singly was of no great consequence, but the controversy was a long time developing. The personality and character of the two men added to the conflict. Their backgrounds, training, and interests were entirely different, and their ideas and methods of operation opposite.

Howson was a bookman, interested in the work of book selection and acquisition. He was very much involved in working with the general public and the university faculty. He was an extrovert, outspoken, with a ready answer to everything—traits extremely annoying to Williamson. Although he, too, could be outspoken, Williamson basically was an introvert, prone to inner examination, and probing. He was discreet, polite, even reticent at times. Howson was extremely popular with the university faculty, while Williamson never really cultivated them to the extent Howson did. Howson was poorly organized; Williamson was highly organized. Howson was always ready with a quick and snappy reply; Williamson was much too restrained for repartee. Howson tended to ignore rules and regulations when they did not suit him; Williamson generally was a stickler for correct procedure, although he also realized that rules can hinder service and was willing to revise them, but only if the facts were presented and the request was well founded. A clash occurred over Howson's continual appointment of staff without Williamson's approval. Howson also acted independently in other matters, often proceeding without Williamson's knowledge or consent.

When Williamson took office in 1926 as Director of Libraries, the administrative control and machinery for efficient administration did not exist—much to his annoyance. He set out to correct this deficiency, hoping, with his abilities as an administrator and organizer, to reorganize the work of the University Libraries. Howson either retained or assumed duties and control, until by 1934 he actually was running the libraries.

DETERIORATION DURING WILLIAMSON'S ABSENCE

The situation from 1926 to 1933 was tolerable, if not particularly pleasant. In 1933, however, Williamson began to suffer from a back condition, which became very serious in the following year. This illness was diagnosed as a spinal abscess causing back pain, fever, and problems with his back muscles and right leg. This illness lasted for about a year and a half, requiring a long period of convalescence; at one point he was not expected to live. During the convalescence he went to Florida. Williamson was granted a leave of absence which, on January 25, 1935, President Butler extended until the first of March.

Any time Williamson was away from the library Howson was in charge, and during this extended period he was in actuality the head of the libraries. When Williamson returned in 1935, he decided to exercise his authority in approving all appointments to the library staff. By 1937 he had "made no progress at all."

In a memorandum of January 6, 1937, to President Butler he described the situation and his problems with Howson.

> A standard procedure in the making of appointments and promotions in the library staff was devised and is being half-heartedly followed, so far as the use of paper forms is concerned. Actually I have no more influence over the personnel policy or the making of most appointments than has the janitor of the building. Appointment papers for my approval in almost all cases reach me after the person has been appointed and is at work. Even when the appointee is

not already at work when the papers reach me for approval the appointment has been settled and no attention is paid to my refusal to approve. I can either approve as pure matter of form or have my disapproval ignored.

Williamson felt an essential step was a direct order from President Butler to the bursar that no one be put on the library payroll without specific approval in writing from the Director of Libraries. He hoped that such a directive from Butler would put into effect the provision of the university statutes, which Williamson confessed he "has not been able to enforce." Williamson made a direct appeal to Butler for help in resolving this matter, for he could see no other way to "get away from our planless personnel practice." He was pessimistic about the solution to the problem.

> I am not too sanguine that such a presidential order will bring about the desired result, but under present conditions it seems to me to offer the only hope. I would be far better if the thing could be done simply because everyone concerned agrees that it should be done. The number of ways of complying with the letter of the law, repudiating it in spirit and nullifying the hoped-for results of any change, are infinite. Compulsion is a puny substitute for desire to cooperate, based on understanding and approval. Left to themselves some department heads would gladly fall in line but they cannot go in two directions at once.

Williamson confessed he had done little in the past about this problem and was not "happy or proud over the results, but perhaps greater unhappiness and humiliation would come from any other course." He suggested it might be better for him to resign and let somebody else shoulder the responsibility.

AGGRAVATION OF EXTERNAL PRESSURES

Another factor which changed the latent controversy into open conflict was the external pressure unknowingly exerted on the Library School by the Carnegie Corporation, which criticized the school for not "having utilized the Columbia library system full enough or definitely enough in [your] training program."[27] This criticism came as a result of the Library School's request to the corporation for funds. Dr. Frederick Keppel, President of the corporation, was critical of this "weak spot." Williamson revealed to Keppel "quite frankly that I would have to admit it was our most serious shortcoming, that I had myself long been conscious of a degree of failure at this point, but that in spite of my efforts I have been able to accomplish very little in this direction."[28]

Now that Keppel had identified and criticized the problem, Williamson wanted to take the necessary steps to eliminate it. However, he confessed, "I fear I have been culpably negligent in this matter for no worse a motive than a desire to avoid unpleasant personal situations almost certain to follow any greater effort than I have already made to bring about improvement."[29]

Williamson's concern with the problem of cooperation between the Library School and the Library at Columbia was evident in his attempts to improve the situation. Following Keppel's criticism he exerted great effort to bring about closer cooperation between the two. Keppel acknowledged in his letter of October 12, 1937, that he was at least partly successful. "I'm very glad to learn about the closer relationship between the School of Library Service and the Library itself."

DIFFERENCES IN POLICY AND PROCEDURE

Another aspect of the problem regarding the cooperation between the Library School and the University involved the training of Library School students. On January 6, 1937, Williamson prepared a "Memorandum on the Administration of the Library Personnel and Its Relation to the School of Library Service." In this document he discussed the goal for the Library School of blending on-the-job and classroom experience into a program which would combine theory and practice. He felt that there were pressures at Columbia to put the new University Library School on a graduate university basis and cut completely loose from the outgrown apprenticeship methods which still dominated library schools. He regretted that because of this pressure, as well as the local conditions at Columbia, "the programs tended from the beginning to be too exclusively academic." He hoped to develop a library school that

> needs to be intimately associated with a large and well conducted library as certainly as a nursing school needs a hospital, and for much the same reason, although the two situations are not fully analogous. Undoubtedly the apprenticeship method, the learn by doing plan, is relatively much more important and the academic instruction less important in the training of a nurse than in the training of a librarian. A good proportion of the library school students, when they come, have already learned by experiences in a library many of the things which are better learned on the job than in the class room. Even they, however, need to participate in the work of a good library to broaden their experience, to become acquainted with new types of service, and to give concreteness to their professional studies.

Williamson understood the real danger—a danger not fully realized—that the "School of Library Service now seems likely to be cited as an example of too great a swing away from the kind of training provided by the library schools conducted by librarians, mainly public libraries, before 1926, or before the publication of the Carnegie Corporation report on library schools published in 1923."

He thought that the University Library provided an excellent place to employ students of the Library School, whom he considered to be a "picked lot, above the average in both ability and in the aptitude they have already shown when admitted." He also believed that since they had a professional interest in the work, they would consider their earnings incidental and would give more than the usual service, if carefully administered. However, very few Library School students were employed by the library at Columbia. He deplored this situation and wanted the University

Libraries to rely on the placement service of the Library School. He felt this procedure "would probably not be easy as the present happy-go-lucky way of making appointments."

Supposedly Williamson approved all appointments to the University Library, but in reality this was not the case. In one instance, when Williamson received a notice of an appointment prior to the hiring of a young man, he wrote Howson that he was elated to know "what is in your mind before the appointment is made."

Williamson commented in his "Memorandum on the Administration" of January 6, 1937:

> The establishment of the School at Columbia in 1926 marked the appearance of the true university school which could no longer permit its students to be exploited in the name of professional training. The School of Library Service has necessarily, therefore, not been serviceable to the University in the ways or to the extent that might have been expected. It has nevertheless put the library staff on a considerably higher professional level by bringing into responsible positions more trained people than would have been appointed had there been no library school on the campus.

He maintained that the University Libraries had not taken full advantage of the School in the "entirely legitimate and mutually advantageous ways that could have been opened up."

Williamson commented on employment procedures, "We have nothing that can be called a policy." At that time the Columbia University Libraries lacked any definite and recognized grades of service with appropriate titles and stated requirements in the way of general and technical training and experience.

Why did Williamson permit such a situation to continue, considering that he held the position of Director of Libraries and supposedly was in a position of authority? In this same memorandum he confessed: "It may seem strange that I, as Director of Libraries, permit conditions to exist which I so heartily disapprove. As administrative head of both the

University Library and of the Library School it would seem that adequate remedy for the situation lies in my own hands." He continued: "Theoretically the Director of Libraries should be able to develop a policy and see that it is carried out. Practically this has proved impossible." Williamson had hoped the move to the new building might help the situation, but "we are apparently farther from reaching a satisfactory adjustment than ever."

Intervention of President Butler

By 1937 the situation was so severe that Williamson even suggested in his letter of February 10, 1937, to Dean George B. Pegram that Roger Howson be put in full charge of the University Libraries for one year and that he remain as Dean of the Library School.

> While I personally believe, as I have stated repeatedly, that the University Libraries and the Library School should be under a unified director, it could do us no great harm to go ahead for a single year with an entirely separate and even unharmonious and unsympathetic relations. The conditions could not be much worse than what we have at present. A year of experimentation might even prove that complete separation of the two is desirable as a permanent policy.

It would appear that this suggestion was made out of desperation rather than for its feasibility.

When President Butler became aware of the extent and seriousness of the situation, he was annoyed. He expressed his reaction in a letter to Williamson on January 18, 1937.

> I had taken it for granted that the relationship between the School of Library Service, its staff and its students, and the various libraries of the University was to all intents and purposes identical with the relationship existing between the Medical School and our various associated hospitals. I did not know until a few days ago that here at Columbia our Library Staff is appointed without reference to the School of Library

Service, its students or its graduates, and that we are not giving our students in our School of Library Service the practical opportunities for usefulness and training which our libraries so amply afford. . . .

In my judgement it is highly desirable that steps be taken without delay to develop a relationship between the School of Library Service and the administration of these various libraries which would be as ideal and as helpful as the relationship between the Medical School and the hospitals.

Events in 1937 moved fast and furiously. On January 22, Williamson answered Butler.

I have never had the slightest doubt as to what your attitude would be in such a matter. The reason I did not bring this particular situation to your attention long ago is simply that I have never been able to see any satisfactory solution to the problem, which seems to me much more fundamental than merely a clear understanding on the part of all concerned of what the Director of University Libraries is authorized or expected to do.

Three months earlier Williamson had decided to resign but postponed the decision. However, by January 22, 1937, he wrote Butler, "It is with the greatest possible regret that I tender my resignation as Director of University Libraries and Dean of the School of Library Service, to become effective at your pleasure, but I sincerely hope no later in any case than the end of the present academic year." Butler immediately took action to have the matter examined.

REVIEW BY THE COMMITTEES

President Nicholas Murray Butler appointed two university committees to investigate the situation, including one chaired by Dean George B. Pegram. Williamson was more than willing to cooperate in any way possible to help resolve the situation. He prepared a detailed plan which might be helpful to the committees; in its introduction he revealed the heart of the controversy as he saw it.

This proposed plan obviously must represent at least in certain of its parts, a material modification of the practice of the past few years. Since the Director of Libraries is the executive officer, and as such must accept responsibility to the University for the administration of the Library, he feels it is essential that there should be, on the part of all, a recognition of that primary responsibility and an acquiescence in such administrative reorganization as accords with his conception of orderly and efficient practice, and makes it possible for him to keep effectively in touch with the various parts of the administration. To this end it has seemed necessary to emphasize the responsibility of the Librarian and of the department heads of the staff to him as Director. This is done with no wish to assert authority *per se*, but merely in the interests of effective administration and the avoidance of possible causes of friction attendant upon a dual administration such as has in practice developed during the past ten years. It is not necessary here to enter upon the causes of the the present situation, it is sufficient to say that the whole aim of the plan is to obviate those causes, that the Library may to its fullest capacity serve the University Community and that to this end each member of the staff may be given opportunity to render his or her best effort.

Butler believed the problem lay in the University Statutes and in the definition of the function of the director of libraries and the librarian of the University; he thought that the situation would be resolved if the trustees revised the statutes. Williamson did not agree: "But I do want to make it perfectly clear and emphatic that in my judgment the possible ambiguity in the statutes has comparatively little to do with the present situation. . . . In other words, the reasons for my decision are just as valid under any revised statute as under the old."

Dean Pegram's committee met during January and February of 1937. Its only recommendation was that Howson must remain as Librarian. Williamson felt defeated and in a strongly worded letter to Butler stated that he could not go along with the committee's recommendation.

This is precisely what has always seemed to me to be impossible. It is extremely difficult for the members of the

> Committee to put themselves in my place. The policies and practices which I would wish to adopt in all matters of personnel, finances, and general administration are radically different from those in force today. I do not see how I can effect the reforms which seem to me necessary through the agency of the persons who are responsible for the present practice and conditions, eager to defend them at every point and actively opposed to the ideas and policies I wish to inaugurate. Failure—total or comparative—seems to me under such conditions to be inevitable, and even partial success at any point to be won only by enormous and unnecessary expenditure of time and nervous strain.

Williamson wished to present Pegram's committee with evidence to "show you concretely what I mean when I say that Mr. Howson's ideas and methods are diametrically opposed to mine on many, if not all, matters which are fundamental in library administration."

On February 8, 1937, Williamson wrote Butler inquiring if he has "any doubt whatever of the adequacy of my reasons for resigning." He suggested that he would like to sit down with a suitable person delegated by the President to go over some of the "material bearing on the situation which seemed to me to leave but one course open to me."

On the same day, Williamson wrote Secretary Fackenthal complaining that the committee did not seem to "understand my point of view." He was upset because of what he felt was their "refusal to accept my resignation coupled with a plan to brand me as the offending person. The future is black indeed." He concluded, "If you think this is an unwarranted pessimistic view I would like to have help to see the brighter side."

A member of the faculty wrote Williamson on February 9, 1937, in an attempt to resolve the problem: "I really do not see why two gentleman of the best intentions will not have at least a good chance of working harmoniously to one desirable end and if a proper definition of their duties and regulations, agreeable to both, is drawn up for their guidance. In the opinion that there would be a reasonable chance for harmony under such conditions, I am inclined to think that almost the entire faculty would agree with me. I therefore believe that both gentlemen ought to be willing to make an attempt in all good will." This letter reveals that the controversy had an impact on all levels of university activity.

Williamson feared that the arguments in the case would be made to appear as a series of petty and trivial incidents of no great importance. Apprehensive of the attitude of the committee he sent a memorandum on February 14, 1937.

> The Committee may say that none of these things are of great importance. Remember that I am looking at the finished fabric itself—these individual threads pulled out here and there may not be impressive. These are only part of the warp and woof of a fabric which was slowly woven before my eyes and to me at least is of such sinister design that I want to dismiss it from my sight forever.
>
> It should be understood, if possible, that each of these items stands for me as a symbol of many others of the same sort running back through several years. Each one brings before me situations and problems with which I have struggled in vain, almost never emerging with any feeling of having accomplished something worthwhile, but only with a sense of defeat and frustration. All I have asked is a chance to get away from it all and to start anew in an atmosphere free from the poisons that pervade both soul and body. This of course has no application to the Library School.

He did not expect Howson to observe revised statutes any more than he had the old ones, which already indicated the Director to be Head of the library. Williamson commented: "I do not believe that before my illness came on Mr. Howson ever thought of any doubt that he was by Statute subject to my authority. I was not expected to recover; the control of the Libraries would, he thought fall into his hands." The problem developed rapidly after October 1933, when Williamson's full recovery was first in doubt. Williamson feared that his absence would provide Howson with the opportunity to "take advantage of my leave." On his return to work, Williamson found that many of his plans had been scrapped and that he was out of the library picture.

INVOLVEMENT OF THE LIBRARY SCHOOL FACULTY

The faculty of the School of Library Service was greatly distressed at the news of Williamson's resignation and wrote President Butler on February 2, 1937, expressing confidence in Williamson and "whole-hearted support of his aim to improve conditions in the University Libraries." The faculty expressed its concern that the Libraries should stand for "the best in library service." They felt it was time for a "radical change of policy and attitude." They discussed frankly the current problems.

> Despite the presence on the Library staff of splendid people, the basis of administration and service in the libraries has seemed unplanned, personal, and even whimsical. Members of the staff apparently have been chosen and placed at times without references to the qualifications required. These practices on the part of the Librarian, together with his obvious cynicism toward the aim of library service, have tended to impair efficiency, have created a gap between the libraries and the School of Library Service, and have spread an unfortunate impression among libraries generally.

On February 2, 1937, Harriet D. MacPherson, a member of the faculty of the School of Library Service, wrote Williamson expressing the feeling of his supporters: "We are all shocked. . . . There is no doubt that every member of your faculty is standing behind you in this crisis."

Williamson's resignation was not accepted. He did not want to seem to shirk "what apparently everyone else thinks is my duty." He decided to make another effort to resolve the situation. Butler agreed that this was the wise course and Howson should be given the chance to cooperate under the amended statutes. Butler felt it only fair to "test the question whether or not . . . he cannot and will not conform to it," and that if after a reasonable trial, "he cannot or will not follow this course, then I think it is plain what must be done." The trustees amended the statutes on May 3, 1937.

In a letter to Butler on May 20, 1937, Williamson revealed the heart of the problem "of bringing about a unified administration in spite of having two officers with titles carrying the implication of chief administrative authority"—a reference to Howson's title as Librarian and Williamson's as Director of Libraries.

As a result of these revisions some changes were made in the libraries. David Clift was hired to assume the duties of Administrative Assistant, taking over Howson's office. Clift had indicated that by the end of 1937 Howson and Williamson were not on speaking terms. Clift took over a number of Howson's duties, especially those relating to personnel, but he was not "in on the long-standing controversy."

Although things did settle down, the animosity still was there; it was felt by the library staff and the faculty of the Library School. By August 9, 1938, Williamson again had decided to leave Columbia, and he wrote President Butler: "It is somewhat over a year now since our present plan of administering the University libraries was put into effect. I believe it was understood at the outset that this compromise arrangement was in the nature of an experiment and that it would be subject to review after a year's experience." Williamson's task during this year was to put into effect in the library some "elementary principles of efficient organization." This meant that he could not devote much time and effort to the Library School or to proceeding "forward in several ways that seemed desirable." However, he felt he had "accomplished as much as could reasonably be expected under the quite extraordinary handicaps."

Improvements had been made but "a great deal remains to be done at nearly every point." Williamson believed the objectives of better methods of training, stimulating interest and improving staff morale, and giving every member of the staff opportunity and incentive to broaden his knowledge and experience are not achieved by "change, but require skillful planning and patient and persistent effort."

> In my effort to visualize what lies ahead and to view the path of progress in the light of the past year's experience I have come to the very clear conclusion that I should again ask permission to withdraw from active service and be relieved of all responsibility. I felt very strongly a year and a half ago that it was advisable for me to insist on my resignation. The

principal reason that I finally yielded was the possibility that a change in the deanship of the School at that time might jeopardize the hoped-for endowment from the Carnegie Corporation. That matter has now been settled.

He told Butler he needed a long period of rest and relaxation; he asked to be permitted to "withdraw from both positions at the close of the present academic year." Butler was not prepared to accept this resignation without further discussion.

The situation was still a burden to Williamson, as he wrote on August 14, 1938, to Fackenthal: "I am extremely sorry to make the break. I do feel, however, that the present situation is an impossible one to face for more than a few months." Williamson pointed out that much had been done toward reorganizing the library; he felt he had accomplished all he could without "too much stress and strain." He continued:

> In any case I suppose I would be good for only two or three years more and then somebody else would have to carry on anyway. This seems to be the easiest and most practicable solution, not only of my personal problem, but of an extremely difficult situation for the University.

Butler Resolves the Controversy

Butler again refused to accept Williamson's resignation. On December 16, 1938, he wrote Howson that to his great regret the difficulties and embarrassments which have attended the administration of the University Libraries for a number of years "have not been removed or ended." Butler had hoped the amendment to the university statutes would resolve the problem. He was concerned because the problems "have become a constant and unfortunate subject of comment and criticism, not only within the University itself but on the part of officers of other important libraries who are familiar with the situation."

In the same letter Butler informed Howson that it was

not possible to continue the services of Williamson and 'yourself' in one and the same system of library administration. He indicated this was "no criticism of your ability or of your character. You have many and warm friends in the University."

Butler indicated that the nature of the trouble arose

> from the constant clash of two different points of view, two different methods of work, and two different ideals of service. It is not a question of which is right or which is wrong. The fact that these two exist and are represented by strong personalities, makes it impossible for the present situation to continue without grave and growing damage to the University, since the incompatibility is complete.

Howson was told: "Your relationship to the Administration of the University Libraries must be terminated and work sought for you elsewhere. It is our desire to effect this change in a spirit of the utmost kindliness."

Howson was granted a leave of absence from December 19, 1938, until December 31, 1939, at full salary. Butler indicated that during that time they would assist him in searching for a suitable post elsewhere or else a bibliographical post might be found at Columbia, "quite apart from the University Library administration."

Butler sincerely regretted having to make this decision. "Your years of devoted service make us all feel highly regretful that this step must be taken; yet there is no escape from it unless our Library administration is to get steadily more and more involved in the clash of personalities and ideals which has already been permitted to exist too long."

With this letter, Butler closed the pages on these rather turbulent times. Roger Howson left the library and was appointed an Associate in History at Columbia.

Williamson wrote Butler on December 20, 1938, stating that he was sorry "this step has seemed to be necessary [and] how keenly I feel the heavy responsibility I am assuming in accepting this, the only possible alternative to the solution I had proposed for a very difficult situation." The controversy had been long, arduous, and painful for all.

The Controversy in Retrospect

Dr. Carl M. White, who became Director of Libraries and Dean of the School of Library Service at Columbia upon Williamson's retirement in 1943, was in a position to know at firsthand of the controversy, since he inherited many of the problems it generated. White felt that the struggle affected the mental, physical, and spiritual well-being of both men. In White's opinion, Williamson was able to come out of the struggle without too many scars and with his ideals pertaining to library service and librarianship intact. This controversy was a classic example of academic warfare—almost along the line of a Greek tragedy. However, Williamson had achieved "a concept of the importance of the professional librarian."[30]

On the surface, the controversy was reflected in an accumulation of petty matters, but it had deeper roots involving two different and at times opposing views of librarianship. Wiliamson believed "the present issue is not merely one between two men." The concept of professionalism in library service was in the balance and the battleground was at Columbia in what was a complex and, at best, extremely difficult situation. Howson and Williamson were both gentlemen, but both were forceful men with strong wills and convinced of their own beliefs.

It is to Williamson's credit that many of his ideas regarding the professional aspects of librarianship survived during these times of personal hardship, high emotion, and continuing tension.

Epilogue to the Controversy

Probably no part of this research has been more time-consuming and difficult than the events of the Howson controversy. The examination of the facts in this situation involved numerous letters and memorandums from all parties to reconstruct what actually happened fifty years ago. This examination of the controversy is based mainly on the Williamson Papers and reflects his view of the situation. Howson's side cannot be presented fully because few of

Howson's papers are extant. According to Williamson, "When he suddenly left he took with him or destroyed much of his correspondence, as I recall."[31] It is doubtful if this controversy can or ever will be completely recorded.

Both Howson and Williamson have been criticized for their part in the controversy. However, this must be examined within the context of the times and the events as they unfolded in a slow but determined pace. Unfortunately the situation could only be settled when "the other individual in this bitter contest left or was transferred to another part of the University."

It is futile to attempt to evaluate the impact of the Howson-Williamson controversy because, in President Butler's own words, "It is not a question of which is right or which is wrong."

WILLIAMSON'S ADMINISTRATION AS DEAN OF THE SCHOOL OF LIBRARY SERVICE

Williamson served the School of Library Service as Director from 1926 through 1930 when the title was changed to Dean; he continued in this post until his retirement in 1943.

In his "Training for Library Work," which was the 1921 typewritten report to the Carnegie Corporation, Williamson commented, "A library school affiliated with Columbia University would not only have the general advantages of the university relation pointed out elsewhere in this report but would also have special advantages in New York City over a school conducted as a part of the New York Public Library." Williamson suggested in this report that the Carnegie Corporation should provide funds for the proposed library school. "If the Carnegie Corporation is prepared to assist in any way in promoting training for library work, it is the writer's opinion that it would be better to develop one strong school than to continue indefinitely to grant small subsidies to many." The chapter entitled "The Library School Situation in New York City" was not included in the printed 1923 report. The idea, however, was presented formally to the corporation and would bear fruit in 1926, when the New

York State Library School and that of the New York Public Library would merge to form the School of Library Service at Columbia University. The Library School was reestablished at Columbia after a hiatus of thirty-seven years when Melvil Dewey had established the Columbia College School of Library Economy, which existed from 1887 to 1889. Dewey left Columbia and was able to transfer the School to Albany, New York, as the New York State Library School.

In addition, "there was acquired at the same time [from 1926 to 1938] a substantial dowry from the Carnegie Corporation."[32] The corporation designated a total of $375,000 to support the Columbia University School of Library Service; an endowed professorship of $150,000 was established in 1938.[33]

Williamson realized that his background and work in library education put him in a difficult situation regarding the Library School. He had advocated changes and made recommendations to improve library education in his 1923 report; he was considered the outspoken critic of professional library education. Now, in his position at Columbia, the library world could scrutinize him and his work. He revealed his thoughts in an undated typescript of a brief talk he gave to the alumni of the New York State Library School:

> A few years ago I had the temerity to tell the library schools what they ought and ought not to do and to be. Not dreaming that I should ever have to prove that I was right in any particular, I could be as critical and as Utopian as I liked. Now reflect on my predicament. Poetic justice you call it or fitting the punishment to the crime. For I have been maneuvered into a position where everybody can make the silencing challenge—"Put up or shut up."

In his new position at Columbia he "attempted to develop in practice many of the ideas contained in his report."[34]

In 1926 his immediate task was to examine and incorporate the scheme of professional education into the new program and curriculum of the School of Library Service. Williamson now had the opportunity to assemble a faculty, plan the curriculum, acquire equipment, and develop a new program of library education. Since most of the faculty were selected from the Albany and New York Public Library Schools, there was not too much of a problem regarding that aspect of the task.

> All invitations to members of the faculty of both predecessor library schools to join the Columbia staff were accepted. E. J. Reece, Principal of the Library School of the New York Public Library since 1917, became Associate Professor of Library Administration; Mary L. Sutliff, an instructor there during the entire life of the School from 1911-26, was appointed Assistant Professor of Classification. From the New York State Library School, where she had been Vice-Director since 1920, came Edna M. Sanderson to be Assistant Professor of Library Administration and Assistant to the Director. She also brought two of her assistants, Gertrude P. Thorpe, as Curator of Collections, and Dorothy A. Plum, as Reviser. Isabella K. Rhodes, also from the Albany School, became Assistant Professor of Cataloging. To round out the staff, John S. Cleavinger, Librarian of the Saginaw, Michigan, Public Library, was appointed Associate Professor of Bibliography.[35]

The original plan was to enroll about fifty students, but by August it was apparent this number would be doubled. In order to meet the increased enrollment, Lucy E. Fay, instructor at the Carnegie Library School at Pittsburgh joined the faculty as Assistant Professor of Bibliography, and Margaret S. Williams, an instructor at Albany, became an Associate in Bibliography.

The Administrative Board of the Library School was established by President Butler, and the first board consisted of Williamson, Professors Robert E. Leonard, John J. Coss, and Robert H. Fife, Trustee Frederick Coykendall, Secretary Frank D. Fackenthal, and Librarian Roger Howson.

Some changes were instituted during the school's first year. The original program granted a certificate on the completion of the first year's work, but this plan was changed to permit the Library School to grant the degree of Bachelor of Science to students completing the first year's work. Those who completed the second year's work were awarded the degree of Master of Science. Students who completed courses through the summer session or university extension were given a certificate.

The problem of a proper degree structure for librarianship was under constant study. At the time the granting of a bachelor's degree for a fifth year of study generally was deplored; however, nothing was done to establish a master's degree for the same work. Williamson did not approve a master's degree for a fifth year, although he felt the selection of students of superior ability might justify such a change. In 1926 he suggested the desirability of a program leading to the doctorate, but no workable scheme was developed. As previously stated not one doctorate in librarianship was granted during the seventeen-year period of Williamson's regime.[36] He wrote to Milton Fairchild on November 18, 1931: "The problem of a doctorate in Library Science presents many difficulties, unfortunately. Thus far very few of the best students have shown any inclination to work for a doctorate, but I think this situation will gradually change."

The School of Library Service officially opened on October 1, 1926, although classes had already started on September 23. At the dedication ceremony, brief addresses were delivered by Williamson and three former directors of the New York State Library School, including James I. Wyer, Edwin H. Anderson, and Melvil Dewey.

President Butler stated:

> By the act of the authorities of the New York Public Library and on the recommendation and instigation of a distinguished member of this University whom we always delight to honor, Dr. Anderson; and by the consent and approval of the Regents of the University of the State of New York on the recommendation and on the instigation of Dr. Wyer; and with the blessing of Mr. Bowker, whose great service to library knowledge, library administration, and library schools has been emphasized by Dr. Dewey and rejoiced in by all of us; and with the approval and personal presence of Dr. Dewey, himself the originator of the idea and the first formulator of all those instrumentalities that he so imperfectly described— he could have told you much more about them had time served—which together made up a great group of carefully planned and well-thought-out agencies for advancement of

adult education in the United States; with all these and the unanimous approval and satisfaction of the Trustees of Columbia University in this year of grace, 1926, this School of Library Service, well organized, well staffed, and well administered, opens its doors.

In his address Williamson remarked, "This is a notable step in the movement toward university status and organization for library training." He also reiterated the idea he had expressed previously:

> The library schools are therefore merely following in the path of evolution of all types of professional education. One of the forces behind the change is the growth of specialization in every field of intellectual effort, which has greatly increased the importance of libraries of various kinds and has forced upon them a specialization of their services. This in turn has created a demand for specialized training which the original type of library school is not prepared to supply.

In the first year the student body totaled 109. Problems of space, which always plagued the Library School, were extremely difficult in the first year when temporary quarters were established in Earl Hall. In the following year the school moved to East Hall, where more suitable quarters were set up.

From the beginning the growth of the Library School Library was considered of the utmost importance. A collection of 2,500 children's books came from Albany and were housed in the Main Library. In addition, 6,000 books from the New York State Library and other items from the Library School of the New York Public Library became part of the new Library School's collection. During the first year $1,000 was spent for books; the budget was $3,000 for the second year.[37]

From 1927 through 1943 a total of 3,069 bachelors' and masters' degrees and certificates were awarded by Columbia University during Williamson's tenure as Dean of the School of Library Service. Many of these graduates became leaders in the library profession.

Louis Shores, prominent author, editor, educator, and

librarian, commented on his years as a student at the Library School under Dean Williamson:

> When I entered Columbia's School of Library Service in September 1927, C. C. Williamson was dean; Edna Sanderson assistant dean. Both were personally concerned with my objectives throughout the year, although the enrollment in the school was very large by library school standards then. Indeed it was necessary to organize the 1926/27 class into four sections, which was done according to previous library experience.
>
> Comparatively, that Columbia library school faculty had proportionately more good teachers than any other faculty of any of the colleges I had studied in to that time. Dr. Williamson was not a library school graduate, his specialty having been the social sciences in general, and economics particularly. His approach to librarianship was freshly different from that of the librarian practitioners. He encouraged me in my earliest crusade for teaching library use to students and teachers more effectively than it had been taught to us in high school and college. As a result of his encouragement, my series of articles for *Scholastic* magazine was published and later republished as a pamphlet.[38]

Williamson felt that the Library School should admit all who were able to meet the entrance requirements and were able to complete successfully the program of study. He felt strongly that no one should be excluded because of race, creed, or color. He was especially eager to foster the training of black librarians. He was a member of the Conference of Negro Librarians, where he spoke on Edward C. Williams and his contributions to librarianship and his influence on him during their days at Western Reserve University.

Developments During Williamson's Administration

Williamson established *Library Service News* in 1929 in order to maintain contact with the graduates of the Library School as well as with the alumni of the two predecessor schools. In June 1930, an alumni association, known as the Association of the Columbia School of Library Service and Its Predecessors, was organized to aid the library profession and the Columbia Library School and maintain an alumni spirit among its members.[39]

The next major event was the move to South Hall in 1934, which both faculty and students hailed as the "greatest event in the development of the School of Library Service since its re-establishment at Columbia in 1926."[40]

Williamson's bibliographical interests were reflected in his work in the School of Library Service. In 1934 he instituted a series entitled "Columbia University Studies in Library Service," which was published by the Columbia University Press. The first book in the series was Georg Schneider's *Handbuch der Bibliographie*, translated by Ralph R. Shaw as *Theory and History of Bibliography*, which appeared in 1925. The second, published in the same year, was *Living with Books*, by Helen E. Haines, with a second edition appearing in 1951. Other books in this series included Lucile F. Fargo, *Preparation for School Library Work*, 1926; Ernest J. Reece, *The Curriculum in Library Schools*, 1936; T. F. Hamlin, *Some European Architectural Libraries*, 1939; Helen E. Haines, *What's in a Novel?* 1942; Maurice F. Tauber, *Technical Services in Libraries*, 1953; Louis Round Wilson, *The University Library*, 1956; the 1958 publication in this series was *The Columbia University Libraries: A Report on Present and Future Needs* (which was the study of the President's Committee on the Educational Future of the University); Mortimer Taube, *Information Storage and Retrieval: Theory, Systems, and Devices*, 1958; and Melville J. Ruggles, *Russian and East European Publications in the Libraries of the United States*, in 1960.

In 1936 major changes were made in the curriculum.

> The first-year curriculum, which had been under study for two years, was reorganized by placing less emphasis on the technical aspects and attempting to provide a wider view of librarianship in general. For the first time, in 1936, the training given to those preparing for the professional certificate or the B.S. degree were identical. Also, plans were made to construct a new series of achievement tests to be admini-

stered in 1937 as comprehensive examinations to supplement the accumulation of credits for course work.[41]

The revised curriculum received praise from Emma V. Baldwin, one of the pioneers in library education who had proposed a plan, in 1919, for the training of librarians. She wrote to Williamson on January 21, 1936: "Congratulations upon the plans for the new curriculum for the Library School as outlined in the December Library Journal. This is the sort of thing which I have hoped for many years, as you will remember, would sometime develop."

Williamson was always interested in tests and measurements, especially as they applied to library education. With the faculty he developed objective achievement tests for first-year students, which were used beginning in 1936-1937. He also encouraged the establishment of syllabi for most of the library science courses, which were published and used for the first time in 1936.

> Dean Williamson's interest in the development and extension of the objective-type achievement tests continued even though this work required the full time of at least one member of the Faculty and the part-time efforts of several others. He hoped that some day a nation-wide system of standard tests might be devised for use as a comprehensive measuring tool for the entire library profession. Therefore, in 1942 an invitation was sent to all accredited library schools asking them to cooperate in the further development of the tests by administering one or more of the examinations prepared by the School of Library Service. Of the eighteen schools which indicated an interest in the project, only four actually availed themselves of the offer. The next year eight schools cooperated by giving a total of 441 examinations. Valuable suggestions and comments on the examinations were made by faculty members and students which enabled the examining division of the School of Library Service to make further improvements in their work.[42]

Another important event in the school's history was Williamson's work toward the establishment of the Melvil Dewey Professorship of Library Service, endowed by the Carnegie Corporation of New York.

Columbia University proudly announced the establishment of the Melvil Dewey endowed Professorship of Library Service on April 5, 1938, with a gift of $150,000 from the Carnegie Corporation of New York. . . . At the same time the Corporation made an additional gift of $100,000 for the general purposes of the School of Library Service. This combined sum of $250,000 was donated by the Carnegie Corporation instead of the Corporation continuing its annual $25,000 grant, which had been in effect since 1926.[43]

In his "Annual Report of the Dean . . . for 1938" Williamson remarked, "No one has failed to note how fitting it is that the first endowed chair of librarianship should bear the name of Melvil Dewey, and be established at Columbia where Dewey over fifty years ago established the first school for the professional training of librarians." Dr. Ernest J. Reece was the first incumbent of the first endowed chair in any library school.

Emily Dewey wrote Williamson on April 10, 1938, of her pleasure: "The article in the New York Herald Tribune announcing the establishment of the new Melvil Dewey Library School Chair at Columbia filled me with gratitude. I have written to Dr. Butler a little note expressing my appreciation but I want to thank you personally for your part also."

Other congratulations came from Ethel M. Fair, former Director, Library School, New Jersey College for Women. She wrote to him on April 29, 1938: "Sincere congratulations upon the establishing of the Melvil Dewey professorship and the accompanying grant from the Carnegie Corporation. Such a gift and its application are eminent recognition of leadership of the School of Library Service. I like to think also that the funds mark the beginning of the second fifty years of education for librarianship."

Until 1941 the faculty of the School of Library Service had been quite stable, but in that year several changes were made:

> Associate Dean Edna M. Sanderson, who had been connected with the Albany and Columbia Library Schools since 1900 and had served as Associate Dean since 1931, retired in 1942, as did Associate Professor Lucy E. Fay after sixteen

years. Both had continued their work two years beyond the normal retiring age. Assistant Professor Mary Shaver-Brown, a member of the faculty since 1927, died on January 31, 1942. Assistant Professor Alice I. Hazeltine, who came to Columbia as a member of the newly established School of Library Service in 1926, retired in 1943. Assistant Professor Harriet D. MacPherson resigned in 1943 to become Librarian of Smith College.[44]

EVALUATION OF WILLIAMSON ADMINISTRATION

Ray Trautman, Professor, School of Library Service, Columbia University, has mentioned some of the major problems which beset the school during its seventeen years under Williamson. The school went through a period of early and rapid growth from 109 students in 1926 to 911 in 1929. In his "Annual Report of the Director of the School . . . 1930," Williamson commented, "It is apparent that, at least in respect to the number of students, the School had far exceeded the wildest forecasts made by anyone when it was established four years ago." The growing pains were the usual ones, including inadequate quarters and heavy staff responsibilities.[45] Until the move in 1934, the facilities of the Library School were woefully inadequate. In addition, the Library School had no endowments other than the Carnegie grant. Williamson felt that the school never had the financial support which was "necessary to develop the School properly."[46] The demands made on the school by increased enrollment were never adequately met with additional faculty or staff.

The following comment by Trautman was indicative of the criticism directed at Williamson's administration:

> The decision of President Butler in 1925 to combine the directorship of the library school with that of the University Libraries was widely hailed at the time, since it was considered to be the only way the University could justify and obtain the services of an outstanding person. Some critics urged that the two positions should be filled with two good persons rather than one, even if that one person had a good assistant in direct charge of each. It was inevitable that no one individual could give all of the time and attention required in

two such responsible administrative posts even under optimum conditions. With inadequate staffs the problem at times became acute. It is known that the feelings of the student body under Dean Williamson, shared in some degree by the Faculty and staff of the School, were that the School was being neglected in favor of the Libraries and that its direction was mainly by remote control.[47]

This criticism must be viewed in relation to Williamson's dual responsibilities and his prolonged illness. He became ill in 1933 and by early 1936 was working only part time. The internal problems in the library continued. These factors must be taken into consideration in evaluating the situation and Williamson's contributions at Columbia. Trautman's charge was not the only criticism of Williamson's work in the dual posts; he also was accused of favoring the Library School and neglecting the libraries.

Handicap of Inadequate Finances

Any evaluation of Williamson's successes and failures at Columbia must be based on an understanding of the financial situation. Trautman states that funds were limited and faculty salaries and operating expenses had to be spread thinly in order to maintain the extensive and varied offerings of the school. The curriculum covered every type of library work in addition to the usual subjects; "needless to say, too much was attempted with too little."[48]

Additions to the Curriculum

Williamson also established new courses relating to specialized training in various fields of library work; by the 1930s one new course was added each year. Trautman analyzed the pattern of these offerings and the development of the program.

> These additions to the curriculum were always begun on an experimental basis but tended to be frozen into the pattern of regular offerings. Some examples of these courses are the

following: County and Regional Library Service, and Bibliographic and Reference Service in Science and Technology, 1936; Microphotography and Law Library Administration, 1937; Music Library Administration, 1938, and Bibliographic and Reference Service in the Medical Sciences, 1939.[49]

Trautman thought that the course offerings of the school demonstrated the degree of fragmentation to which the original curriculum had been subjected and the large number of peripheral studies which had been added to the already impressive listing of courses.

Williamson's desire for correspondence courses never really materialized beyond a brief attempt in the Home Study Program at Columbia. The fact that the American Library Association was not favorably inclined to the idea was revealed in a letter of November 22, 1939, from Margaret E. Vinton, Assistant, Board of Education for Librarianship, to Sister de Pazzi of Chicago, who had written for information about correspondence courses in library work. Vinton indicated that the association was not in favor of this method since "it did not offer adequate instruction in library science." Williamson felt adequate instruction could be offered, if properly handled and administered, but the profession never accepted his view on correspondence courses.

From its beginnings the school "embraced features which by that time librarians were coming to consider essential, such as a large student body, an expanded faculty, a diversified program, a university connection, improved resources, and generous physical facilities."[50] Williamson tried to see that the Library School was responsive to the demands and currents of thought in the library field. He introduced the scheme of the courses, syllabi, and examinations which "liberalized markedly its already extensive offerings and rendered them more adaptable to the individual interests of students."[51]

Paul North Rice believed that Williamson made his major contribution to librarianship not in the University Libraries but as Dean of the Columbia University School of Library Service, which provided him with an "unusual challenge and opportunity. How well he met that challenge is proved by the work now being done by the more than three thousand librarians who have received their training under his direction."[52]

Rice summarized Williamson's contributions to the Library School.

> In South Hall, he planned library school quarters that far excelled anything known elsewhere. To a faculty chosen in the first place from the already seasoned faculties at Albany and The New York Public Library, he added leaders in various fields of Library activity. The School of Library Service will long remain a monument to its first Dean.[53]

Metcalf maintained that Williamson's contributions were many, but building up the "largest library school, even if it had 'predecessors' was no mean task, and by many it will be considered his most important achievement." Of course, "he was not a one-achievement man."[54]

Wilson and Tauber also commented on Williamson's contribution to library education in the period after 1926.

> The merging of the library schools of the New York State Library and the New York Public Library in 1926 under Williamson's direction, the reorganization of the curriculum of the School of Library Service, the publication of syllabi for the various courses offered by the school, the development of extensive apparatus and procedures for examinations, experimentation in the development of tests applicable to prospective librarians, the establishment of a series of "Studies in Library Service," the development of a plan of part-time employment of students of the schools of New York and other libraries, and the securing of the endowment for the Melvil Dewey Professorship by the Carnegie Corporation represent other aspects of Williamson's interest in education for librarianship.[55]

OTHER ACTIVITIES RELATED TO LIBRARIANSHIP

As head of the School of Library Service, Williamson was involved in many activities which reflected his constant interest in library work at Columbia, the Library School, its faculty, and students. A picture of this active program evolved in the many letters to and from librarians, organizations, institutions, scholars, alumni, and students pertaining to activities and programs of the School of Library Service.

During this time many people wrote to ask for advice and reaction to their ideas, plans, surveys, studies, or work. His advice was frequently requested on professional matters involving librarianship, library service, and especially library education. The American Library Association and particularly the Board of Education for Librarianship wrote him frequently for suggestions. The files of the School of Library Service disclosed extensive correspondence with the association and its activities in public relations, membership, recruiting, the American Library Association *Bulletin*, publishing, personnel, the International Relations Board, and other divisions of the association.

Williamson also maintained an interest in international librarianship projects through the American Library Association. He encouraged visits from foreign visitors and the enrollment of foreign students in the Library School.

Many librarians and educators included visits to Columbia in their itineraries. Some of these visitors were Monsignor Eugene Tisserant, Vatican Librarian and later Dean of the Sacred College of Cardinals; Dr. T. L. Yuan, Director of the National Library of Peking; Dr. Rubens Borba de Moraes, Chief of Division of Libraries and President of the Library Council of São Paulo, Brazil; and Dr. Josip Badalic, Librarian of the University of Yugoslavia.

Williamson was most cooperative with and interested in closer ties with international librarians and foreign students. He supported the work of Dr. Igino Giordani and Dr. Gerardo Bruni of the Vatican Library who visited Michigan and Columbia. He was informed on August 20, 1927, of their coming by Monsignor Eugene Tisserant: "Our men leave Rome today and I have nothing more to say about them, they will speak for themselves. But I want to send you my best greetings and my thanks."

Relations with the Library School Faculty

In his "Annual Report of the Director of the School . . . 1928-1929," Williamson observed that in the three years since the "School was established we have lost no teacher of professorial rank, and but one instructor."

The faculty members of the Library School were satisfied with the situation, even though several were offered tempting faculty or administrative posts in other institutions. Williamson stated in the same annual report that the fact that "they prefer to remain at Columbia is cause for genuine satisfaction. We have our own problems and difficulties; conditions are by no means ideal, but it may fairly be assumed that the opportunities and advantages at Columbia compare favorably with those offered in other library schools."

Alice I. Hazeltine commented on her experience and work with Williamson. She recalled in a letter of June 9, 1948, the day in 1927 when she visited him to discuss joining the faculty.

> I had wondered, before that, whether you "understood" children's work. After that, I had no hesitation, for I knew at once that your vision included the boys and girls as well as the older people. I have never had reason to change my mind, since your comprehension of the rightful place of work with children as the foundation of all book services was made evident all during the time I taught in the School of Library Service.

Bertha Frick also was a member of the Columbia faculty. She wrote the author on June 16, 1966, that she felt Williamson had "vision and imagination." In describing his personal characteristics and habits she observed that he had "enormous energy and capacity for sustained work, thoroughly familiar with details, complete loyalty to his staff and faculty."

On October 15, 1959, Isabella K. Rhodes, former Assistant Professor of Cataloging, wrote to him reminiscently and observed she had been going over files of letters and documents from the old days in the School of Library Service.

> Such wise and reasonable and friendly letters—even when they were reproving me for some of my shortcomings. Reading them again makes me realize anew what a privilege it was to work with you as chief, and how I have always appreciated that privilege.
>
> They were good days, weren't they, in spite of some trials and tribulations and disappointments. You laid a good foundation in that school, which will be evident for many years to come.

The faculty of the School of Library Service considered Williamson a capable administrator, a man of vision, and a leader. Miriam D. Tompkins, Associate Professor at Columbia from 1936 to 1954 wrote to Williamson on December 31, 1951: "You will be interested in a remark of one our most capable advanced students . . . 'I never could see what was wrong with the program. . . . It seemed pretty good to me.' So say all of us who had the privilege of teaching the courses under your leadership."

Williamson firmly believed that librarians need not be limited to work and activities solely related to their profession. He wrote Louis Round Wilson on January 4, 1943, that the librarian should "take a hand in activities of various kinds that need not be considered a part of his library duties in the ordinary sense." He continued in the same letter expressing his belief that such opportunities were unlimited, or "rather they were limited only by the librarian's time, imagination, and energy."

ATTITUDES OF THE PROFESSION ABOUT APPOINTMENT OF ARCHIBALD MCLEISH

Williamson was concerned about the professional aspects of library work and its emergence as a true profession. He was one of the many people who attempted to raise library work from the level of apprenticeship to that of a profession.

William Warner Bishop observed in his letter of August 18, 1928: "I feel that we suffer in a good many respects because of the fact that librarianship has not yet reached a full professional status, particularly in the mental attitudes of librarians toward their calling. We are still in the pioneer state, and our work is very much more an art than a science."

Even today the attitude of many people toward library service as professional work is often negative. In his annual report of 1931 Williamson remarked on this constant struggle.

> It is not at all an uncommon occurrence to find men of high standing and influence in the educational world who deny to librarianship the status of a profession and refuse to recognize that special training for library service has a legitimate place within the university. Such an attitude indicates complete ignorance of the duties, responsibilities, and opportunities of workers on higher levels of librarianship. Because library service requires much routine and clerical work for which even a college education is not necessary it is often ignorantly assumed that librarianship is on a lower intellectual level than teaching, or engineering, or any of the other professions. No matter what the self-appointed guardians of university standards may say to the contrary, the essentially professional character of librarianship must be apparent to anyone who will take the trouble to look at the facts. It will also be found to require both general education of collegiate grade and an extended period of technical training on a university level.

Professional library training was momentarily shaken on June 7, 1939, when President Franklin D. Roosevelt sent to the United States Senate his nomination of Archibald McLeish for Librarian of Congress. McLeish had no professional library training and his appointment to the top library position in the United States was "destined to fall like a bombshell upon the sensitive ears of librarians in many quarters, reverberating with special distinction in those circles where certain officials of the American Library Association waited and listened expectantly."[56] The "controversy over a poet" was heightened by Milton J. Ferguson, then President of the American Library Association: "Librarians throughout the country would protest the nomination of Archibald McLeish as Librarian of Congress because of his lack of technical training."[57] Dr. Ferguson continued his attack in a letter to President Roosevelt: "We think that the confirmation of Archibald McLeish as Librarian of Congress would be a calamity."

The American Library Association and many librarians were especially annoyed that McLeish's appointment was a "denial of the value of professional training and experience."[58] The American Library Association sent two representatives before the United States Senate on June 21; the next day the matter of the appointment came to the floor. Senator Alben W. Barkley of Kentucky stated the association's position, which was "that a trained professional librarian should have been selected rather than somebody who was not."[59] The Senate, however, confirmed McLeish's appointment on June 29, 1939.

The American Library Association became reconciled to McLeish; the new President of the association, Ralph Munn, wrote him, "For the Association, and for myself, I wish you well in your new duties."[60]

Williamson expressed his own feeling about the controversy and the appointment of a nonprofessional as Librarian of Congress in a letter to Asa D. Dickinson, then Librarian of Brooklyn College Library and former Director, University of Pennsylvania Libraries, on June 28, 1939:

> The news from Washington is, I suppose, susceptible of various interpretations. . . . The new Librarian of Congress will have to get both training and experience before he can be anything except a figurehead. The process of getting that training and experience is going to be slow and costly to the nation: The appointment seems to me not to show that training is unnecessary but that there is a wrong way and a right way of getting it.

CRITICISM OF LIBRARY SCHOOLS

Criticism of library schools had been heard for years, and Williamson found such comments annoying. In 1934 an Appraisal Committee was appointed by the Carnegie Corporation of New York to "make an appraisal of the library school, to determine if possible the direction of its growth, its outstanding strength, its weakness capable of conscious remedy, its adequacy in selecting and training the right number and quality of librarians whose presence in professional ranks may be counted upon to make this instrument one of distinct human service." The committee consisted of Milton E. Lord, Mary U. Rothrock, Charles E. Rush, George B. Utley, and Milton J. Ferguson, Chairman.

Williamson, in answering their questionnaire on February 14, 1934, expressed his attitude toward the constant criticism of library schools.

> Librarians have talked a great deal about the deficiencies of the library schools, and the library schools have meekly let it pass. I often wonder whether it would not be a good thing for the library schools to turn the tables for awhile and say what they think of librarians as they see them. It might be a good thing if the schools were to put on record some of the defects which they see in librarians' personnel practices, but the schools won't do that for they are unwilling, in the first place, to incur the displeasure of library administrators, and secondly, I fear that library school administrators and faculties have acquired a well-developed inferiority complex. They have become so accustomed to all kinds of criticism of themselves and their product that they have apparently come to think that it must be true that they are a poor lot. I admit that I have in the past contributed my share of such criticism of the schools. In recent years, however, I have come to see more clearly the need of airing the other side of the question. Certainly I don't mean to say that the schools should be free from criticism, but I should not be surprised if a moderate amount of well-deserved appreciation and encouragement might not at the present time be more helpful to the whole profession.

The Decision to Retire

By September 1941, Williamson indicated his desire to retire. Action was delayed one year; his retirement did not become effective until 1943.

President Butler notified Williamson on April 5, 1943, that the Trustees of Columbia University had designated him to be Director Emeritus of Libraries following his retirement from active service on June 30, 1943. Butler congratulated Williamson on this "new and well-won distinction." Williamson's final act at Columbia University was to write to Butler on April 8, 1943:

> Nothing within the power of the Trustees could have given me greater personal pleasure and satisfaction than the designation of Director Emeritus of Libraries. Please convey to the Trustees and accept for yourself my grateful appreciation of this generous action.

When his retirement was announced, Williamson received many letters which were sent to the School of Library Service to be included in a bound volume as a testimonial to him and his work. These included letters, telegrams, and notes, all indicating the good wishes of friends, former students, colleagues, and well-wishers on his completion of seventeen years of service at Columbia University.

On May 19, 1943, a reception was held in his honor in the rotunda of Low Memorial Library. Over four hundred people attended. President Butler presented Williamson with the testimonial volume.

SUMMARY OF WILLIAMSON'S TERM AT COLUMBIA

The work which Williamson accomplished as Dean of the School of Library Service was reviewed by Louis Round Wilson in a statement to the author on July 31, 1966.

> Williamson believed in sound basic education, a solid foundation in library technology and service. He insisted on strict admission requirements to the School, and thought that performance in the School would be heightened if it was based on experience in a library before admission. The adoption of the Master's program in librarianship did not go into effect until 1927-28. His *Report* showed his interest in sound scholarship, and he believed it could be best assured if

Columbia University in the City of New York

it was provided under the auspices of a university. He did not think that a school backed by anything less could produce the kind of librarian desired.

He believed in research in librarianship but found little acceptance of the idea by librarians. He was convinced that the scientific point of view was essential to sound thinking and was necessary to the discovery of new truth.

In summing up Williamson's contributions to the Library School, Wilson continued:

> He was clear in his thinking about the status of library schools and their need for the contribution from other schools and departments in a strong university. He had the ability to work out the merger of the New York State and New York Public Library Schools, build up a staff for the new school, develop a balanced curriculum with some inclusion of courses from other disciplines, project a Master's program, and work out syllabi and comprehensive examinations, all of which required the ability to plan, and to be sufficiently tough-minded to see them effectively at work.

In his last report as Director of Libraries for 1942-1943, Williamson looked back on his work at Columbia University and his feelings after these many years of service. Although this report relates specifically to the work in the University Libraries, it also sums up his entire career at Columbia in his dual position as Director of Libraries and Dean of the School of Library Service.

> For two acknowledgements which it is my pleasant duty to make in this my final report, I do not need to refer to documents on file. The facts are ever present in my mind and heart. The first of these is my gratitude to you, Mr. President, for the personal interest and full understanding you have never failed to show in the work of the Libraries and for the strong support you have given me in the performance of my official duties in all of the seventeen years I have had the honor to serve as Director of Libraries. Also, I must record my grateful appreciation of the loyalty and devoted service of members of the library staffs, which make it possible for me to look back with some modest satisfaction over the record of achievement in these seventeen years—satisfaction duly

temperated with the consciousness that much more should have been accomplished with the means which the University placed at our disposal. Had time and space permitted I would have attempted in this last of my annual reports to review the work of these seventeen years. That, however, will have to be left, if it is worth doing at all, to some hand which can impartially set down the record of failure as well as of accomplishment.

The philosophy of library education and library service as expressed in Williamson's *Training for Library Service* in 1923 had been applied to the activities of the School of Library Service at Columbia University. This was the testing place for Williamson's wider vision of the profession. His concept of library education needed a person of zeal, energy, and persistence. It is to his credit that the development of librarianship as a professional field of endeavor was accomplished. As David Clift stated, "The real history of library education begins with him."

NOTES

1. Ray Trautman, *A History of the School of Library Service, Columbia University*, pp. 34-35.
2. Richard B. Morris, ed., *Encyclopedia of American History*, p. 682.
3. Ray Trautman, *op. cit.*, p. 33.
4. *Ibid.*, p. 67.
5. *Loc. cit.*
6. Paul North Rice, "Editorial Forum: Charles C. Williamson," *Library Journal* 68 (June 15, 1943), 522.
7. Ernest J. Reece, "C. C. Williamson: A Record of Service to American Librarianship," *College and Research Libraries* 4 (September 1943), 307.
8. Trusten W. Russell, "A Library of the New Era," *New York Times*, July 8, 1934, p. 6.
9. *Loc. cit.*
10. *Loc. cit.*
11. *Loc. cit.*
12. *Loc. cit.*

13. "Columbia Plans Library Opening," *New York Times*, October 7, 1934, Sec. 2, p. 1.
14. *Loc. cit.*
15. Letter to the author, July 20, 1966, p. 1.
16. *Loc. cit.*
17. Keyes D. Metcalf, "Charles C. Williamson," *Library Service News* 11 (November 1943), 23.
18. Paul North Rice, *op. cit.*, p. 522.
19. Letter from David Clift to Genevieve H. Williamson, May 17, 1965.
20. Winifred B. Linderman, "History of the Columbia University Library, 1876-1926" (Ph.D. diss., Columbia University, 1959), p. 456.
21. *Loc. cit.*
22. "Roger Howson, 79, Retired Librarian at Columbia University, Served 22 Years" (Obituary), *New York Times*, April 23, 1962, p. 29.
23. Linderman, *op. cit.*, p. 537.
24. *Ibid.*, p. 540.
25. *Ibid.*, p. 543.
26. *Loc. cit.*
27. "Memorandum of Interview of Charles C. Williamson with Dr. Keppel," December 21, 1936, p. 2.
28. *Loc. cit.*
29. *Ibid.*, p. 3.
30. Interview with Carl M. White, July 11, 1966.
31. Letter from Charles C. Williamson to Carl M. White, April 4, 1952, p. 1.
32. Ray Trautman, *op. cit.*, p. 34.
33. Florence Anderson, *Library Program, 1911-1961*, pp. 72-73.
34. Robert D. Leigh, "The Education of Librarians," in Alice I. Bryan, *The Public Librarian*, p. 309.
35. Ray Trautman, *op. cit.*, p. 35.
36. *Ibid.*, p. 48.
37. *Ibid.*, p. 34.
38. Louis Shores, *Quiet World: A Librarian's Crusade for Destiny*, p. 21.
39. Ray Trautman, *op. cit.*, p. 39.
40. *Ibid.*, p. 41.
41. *Ibid.*, p. 42.
42. *Ibid.*, p. 45.
43. *Ibid.*, p. 43.
44. *Ibid.*, p. 46.

45. *Loc. cit.*
46. *Loc. cit.*
47. *Ibid.*, p. 47.
48. *Ibid.*, p. 48.
49. *Loc. cit.*
50. Ernest J. Reece, *op. cit.*, p. 307.
51. *Loc. cit.*
52. Paul North Rice, *op. cit.*, p. 522.
53. *Loc. cit.*
54. Keyes D. Metcalf, *op. cit.*, p. 23.
55. Louis Round Wilson and Maurice F. Tauber, *The University Library*, 2nd ed., pp. 545-546.
56. Lucy Salamanca, *Fortress of Freedom: The Story of the Library of Congress*, p. 364.
57. *Ibid.*, p. 365.
58. *Ibid.*, p. 374.
59. *Ibid.*, p. 375.
60. David Mearns, *The Story Up to Now: The Library of Congress, 1800-1946*, p. 209.

13

RELATED PROFESSIONAL ACTIVITIES

ACTIVITIES IN PROFESSIONAL ORGANIZATIONS
AND ASSOCIATIONS

DR. ERNEST J. REECE summed up the work Williamson did for library, scholarly, and professional organizations.

> He has been the mainspring of the annual Thanksgiving time conference of eastern college librarians; he was a prime mover in marshaling support in the United States for the completion of the printed catalog of the Bibliothèque Nationale; he was president from 1929 to 1931 of the Association of American Library Schools; he has served a term on the Executive Board of the American Library Association; and he has been active in the Association of Research Libraries.[1]

Williamson was a member, at various times, of the American Library Association, Special Libraries Association, Manhattan Special Libraries Association, New York Library Association, American Library Institute, Bibliographical Society of America, Association of College and Research Libraries, Association of American Library Schools, and the New York Library Club. In addition, he also belonged to the American Association of University Professors, American Economic Association, American Political Science Association, Academy of Political Science in the City of New York, National Municipal League, American Statistical Society, American Sociological Society, National Arts Club, American Humanist Association, Rational Free Press of London, and the American Council for Better Broadcasts. He was elected to Phi Beta Kappa and Phi

Gamma Delta. In 1964 he was awarded the Beta Phi Mu Award for his contribution to library education.

The New York Library Association: Williamson was elected President of the New York Library Association, serving in that capacity for 1920-1921.

The American Library Association: Prior to his work at Columbia, Williamson had been active in the American Library Association. He became a member in 1913. In 1917-1918, 1919-1923, and 1927-1931 he was a Member of the Council of the Association. He also served on several committees, evidence of his continuing interest in the work and programs of the association. His committee work included Chairman of the Committee on National Certification and Training (1920-1922), Chairman of the Committee on Study and Development of Reading Habits (1926-1927 and 1928-1931), Chairman and Member of the Committee on Journal of Discussion (1927-1929, 1932-1934, and 1936-1938), Member of the Committee on Recruiting for Library Service (1930-1931), Member of the Committee on Coordination of Conference Programs (1930), Member of the Committee of Research Studies, Surveys, and Special Projects (1932-1933), and in 1940 he was appointed to the Advisory Board for the Study of Special Projects, Dr. Leon Carnovsky, Chairman.

The American Library Association appointed Williamson and Edwin Hatfield Anderson as delegates to represent the association at the Fiftieth Anniversary of the American Society of Mechanical Engineers at their convention in Washington, D.C., in April 1930.

In 1937 Williamson was nominated for the position of First Vice-President (President-elect) on the 1938 ballot of the American Library Association. He was opposed by Ralph Munn, who was then Librarian of the Carnegie Library of Pittsburgh, Pennsylvania.

Williamson had been advised by friends and colleagues that his chances for election were slim and that the possibility of electing a third New Yorker in succession to this position was most unlikely. Paul North Rice, then Chief of the Reference Department of the New York Public Library wrote him on April 11, 1938:

Related Professional Activities

> Ever since I knew you were nominated for president of the American Library Association I have been meaning to write to you to express both my delight and my regret. Two years ago I hoped very much they would nominate you, and I can think of no one who deserves the honor more. I do feel very regretful, however, that you have been nominated now as the third New Yorker in succession. With the natural feeling of jealousy of New York which is always prevalent in the Middle West, it puts you at such a disadvantage that it will be a most conspicuous recognition if you are elected. Your friends . . . expect you to be defeated, as they do not think even you can overcome that disadvantage. If we are wrong, however, we shall be all the more delighted.

Williamson agreed with this prediction and wrote to Carl Milam, Secretary of the American Library Association on May 10, 1938.

> It does not seem probable at this moment that I shall get to Kansas City. . . . I have an easy conscience about being absent from the Conference because it does not seem probable that I shall find myself a member of the Executive Board. My best friends tell me that there is no chance in the world that I or any other New Yorker can be elected this year. It is just as well, for various reasons. I really should have thought the matter through a little more carefully before accepting the nomination.

Ralph Munn won the election as had been predicted, and Williamson wrote him on August 8, 1938:

> As soon as I heard the result of the A.L.A. election I meant to send you my heartiest congratulations and best wishes for your presidential term. Your election was a great relief to me and still more so to many of my friends who have scolded me to my face (and no telling what they have said to my back) for accepting the nomination in face of the heavy burden I am carrying here. Of course they do not know some of the things I know. Nevertheless they are entitled to assume I was foolhardy, not to use a harsher term.
>
> Well I believe the present system of letting the Association elect its own president is an excellent one and the success of the system depends on cooperation all around, including

members nominated for office. If no one accepts a nomination unless assured of election the plan breaks down. So I think it is the duty of people who are asked by a nominating committee to stand for election to do so. I am glad I did and I'm glad you were elected. The system is vindicated and the Association will have an excellent president.

By the way, you will be the youngest man to serve as president in the history of the Association, will you not? That is a fine tribute.

A few weeks later on August 22, Munn answered.

Yes I do realize that I am the youngest man ever elected, and I am convinced that there is a great deal of significance in that fact. It appears to me that the A.L.A. membership fell into the error of adopting industry's principle that "no one over 45 need apply." No other explanation is satisfactory to my mind.

If your health is still anything less than a full 100 percent, you are indeed lucky that I am the one to carry the burden. Having worked for Jennings while he was president, I am looking forward to next year with more than a little fear.

With many thanks for your good wishes—and I'll need them.

Williamson's other work within the American Library Association was to serve on the Committee for the Herbert Putnam Honor Fund. This fund was established in 1939 to honor Dr. Putnam and to inspire librarians by providing them some income as a grant-in-aid. The fund was established to honor Putnam's fortieth anniversary as Librarian of Congress, which he celebrated on April 5, 1939.

Association of American Library Schools: Williamson also was active in the Association of American Library Schools. From 1929 to 1931 he served as president; receiving a telegram on April 23, 1929, from William Warner Bishop: "HOPE YOU WILL ACCEPT STOP THIS SEEMS EXCELLENT OPPORTUNITY TO PUT NEW LIFE AND VIGOR IN THIS PROFESSIONAL ASSOCIATION." In 1940 he was a member of the association's

Related Professional Activities

Committee on Tests and Measurements, serving for one year.

Catalog of the Bibliothèque Nationale and Legion of Honor: Williamson was concerned about the delays in completing the printed catalog of the Bibliothèque Nationale of France. He was eager to have this reference work completed and expended much energy and effort toward achieving this goal.

He convinced the Rockefeller Foundation of the value of the project. He was able to obtain support from libraries in the United States who agreed to subscribe to the catalog. This evidence of increased interest and assistance caused the French government to increase its aid. Williamson wrote an article, "Can the Catalogue of the Bibliothèque Nationale Be Completed in Ten Years?" which appeared in the *Library Journal* and the *American Library Association Bulletin* and was written specifically to stimulate interest in this project and obtain wider support.

Wilson and Tauber commented on this aspect of his bibliographical activity.

> Soon after he went to Columbia he found that the publication of the highly important catalog of the Bibliothèque Nationale was dragging on interminably. He went to Paris to discuss the matter with the director, Roland Marcel, and secured a grant from the Rockefeller Foundation for Marcel to come to America to consider the matter further. An agreement was worked out with American subscribers to speed up the rate of publication, and a grant was received from the Rockefeller Foundation to supplement library support. As a result of this activity the French Government agreed to increase the appropriation for the catalog. In recognition of his interest and the aid he secured for the undertaking through him, Williamson was made a Chevalier de la Légion d'Honneur in 1929.[2]

On July 1, 1929, he received a letter from the Consul General of France at New York, announcing: "I have the honour to inform you confidentially that you have been proposed for a French honorific distinction." Roland Marcel, Administrator General of the Bibliothèque Nationale had proposed him as a member of the French Legion of Honor. On August 20, 1929, Marcel received a letter from M. Carré of the Ministère des Affaires Etrangères of the French government, which stated:

> *Vous avez bien voulu me recommander pour la croix de CHEVALIER de la Légion d'Honneur M. Charles Clarence Williamson, citoyen américain.*
>
> *Je suis heureux de vous annoncer que M. le Président de la République vient, sur ma proposition, de lui conférer cette distinction.*
>
> *Agréez, Monsieur, les assurances de ma considération la plus distinguée.*

> You have recommended to me Mr. Charles Clarence Williamson, an American citizen, for the cross of KNIGHT of the Legion of Honor. I am happy to announce to you that the President of the Republic has just conferred this distinction upon him, on my proposal.
>
> Please accept my most honored esteem. [ed. trans.]

Marcel wrote Williamson on August 22, enclosing the above letter and advising him "of the honor bestowed upon him." Marcel congratulated Williamson on receiving this honor for the work he did for the Bibliothèque Nationale.

> *Sans doute, je ne vous avais pas parlé de ma proposition, mais je tenais beaucoup à ce que le Gouvernement Français reconnût le service qu'avec tant d'intelligence et de coeur vous avez rendu à la Bibliothèque Nationale. C'est pour moi une grande joie de vous féliciter, Madame C. C. Williamson et vous, d'une haute décoration que vous avez bien méritée.*

> Probably I had not spoken to you about my proposal, but I was very anxious that the French government recognize the service you have rendered with so much intelligence and heart to the National Library. It is a great joy for me to congratulate you and your wife for a high decoration that you have certainly earned. [ed. trans.]

Related Professional Activities

Williamson, pleased at the honor from the French government, wrote to Marcel on September 14, 1929: "I cannot avoid feeling that you have been over generous in your interpretation of my service to the Bibliothèque Nationale; nevertheless, I am very glad to accept this high distinction and shall always look upon our association with the greatest satisfaction. . . . Thanking you for your courtesy which I greatly fear exceeds my deserts."

The award from the French Government read:

ORDRE NATIONAL DE LA LEGION D'HONNEUR
Honneur-Patrie

Le Grand Chancelier de l'Ordre National de la Légion d'Honneur certifie que, par Décret de Six Août, mil neuf cent vingt neuf.

Le Président de la République Française a conféré à M. Charles Clarence WILLIAMSON, citoyen américain, Directeur des Bibliothèques et de l'Ecole du Service des Bibliothèques, à l'Université de Columbia à New York, la Décoration de CHEVALIER de l'Ordre National de la Légion d'Honneur.

Fait à Paris, le 12 Août, 1929.

Vu, scellé et enregistré, No 39.90F
Le Chef du 1er Bureau

[J. Renault]

NATIONAL ORDER OF THE LEGION OF HONOR
Honor-Fatherland

The Lord Chancellor of the National Order of the Legion of Honor certifies by Decree of the sixth of August, nineteen hundred twenty-nine:

The President of the French Republic has conferred upon Mr. Charles Clarence WILLIAMSON, American citizen, Director of Libraries and of the School of Library Service of Columbia University in the City of New York, the Decoration of KNIGHT of the National Order of the Legion of Honor.

Paris, August 12, 1929.

Witnessed, sealed, and registered, No. 39.90F
Senior Clerk

[J. Renault] [ed. trans.]

The *New York Times,* in its November 17, 1929, issue, carried the news of the award:

> France Honors Dr. C. C. Williamson
>
> The President of the French Republic has conferred upon Dr. C. C. Williamson, Director of Libraries and Director of the School of Library Service of Columbia University, the decoration of Chevalier of the Legion of Honor in recognition of his successful efforts to organize American support for the rapid completion of the printed catalogue of the Bibliothèque Nationale.

Williamson also received the medal of Grands Bienfaiteurs de la Bibliothèque Nationale. He acknowledged this further evidence of the generous interpretation of the Bibliothèque Nationale for his "slight service": "I shall treasure the medal above anything of the sort that I have ever received and am ever likely to receive. In the course of time perhaps I shall be able to live down the feeling that I have done nothing at all to deserve so great an honor." Williamson was also made a Membre Perpétuel and Membre Titulaire à Vie by the Société des Amis de la Bibliothèque Nationale et des Grandes Bibliothèques de France.

Williamson received many congratulatory letters on his receipt of the Legion of Honor, including one on October 19 from President Thwing: "I rejoice in your receiving the decoration of the chevalier of the Légion d'Honneur. I feel a sense of pride in your new honor."

BIBLIOGRAPHICAL AND REFERENCE BOOK INTERESTS

John Fall, of the Public Affairs Information Service, discussed some of Williamson's activities in bibliographical and reference book production. Williamson felt this kind of material was needed by librarians and encouraged such

Related Professional Activities

research and publication. Fall stated, "He worked for the establishment of the *Index* of the *New York Times*, to serve as a founder of *Facts on File*, to edit *Who's Who in Library Service*, and to advise the Bibliothèque Nationale on a more rapid method for the production of its catalog."[3]

Although there is no material to document Williamson's work relating to the *New York Times Index*, he was probably involved around 1913 during the time when the publication was going through a period of reorganization. The *New York Times Index* found no record of his role. Williamson, however, commented to the author during a personal interview in 1964 that he had been involved in work with the *New York Times Index*.

Williamson's work with *Facts on File* was documented in a letter of May 17, 1965, written to his widow by Howard M. Epstein, then Managing Editor.

> We at Facts on File were terribly saddened to hear of Dr. Williamson's death. We last had seen him some two years ago, when he kindly agreed to come to New York to discuss the problems faced by today's librarians and the devising of new services to meet contemporary library needs.
>
> Dr. Williamson was associated with Facts on File from its inception in 1941, when it was an idea struggling to become a business. We will not forget him.

In 1940 Williamson expressed his interest in the possibility of an indexed news publication and agreed to serve on the *Facts on File* Advisory Board with William L. Shirer, H. V. Kaltenborn, Dr. Frank Tannenbaum of Columbia, Frances W. Coker of Yale, President Harry D. Gideonse of Brooklyn College, John Gunther, and Elmer Davis.

Williamson was most pleased with *Facts on File* and complimented the organization in a letter to them on March 31, 1954, regarding the handling of the previous years' news and publication of the latest volume of its *Yearbook*: "There ought to be a Pulitzer prize or some more fitting kind of award for this type of service to scholars, writers and every one who deals with the facts that are making history."

Epstein commented in his letter to the author on November 17, 1967:

> Dr. Williamson's association with Facts on File was limited, but provided us with encouragement sorely needed during the years when it was not quite clear whether the publication would catch on or not. While it cannot be documented from correspondence in our files, Mr. Van Westerborg, the successor to Bernard Person as publisher of Facts on File, tells me that Dr. Williamson was very emphatic about the academic community's need for this type of publication.

WILLIAMSON'S CONCERN WITH *LIBRARY LITERATURE*

Williamson also was involved in the publication of *Library Literature*, the index to professional literature in the field. Harry G. T. Cannons had compiled his *Bibliography of Library Economy, 1876-1920*, which was published by the American Library Association. Plans for a supplement to Cannons were discussed, and Williamson kept urging publication. R. R. Bowker felt that *Library Journal* was doing an adequate job and was unwilling to permit others to undertake such a project. Williamson wrote to Bowker and to H. W. Wilson, hoping to break the deadlock and get an index to current professional library literature compiled and published as soon as possible. Carl Milam, of the American Library Association, did not think the association had to wait but could go right ahead and publish a supplement to Cannons if they found "somebody to compile it." Williamson was critical of Cannons and wanted to make sure that if the American Library Association did publish a supplement it "would be done in a much better way than the Canon [*sic*] list." The association continued with its plans and published *Library Literature: A Supplement to Cannons, 1921-1932*. In 1933 the H. W. Wilson Company took over the publication of *Library Literature* as a quarterly and has maintained this service ever since. Williamson's involvement in this most important index to library materials was further evidence of his continuous work in the improvement and availability of reference materials and tools for librarians.

Conference of Eastern College Librarians

The Conference of Eastern College Librarians was established at Columbia University in 1914 by William D. Johnston, Librarian, and ran for two years under his guidance. From that time until 1930 it was organized by a variety of people, but that year Williamson took over and remained in charge of the annual program until his retirement in 1943.

Harold M. Turner, in his article, "The CECL's First Fifty Years," appearing in *College and Research Libraries* in July 1965, observed:

> His fourteen year stewardship of the Conference was remarkable in many respects. For one, he was simultaneously managing two sizeable enterprises: the Columbia University library system and its school of library service. But more remarkable, I think is the *way* in which he ran the Conference as if it were a kind of third Indian club he kept twirling in the air. And he did so with a sure hand, with flair, and with much dexterity, which make the Conference seem all the more worth celebrating today. As Dr. Williamson cheerfully acknowledged to me not long ago, he has one serious administrative flaw. He found it almost painfully hard to delegate detail. But not for want of faith in his subordinates. Rather, I suspect, because he was so fond of detail himself.
>
> In any case, at his desk, first in Low Library, and then in Butler, he centralized the entire responsibility for the Conference. From there he ran the whole show. He handled the delicate business of speaker, the topic procurement, and incidentally he had quite a knack for that. Almost ingeniously, he would write people asking their suggestions for topics. Then once he had them, he would ask the same people who suggested them to speak on them. And often enough they would.[4]

In addition to the meeting, always held on the Saturday after Thanksgiving, Williamson organized a "Conference within a Conference," which met on Friday evening before the conference for dinner and a smoker. The Friday night dinners were "highly honorific affairs, freighted with status, and hedged all about with restrictions."[5] The people who attended were men like "the Goodriches of the College of the City of New York and Dartmouth; Mark Llewellyn Raney of Johns Hopkins; Otto Kinkeldey of Cornell; Andrew Keogh of Yale; William Warner Bishop of Michigan; Fremont Rider of Wesleyan; Milton Lord of the Boston public library; Harry Lydenberg and Paul North Rice of the New York public library, and Keyes Metcalf of Harvard. In short, The Establishment."[6] The Friday night dinners were informal, but in addition to general conversation the group also discussed problems pertaining to library work.

Williamson's impact on the conference was long lasting because, "Williamson was rarely gifted, especially where the Conference was concerned, and I think it is fair to say, with due respect to all who have followed him since, that much that is best about the Conference today still bears his imprint."[7] The Conference of Eastern College Librarians discontinued its annual meetings in 1970.

AMERICAN LIBRARY INSTITUTE

Williamson was a Fellow of the American Library Institute and in 1933 served on the board. The American Library Institute was established in 1906 in order to encourage the "more scholarly aspects of librarianship, hitherto neglected, and . . . a careful and scientific study and discussion of the more important problems of library science."[8] Munthe refers to the "100 esteemed members of the exalted American Library Institute."[9]

Tse-chien Tai states that "at a glance the organization of the American Library Institute will suggest to us a mental picture of the House of Elders of Japan or the House of Peers of England. Its members consist of all ex-presidents, mem-

Related Professional Activities

bers of the Executive Board, and members of the Council of the American Library Association, and elected Fellows."[10] The objective of the American Library Institute was to "deliberate on difficult questions in connection with library administration and economy. In reality the Institute is a body like the learned societies and scientific academies."[11] The members were considered as powerful elders.

Williamson was a member of the American Library Institute until 1937. Although he had renewed his membership for a ten-year period, he decided he wanted to withdraw from any connection with the organization. On November 19, 1937, he wrote Herbert B. Brigham, Secretary of the institute, giving his reasons for resigning from what he called "a completely unnecessary and futile organization."

Williamson's resignation caused some concern among the members. He wrote to George B. Utley, President of the institute on December 3, 1937, that his decision to resign was not a criticism of Utley's service as President.

> In my judgment no one, even if he gave his entire time to the presidency, could achieve very much that is worth while for the library profession under existing conditions. I quite agree that the idea of a library senate made up of the "elder statesmen" is alluring, but nothing has happened since I have been a member to justify the existence of the Institute, except as a kind of professional club or mutual admiration society.

Williamson was concerned over the fact that the election of Fellows was "a popularity contest, a recognition of past service," rather than based on any contribution the people were making and were certain to make to the profession. He stated:

> I personally enjoy the friendship and personal relations with every member of the Institute. If it were regarded merely as a social club and if we could get together frequently without any pretense of being a professional organization with a serious purpose and definite functions to perform I should probably feel differently about it.

Although he had resigned, he still wanted to attend the December 27 meeting of the institute because he was "deeply interested in the problem of finding a function for the Institute." He warned Utley not to ask him to "ventilate any of the heretical views I have expressed here."

It appears that Williamson was partly right about the institute, because after 1941 it ceased to function as an organization. It held its last meeting on June 21, 1941, at the Harvard Faculty Club in Cambridge. According to George B. Utley, "no meetings of the Institute have been called since this country entered the war."[12]

WILLIAMSON AS A SPEECH-MAKER

On June 15, 1920, Williamson gave the Founder's Day Address at the Library School of Western Reserve University. This commemorative address was entitled "Andrew Carnegie: His Contribution to the Public Library Movement."

In 1926 he gave a brief address to the Professional Training Section of the American Library Association at the Atlantic City meeting, speaking on the training of the library school instructor.

In the 1928 fall term he delivered the Dedication Day Address at the Jones Library at Amherst, Massachusetts.

Williamson also gave the address at the dedication of the new library at Randolph-Macon Women's College in 1929. This speech was delivered to an audience of about 1,000, including members of the college, representatives of the State Library Association, and guests. The ceremony took place on Friday, November 1, 1929. His speech, which lasted forty-five minutes, was entitled "Library Service in a Machine Age." The address was published in the College *Bulletin*. William Black, Assistant to the President, expressed his reaction to Williamson's visit, writing to him on November 5, 1929, and expressing his delight "that you could be with us on such an interesting and inspiring occasion and hope we may have the pleasure of meeting you again."

Williamson was invited again to give the Founder's Day Address at Western Reserve University. On June 10, 1930, he discussed "The Place of Research in Library Service." This address became the lead article in the first volume of *Library Quarterly*, appearing in the January 1931 issue.

Although Williamson was constantly engaged in these and other public speeches, including a great number given at Columbia University to visiting groups and associations, he confessed his attitude toward public speaking in the letter of March 7, 1921, to Edwin Embree of the Rockefeller Foundation: "There is one thing I have to do occasionally which I very much dislike and which I know I do badly, and that is public speaking."

Publication of *Who's Who in Library Service*

During the time Williamson was working on the survey of the library schools, he became aware of the acute need for a clearinghouse regarding people in professional library work. This led to the "suggestion of a librarian's Who's Who," which he included in the 1921 typewritten report of "Training for Library Work"; this recommendation was not included in the printed *Training for Library Service* of 1923. He believed such a publication would

> do much to aid in solving the placement problem by putting at the service of library administrators and library boards information which they find it difficult to now get in regard to the educational qualifications and professional experience of library workers. The problem of selecting those whose names are to appear in such a guide, however, brings us back once more upon the necessity for some certification system for formulating and applying standards for professional library work.

It was not until ten years later that the first edition of *Who's Who in Library Service* appeared; it was edited by Charles C. Williamson and Alice L. Jewett, and published by the H. W. Wilson Company. A second edition was prepared by Williamson and Jewett in 1943. Interest in this publication has continued with later editions and with variation in the title, the third edition was edited by Dorothy Cole and published in 1955 by the Grolier Society, with the fourth edition edited by Lee Ash and published by the Shoe String Press in 1966. The name change appeared in the fifth edition, also edited by Lee Ash but called *A Biographical Directory of Librarians in the United States and Canada*. The sixth edition was edited by Joel Lee in 1972 under another name, *Who's Who in Library and Information Service*; both the fifth and sixth editions were published by the American Library Association. The history of this publication continues to the present-day with the appearance of the *Directory of Library and Information Science Professionals* published in 1988 by J. Dick Publishing Research Publications and sponsored by several professional associations, including the American Library Association, Special Libraries Association, and American Society for Information Science. In addition to the hard copy of this publication, it has been made available on CD-ROM disc.

The publication of this book in 1933 and 1943 was another of Williamson's major accomplishments and reflects the continuing need for such a publication, which has gone through seven editions in a period of fifty-five years. The publication's place in library work is supported by this continued interest and need for a basic reference source of biographical information about members of the library profession.

In commenting on the idea of compiling *Who's Who in Library Service*, Alice L. Jewett said on June 16, 1966, that the idea was Williamson's and it grew

> out of difficulties in seeking qualified personnel with suitable experience for library positions under his direction. It is a matter of record that he had discussion with other library school directors, professional organizations and publishers, all of whom recognized the usefulness of such a publication but were not in a position to undertake it. He felt so strongly about it he decided to undertake it himself.

Assembling the publication involved the task of reaching the librarians to be included in the directory. The first step,

Jewett stated, was to decide the scope of inclusion. Then the library schools were asked to forward application blanks to their graduates. Librarians of large public libraries and other important libraries were asked to submit the names of staff members and nongraduates of library schools who, by reason of the position held or the special quality of their work, should be included. From these application blanks, they recorded the essential biographical information. This material was drawn up for the printer. Decisions had to be made about form, content, and general layout. Reviewing the galleys and the page proofs involved much discussion. Williamson "assumed the financial responsibility, made all contacts with library schools, librarians, university officials, printer, publisher, etc."

In commenting on this contribution, he stated in a letter of January 4, 1943, to Louis Round Wilson, "It did seem to be a real need. The work was hardly a financial success yet it assisted librarians by establishing a guide to members of the profession and lending some dignity to the work of librarianship." Williamson also confessed, "Had I known all the headaches it would cause me, I would never have touched it." He believed this publication gave "librarians a sense of professional status."

Wilson and Tauber considered *Who's Who in Library Service* a pioneer work of great value to librarians and the library profession.

> The publication of *Who's Who in Library Service* in 1933 and of the revised edition in 1943, edited by Williamson and Alice L. Jewett, has been of particular significance to librarians. Through the two editions librarians have been able to secure information concerning members of the profession about whom data would otherwise not be so easily accessible.[13]

Consultant and Advisory Work, and Other Professional Activities

Williamson frequently was involved as a consultant to various libraries and library schools. He also engaged in a good deal of advisory work for various publications.

His consultant work included a request from William K. Brewster about the establishment of the library school in Portland, Oregon. In 1920 Brewster wrote, "I certainly hope that you will be in Portland to give us advice on the library school situation."

In 1921 President James R. Angell, of the Carnegie Corporation of New York, asked Williamson to undertake a study of the Carnegie Library of Pittsburgh, Pennsylvania. The library had requested funds and the corporation did not want to give any until an outside person had examined and reported on the library. Williamson presented this report to President Angell on May 20, 1921.

From 1927 to 1931 W. W. Charters, Editor of the *Journal of Higher Education* was Director of the Library Curriculum Study, which had been established to evaluate the curriculum study textbooks of the American Library Association. Charters asked Williamson to provide him with reactions to these publications. Williamson sent Charters his comments and criticisms, as well as observation from some of the faculty of the School of Library Service at Columbia, with suggestions for improvement of the texts.

On November 17, 1928, he was appointed a member of the Committee on Academic and Professional Higher Degrees of the Association of American Universities.

Williamson's professional activities also included work as Chairman of the Commission on the Library and Adult Education, representing both the American Library Association and the American Association for Adult Education. He was the Chairman of this five-member committee consisting of William S. Gray, Dean of the College of Education, University of Chicago; Effie Power, Director of Work with Children, Cleveland Public Library; E. L. Thorndike, Teachers College, Columbia University; and Dr. Henry Suzzallo. Funds for the study were provided by the Carnegie Corporation of New York. The work of the committee resulted in the publication, in 1929, of *The Reading Interests and Habits of Adults*, by William S. Gray and Ruth Munroe.

President John Hope of Atlanta University, Atlanta, Georgia, requested Williamson's assistance in drawing up plans for their library.

Related Professional Activities

William N. Seaver, Librarian at the Massachusetts Institute of Technology, asked Williamson's advice on a report of the Vail Librarianship (Graduate Physics and Chemistry Library). Williamson commented on the report in October 1931 and sent this to Seaver.

Williamson was called in as a consultant for a new library building at the University of Buffalo, New York. He was critical of the plans and felt the projected building was too small, without sufficient reading accommodations, and did not lend itself to expansion. He submitted a "Draft of a Memorandum" in August 1933.

In 1937 he edited *School of Library Economy of Columbia College, 1887-1889*, which was a compilation of source materials pertaining to the early days of the Library School at Columbia under Melvil Dewey. In the same year, he advised Grace Siewers, Librarian of Salem College, Winston-Salem, North Carolina, regarding its library building.

In 1940 he was appointed a member of the Visiting Committee for the Library of the Massachusetts Institute of Technology. Another honor was his appointment, in 1940, as a Member of the Board of the Columbia University Press.

Williamson's work as a consultant was varied and, if not particularly extensive, certainly indicative of his many interests and desire to assist librarians.

When *Library Quarterly* was established at the University of Chicago in 1931, he was appointed an Associate Editor and a member of the Advisory Board. Williamson also was an Associate Editor of the *Journal of Higher Education*, and after his retirement in 1943 he continued to serve in that capacity. He was involved with this work from the beginning and did all he could to help the journal establish itself. A letter of March 2, 1949, from R. H. Eckelberry, the editor, stated:

> The JOURNAL, now in its twentieth year is deeply indebted to the Associated Editors. With your interest and cooperation, particularly in the early and uncertain years, the JOURNAL has won for itself a place in the national scheme of higher education. The prestige of your professional reputation has

lent the JOURNAL dignity of which it has always tried to be worthy.

Williamson felt that his work had been "microscopic." In 1949 Eckelberry asked Williamson to serve on a new Advisory Board. Williamson refused, telling Eckelberry, "For many years I have had an uneasy conscience about letting my name appear as an Associate Editor."

In 1958 the *Journal of Higher Education* went through a period of reorganization and Williamson was asked to serve in a new position, as Editorial Consultant. Dean Everett Walters, Chairman of the Editorial Board, wrote to ask if he would be willing to continue his support under this title. "The University is grateful for the assistance that you and others have given during the past years and hopes that you will continue. But it is believed that the proposed title Editorial Consultant will reflect more accurately the type of service you have been rendering." Williamson accepted and continued to offer his support "in every possible way."

In 1960, when Professor Robert Patton became Editor of the *Journal of Higher Education*, he wrote to the Editorial Consultants, asking for their continued help. In his answer, Williamson stated he would be happy to be of "the slightest help to you in your editorship of the *Journal of Higher Education*." Williamson then described the work he had done during the early days of the *Journal*.

> As you may know, my contribution for many years has been very slight indeed. The presence of my name among the associate editors, and recently, among the editorial consultants, goes all the way back to the founding of the *Journal* when I had the privilege of working with Professor Charters on some of the problems of launching a new publication.

HONORARY DEGREE FROM COLUMBIA UNIVERSITY

On June 4, 1929, President Butler wrote Williamson informing him that the 175th anniversary of the issuance of the original charter of King's College was to be celebrated with

Related Professional Activities

"becoming ceremonial." Butler announced, "At a public convocation of the University to be held on the afternoon of October 31st, it is proposed to confer the degree of Doctor *honoris causa* upon certain selected members of the faculties who have during the past quarter century contributed by their academic devotion, their scholarship and their research to the fame and influence of the University."

Butler then informed Williamson: "It is with the greatest possible pleasure that I advise you that the Trustees have placed your name upon the list of those who are to be so honored. We trust, therefore, that you will arrange to be present at the convocation on October 31 when the degree will be publicly conferred." Williamson expressed his "very great pleasure and surprise." He felt that his "personal contribution to the fame and influence of the University does not justify so great an honor, but I am glad to accept it as recognition of the place that the library should occupy in a great university."

Williamson "received the degree of Doctor of Letters, *honoris causa*, at the Special Convocation on October 31st, 1929." The citation read:

> Charles Clarence Williamson, Litt.D., Professor of Library Administration and Director of University Libraries and of the School of Library Service.
>
> Books, he knows
> Are a substantial world, both pure and good.
> Round these, with tendrils strong as flesh and blood,
> Our pastimes and our happiness will grow.

Other recipients of honorary degrees at this Convocation were Franz Boas, John Dewey, Edward Charles Eliot of Purdue, Dorothy Canfield Fisher, Robert Morison McIver, and Paul Monroe.

Professional Activities in Retrospect

It was Keyes Metcalf who claimed that Williamson was not a "one-achievement man." He was interested in a great number of things, as seen in the service he gave to many who came to him for advice and help. Although the Williamson report will always remain his major contribution, he certainly did not feel it was his only contribution to librarianship. The professional, bibliographical, and many other activities which filled his life are a testimony to this energetic and dedicated man.

NOTES

1. Ernest J. Reece, "C. C. Williamson: A Record of Service to American Librarianship," *College and Research Libraries* 4 (September 1943), 307-308.
2. Louis Round Wilson and Maurice F. Tauber, *The University Library*, 2nd ed., p. 546.
3. Charles C. Williamson, (biographical sketch). "Charles C. Williamson, 1877-1965." *Public Affairs Information Bulletin* (1965), p. iv.
4. Harold M. Turner, "The CECLs First Fifty Years," *College and Research Libraries* 26 (July 1965), 289-290.
5. *Ibid.*, p. 291.
6. *Loc. cit.*
7. *Ibid.*, p. 292.
8. Wilhelm Munthe, *American Librarianship from a European Angle*, p. 152.
9. *Loc. cit.*
10. Tse-chien Tai, *Professional Education for Librarianship*, pp. 60-61.
11. *Ibid.*, p. 61.
12. George B. Utley, "The American Library Institute: A Historical Sketch," *Library Quarterly* 16 (April 1946), 158.
13. Louis Round Wilson and Maurice F. Tauber, *op. cit.*, p. 546.

14

PERSONALITY AND INTERESTS

ALTHOUGH THIS BIOGRAPHY has emphasized Williamson the librarian and library educator, it is necessary to remember there was also Williamson the man. His personality and interests were a vital part of his work and contributions; it is necessary to blend them into a picture of the complete individual. Of course, this kind of discussion can be little more than a compilation of the personal and sometimes subjective impressions of friends and colleagues. Still, it can aid to round out the picture.

Williamson's personality was molded by his environment, training, education, parents, friends, experiences, and the many other elements which are part of the activities and work of any individual's life. The present study already has revealed some of these influences.

His brother Alfred remarked in a statement to the author on September 30, 1966, that Charles' philosophy of life could have been "Be calm, think deeply, unhurriedly, and . . . Be *sure* you are right; then go ahead."

WILLIAMSON'S PHYSICAL APPEARANCE

Williamson was an energetic, active, alert, rather wiry man. He was strong, able to do heavy work, and skillful in the use of his hands. He enjoyed the outdoors and took delight in hiking and working in his garden. He seldom was sick; except for typhoid fever while at Bryn Mawr College and the severe illness in 1934 while at Columbia University, he was in good physical condition throughout most of his long life.

Genevieve Williamson described her husband in a letter

to the author on November 22, 1967, as a "tall, lean man, weighing about 160 pounds. In the latter part of his life he was a strong and vigorous man with gray-white hair, bright blue eyes, a clear rosy complexion. His smile was bright and kindly."

WILLIAMSON'S FAMILY LIFE

Charles Williamson met his first wife, Bertha L. Torrey, at Western Reserve University. She had been a student and graduate of the College for Women and was Registrar there when he met her in 1904. They were married on June 22, 1907, and had one daughter, Cornelia, who was born on August 15, 1913, in Dobbs Ferry, New York. She married Edward Stiles Watson. Williamson had two grandchildren, Charles S. Watson and Margaret Torrey Watson, and at the time of his death, one great-grandchild, Derrick S. Watson, son of Charles. Bertha Williamson died on September 16, 1939, after a long illness. On August 28, 1940, he married Genevieve Austen Hodge. They had no children.

Genevieve Williamson, his widow, recalled that he enjoyed family life and that his family relations were good. "There were no special family traditions or events, except we nearly always had Thanksgiving dinner and spent Christmas Day with the Watsons and they came to us on the Sunday nearest his birthday, and sometimes at Easter. We took things as they developed. We often spent three days in August with them at their camp."

In answer to the question, What was the general tenor and temper of your life together? she replied, "Good, congenial, and warm. I was immensely proud of him and devoted to him."

WILLIAMSON'S PERSONALITY

Miles Price, in a letter in August 1966 to the author, summed up Williamson's personality and his relations to others, stating that he seemed "to inspire . . . the same feeling that cats inspire in people: you either liked him very much indeed, or you didn't."

Other friends and acquaintances provided the author with comments and impressions to assist in an attempt to record Williamson's personality and general interests. The statements should not be considered separately but as a composite picture of his character drawn by those who knew and worked with him. In addition, statements in the literature also provided data. The author had written to many librarians, library educators, friends, historians, acquaintances, and co-workers with requests for information on their relationships with Williamson. Most were cooperative and provided informative and relevant data.

In describing Williamson, Lucy M. Crissey maintained:

> Probably the most immediately noticeable of his characteristics was his physical vigor. There is nothing unusual in the fact that he played golf, took long hikes with a group of his friends, and was an enthusiastic gardener. What is unusual is that he combined all these activities with working days of fifteen to eighteen hours, and held the conviction that this could normally be expected of anyone genuinely interested in his job. His long stride set a pace that few could keep up with, and he habitually took the stairs two at a time, between his two offices in Butler Library.[1]

She also commented on Williamson's well-disciplined mind and his qualities on the job.

> A more impressive quality however, was the alertness of his well-disciplined mind. He was able to break off an involved piece of work to listen to a problem, give it undivided attention, state his opinion, and return to his original concern as if there had been no interruption. His clarity of thought was such that he could dictate long letters and memoranda with the logical organization and precision associated with many drafts and revisions. The manifold problems of administration obviously stimulated him. . . . Another aspect of his well-ordered mind was his phenomenal memory.[2]

She felt that his most important qualification at Columbia was his "capacity for thorough and logical organization. He was at home in the realm of ideas, had imagination in long-range planning, and possessed a strong practical bent that involved him in the application of his theories down to the smallest detail. He laid strong foundations."[3] She commented in a letter to the author on July 25, 1966:

> Personally he was a man of dignity and reticence, which made for good working relationships. . . . The only thing I can comment on further concerns one of his tremendous assets that also had elements of a drawback. His very active mind and his ability to plan years ahead and in considerable detail meant that he was ready to implement his ideas before those around him had even begun to grasp the first stages of what he had in mind. He had the greatest difficulty in being patient while they caught up.

The attitude of faculty and staff members who worked with him was warm and appreciative, dispelling the myth he was a cold and aloof person. Time and time again the correspondence revealed this warmth. Although only a few of these comments are included in this study, these letters and words of friendship are typical of the attitudes and feelings of many men and women who knew or worked with Charles C. Williamson.

Alice I. Hazeltine wrote him on June 9, 1948:

> As times goes on, I think I appreciate more and more your great contribution to librarianship. Your penetrating analysis of conditions as it appeared in your famous Report—your achievement in bringing together two schools and in creating a third school with its broad outlook and constantly developing ideals and methods—your honest appreciation of the relation of education for librarianship to library service of many types in the so-called "field"—these are some of the reasons why those of us who had the privilege of membership in your faculty value that privilege more highly than can be easily expressed.

John Bassett Moore commented on March 3, 1943, regarding Williamson's retirement: "It is needless to say that my heartfelt best wishes will attend you. . . . I always bear in mind my old colleagues and cherish the recollections of our association."

Alice I. Bryan echoed this thought in a letter to him on December 11, 1945: "Again, may I thank you for help and encouragement. The Faculty misses you terribly and more than one has said that he wishes that his term of service could have come entirely within your administration. These are my sentiments."

Professor Ernest J. Reece knew Williamson for sixty-five years and had the opportunity to observe his personal characteristics and habits. He contended in his letter to the author on August 25, 1966, that Williamson had

> an acute, analytical mind, which it gratified him to use; deliberate judgment; decision, determination and firmness; indefatigable in work, contented only when accomplishing something; interests wide-ranging; friendliness, consideration and attachment in dealing with people.

Reece evaluated Williamson's "ingredients of success."

> His farm life gave him a contact with realities which many men miss. The time he devoted in college days as secretary to the president of Western Reserve University afforded him an insight into the management and financing of an educational institution. His graduate study assured for him a thorough academic equipment. Initiative and capacity for planning and execution are strong in him, as becomes evident when they demanded quicker and more complete fulfillment than seemed likely to be attained in a professor's field of activity. And behind all these are a keenness of mind, a clearness of vision, a quiet but dynamic enthusiasm, an ability to wait as well as to act, a persistence in pressing toward a goal, and a readiness to carry loads of work far beyond the powers of most men, which together could not fail to make him a leader and a builder.[4]

Williamson's personal characteristics also were recalled by Alice Jewett in her reply to the author on June 16, 1966.

> He was a steady, diligent, relaxed worker, always in command of himself and of the work he was engaged in. His mind was phenomenally active and imaginative with a scientific grasp of the facts and problems involved in his varied fields of interest. He was reserved but friendly, cooperative but firm in his convictions, persistent in his efforts to accomplish his purposes. A delightful sense of humor seasoned all his work. Fore-armed with a careful marshalling of supporting facts, he was a master hand at persuasion. He had an amazingly practical turn of mind, which was an advantage in putting his theories to practical work. He was painstaking even meticulous, had little patience with carelessness or stupidity but a controlled patience with less than perfect performance on the part of those less well-equipped than himself.

In commenting on his responsibilities, she observed, "The professional positions held by Dr. Williamson during this period demanded broad general knowledge as well as a thorough background in economics, sociology, statistics and librarianship; also organization and administrative ability of the highest order, both of which were marked attributes."

Dr. Robert B. Downs, in his reply of August 23, 1966, contended that Williamson gave an "impression of reticence and lack of warmth to casual acquaintances, a feeling that was dispelled with better acquaintance."

L. Quincy Mumford, former Librarian of Congress, who was a student at Columbia University School of Library Service in 1928-1929, felt Williamson's particular strengths were his "energy, initiative, high degree of intelligence, broad perspectives, warm, and friendly personality." Mumford in his letter to the author of August 23, 1966, recalled "him as a genial person, with good sense of humor, devoted to work but easily accessible."

David Clift's evaluation of Williamson, revealed in an interview with the author on July 14, 1966, that "he was a great man and one of the finest bosses I ever had." Clift felt that working under Williamson was a privilege and that it was impossible to work with him or under him without learning a

Personality and Interests

great many things. "One of the things he taught me was the value of precision." Clift continued: "There were two ways you did a job for C. C. Williamson: the first was an acceptable job, since the other way didn't count. You didn't stay unless you did an acceptable job."

On the subject of Williamson's personality, Clift agreed he was somewhat aloof in his working relations, since there was very little, if any, idle talk. Williamson was a retiring man. Many thought that he found it difficult to unbend and be immediately and openly pleasant about everything and to everyone. In commenting on Williamson's work with the staff and faculty, Clift maintained that Williamson was not unapproachable but dealt precisely and sternly with people who worked in the library. Many of his staff and faculty sought every opportunity to talk to him, while others found a conference with Williamson "not an easy thing." If the person was unsure what he was talking about, he was sent back to find out. This procedure must have been extremely trying, especially for people who were not particularly competent. Clift always liked Williamson's phrase, "Small craft needs to stay close to shore." Williamson expected the craft to go out into deep waters.

Williamson's letters revealed other aspects of his personality. He was very annoyed at inefficiency. One example was in 1955, when he wrote to the Office of the Superintendent of Documents in Washington, D.C., to obtain an annual report from some governmental agency. The wrong report came in the mail. On April 28, 1955, he wrote to Washington, "Isn't there somebody on your large staff who can read?" He received the correct annual report.

He always was frank, a trait which can be trying for other people and often is interpreted as a lack of tact. His sense of humor was often biting but always direct and to the point. When he disliked something, he was certain to express his displeasure in no uncertain terms. This tactic often obtained the desired result.

Williamson frequently directed his sense of humor at himself. Isabella K. Rhodes found it difficult to locate his address in order to ask him for a contribution for the memory of Miriam Tompkins. She checked in the 1955 edition of

Who's Who in Library Service and wrote on June 9, 1955, "I've been looking up addresses in the new W W in L S and was surprised and shocked not to find you in it!" Williamson sent a donation and indicated he was not in the new edition because he had not been in library service for the past twelve years and, feeling he did not belong in *Who's Who*, consequently never returned the forms sent to him. "Everything that needs to be known about me can easily be found elsewhere. No use to add to the cost of the volume by including obsolete material."

Generosity was another trait which he possessed, even if he held it in check with his concern for thrift. If the cause was good, if the need genuine, he was most generous. He offered assistance to relatives and friends, in the form of both financial help and moral support.

Genevieve Williamson stated in her comments of October 25, 1967, that her husband was "not a demonstrative man and did not show his feelings easily." She also affirmed the view of others in her statement of his personal characteristics:

> Great dignity, wise, patient, kind, gentle, strong, forward-looking, curious, thorough, sense of humor, direct, simple, common sense, very reserved, good listener, interested in everything, meticulous in everything, had integrity, loyalty, honesty, humility, very independent, didn't like to be helped, self-reliant to a marked degree. Never swore except to say one "Damn" at a time. If angry or upset he withdrew within himself. Vigorous, great concentration. There was only one way to do things and that was the right way. Hated to be criticized, sensitive. Felt he was right and he usually was. Never flattered, didn't like frills. Rather egotistical but in an unobtrusive way. Had good judgment.

Mrs. Williamson also revealed he "didn't care for 'society' as such." However, in his social relations he was "friendly, interested, kindly, sense of humor, didn't like any kind of 'night life!' When at Columbia we attended a good many social events and dinners. Sometimes the theatre. After retirement quiet evenings at home or dinner with friends. Seldom watched TV unless it was educational."

She also observed:

> Intellectual and cultural interests during his professional life and retirement: Reading and studying on many subjects. The theatre sometimes. Seldom to the movies. He used to go to the opera during his first marriage, chiefly because his wife liked it, but we didn't go while we were married. He enjoyed art but it was not vital to him. Also enjoyed music.

Regarding Williamson's work habits, Mrs. Williamson commented on the days during his last three years at Columbia and during his retirement:

> He was a very early riser, 5:40 daily. Worked in his study. Read the morning paper and went to work. During his retirement: up at 5:40 as usual. Worked in his study and read the morning paper. He had many interests—interested in almost everything. On various committees, both civic and educational and in connection with the Greenwich Garden Center. He was handy around the house. His time was full. He generally took an hour's nap after lunch.

Williamson was a Quaker in his early life, then a Methodist. In *Who's Who in America* he listed himself as an Episcopalian. Mrs. Williamson observed, "He viewed various religious precepts, compared and evaluated them. Very much interested in philosophy and sociology." In later years he was a humanist.

Mrs. Williamson recalled that during moments of stress he "would generally withdraw within himself and work most things out by himself. He was reserved, a man of few words, especially on personal matters. Somewhat shy too. He had tremendous endurance and courage."

WILLIAMSON'S TRAVELS

Williamson made several trips to Europe, although he was not a frequent traveler. His travels were confined primarily to England and France, where he visited the Bodleian

Library, the British Museum, London Library, the Bibliothèque Nationale, centering his visits in Oxford, London, and Paris. Some of these trips were related to professional activities; others were recreational.

Mrs. Williamson also commented that he "liked to drive. Liked to explore the countryside. For example: we have explored the state of Connecticut visiting every town [169] in the state, many in Massachusetts too."

WILLIAMSON'S GENERAL INTERESTS

Williamson's general interests were as wide and varied as his professional activities. He showed concern for efficiency, honesty, and frankness in municipal and social welfare, community activities, and general improvement of the human condition.

The range of these interests is evident from an examination of the boxes of newspapers and periodical clippings which are in the file of the Williamson Papers at Columbia University. Approximately forty-five of the fifty boxes contain clippings from journals, pamphlets, and newspapers, and are all carefully classified under various subject headings, including attitude of librarians, bookishness, book learning, bibliomanic, leadership, agitation, reform, libraries and evolution, philosophy of life, changing human nature, citizenship, genius, publishers, human nature, teaching, writing, public speaking, book illustration, on being bored, heretics, influence of great books, bibliography, how to read, solitude, specialization, and standardization. There are many more.

Mrs. Williamson listed his general interests as:

> Reading, gardening, carpentering, watch or clock repairs, general household handyman, original ideas for conveniences which he could implement. Electrical and plumbing (limited) jobs. Ingenious. Interested in the do-ers of the community and the world (vs. passive people). . . . I want to stress his great love for knowledge. He also was extremely fond of gardening, about which he knew a great deal.

Personality and Interests

His interests involved him in activities which he felt would be useful to others. In 1916-1917 Williamson was a member of the Board of Administration of the Marquand School for Boys. This school, located at 55 Hanson Place, Brooklyn, New York, was part of the educational work of the Central Branch of the Young Men's Christian Association.

His activities in social clubs were limited but did include membership in the City Club of New York, to which he was appointed a member of the Suburban Class on October 21, 1916. In 1928 he was recommended to be a member of the Century Club by Mr. Edwin H. Anderson of the New York Public Library and Mr. Clyde Furst of the Carnegie Foundation for the Advancement of Teaching. Williamson remained a member of the Century until May 24, 1944.

Williamson's interest in books and publishing led to his membership in a group called the Book Table. This was an informal group of authors, publishers, and librarians who met regularly on the second Wednesday of each month for lunch. Members of the group included Frederic G. Melcher of the R. R. Bowker Company, Alfred A. Knopf, Elmer Adler, Franklin E. Hopper, Elmer Davis, Carl Van Vechten, Harry M. Lydenberg, Milton J. Ferguson, Carl Van Doren, Whitney Darrow, John T. Winterich, Robert de Graff, and others. The Book Table would invite guests to speak informally to the group about their areas of interest, followed by discussion.

Williamson's interest in books extended to his work on the Typographic Library which was established at Columbia in 1936. This collection of some 16,700 items included 6,500 books, 3,500 volumes of periodicals, 5,000 pamphlets, 200 scrapbooks, 500 portfolios and boxes, and at least 1,000 miscellaneous items. Williamson was very much in favor of developing this collection and obtaining additional items and materials which would be useful in making "Columbia University the center of information and research in this important field."

Williamson's political affiliations varied. In his early years he considered himself a Democrat and so indicated in the data he sent to his listing in *Who's Who in America*. On

February 17, 1937, in a letter to the Honorable Robert F. Wagner, United States Senator, he stated, "I consider myself a Democrat." In later life, he "was a Republican," according to his widow.

He always was interested in politics and government. His correspondence contained many letters to various political leaders, voicing opinions and ideas about current legislation. After retirement he wrote frequently to Washington and to representatives in Connecticut concerning his feelings on various issues of the day. He opposed Senator Joseph McCarthy and wrote many letters to members of the Senate Permanent Investigations Subcommittee commenting on the hearings, which he avidly watched on television.

During his retirement he was most active in various educational groups, which included the Greenwich Association for the Public Schools, Connecticut State Educational Television Commission, and the American Council for Better Broadcasts (he served as its President in 1956-1957).

His work with the Greenwich Association for the Public Schools was concerned mainly with alerting the members to the dangers inherent in the anti-intellectual philosophy which he felt was growing strong in the public schools and educational circles. Williamson believed in "intellectual training . . . in the public schools," which he felt had changed and contained "only a faint trace of liberal arts." He considered that the present life-adjustment type of curriculum was especially dangerous and anti-intellectual.

He disliked the Connecticut teachers colleges, which he felt were "mere trade and vocational schools on about the same intellectual level as the state supported schools for training bakers, barbers, plumbers, and printers."

Williamson was extremely interested in the potential of educational television, which he felt should be used but only if and when the concept behind its use was correct and thoughtful. He was pleased to find that some thoughtful promoters of educational television also were concerned with the correct concept of education in television programs and were not confusing it with a hodgepodge of miscellaneous information. He did not want to condemn all "education by air," but wanted to "be more certain that its development will be guided by those who have some concern for intellectual training."

The tribute to Williamson from the Greenwich Garden Center on January 15, 1965, stated: "It was he who kept us up to date, looking and moving forward. He was filled with common sense and . . . humor. His work was everyday; he wore many hats—treasurer, librarian, carpenter, handyman, and mail fetcher."

Concerning other activities and interests, Mrs. Williamson described her husband as a

> great hiker and enjoyed it immensely. Every Fall he and several other good library friends would meet and go together to the Catskills to go mountain climbing. This was part of his life for many years and ended only when some of his friends died and those who were left were not able to exercise so strenuously. He would get himself in good physical condition by walking from Grand Central Terminal down to lower Broadway to his office. Also would walk up to the 27th floor! He played golf sometimes, and occasionally would watch baseball games.

In addition to Williamson, the good library friends, or the Mountaineers, as they called themselves, included Paul North Rice, Harry Miller Lydenberg, Charles S. McCoombs, Keyes D. Metcalf, and Frank Waite. The Mountaineers drove up to the Catskills every fall to hike. They spent their time at Woodlands, which was not really a town, but only a few rustic homes up beyond Kingston, near Phoenicia. They often climbed Mt. Wittenberg (3,802 feet) and also Mt. Slide (4,204). They stayed at a house run by Evelyn Craig and her sister, Mrs. Patrick Murphy. The group met to enjoy the countryside, to relax, to meet socially, and also to permit the men to discuss library business. "They had wonderful times and their reunions meant a lot to all of them. They were a delight to CCW."

Williamson had many and varied personal interests. From his concern with the improvement of public school education to gardening, from better broadcasting and educational television to humanism, from the problems of library education to carpentry, from his keen grasp of library affairs to the repair of clocks, from his administration of the University Library at Columbia to his Garden Center—in all of these aspects of his life he took a genuine interest.

NOTES

1. Lucy M. Crissey, "Charles C. Williamson, 1877-1965," *Library Service News* 26 (March 1965), 1.
2. *Loc. cit.*
3. *Loc. cit.*
4. Ernest J. Reece, "C. C. Williamson: A Record of Service to American Librarianship," *College and Research Libraries* 4 (September 1943), 308.

15
RETIREMENT AND DEATH (1943-1965)

UNTIL THE END OF HIS LIFE Williamson was active, alert, vital, and keenly interested in people and life.

Lucy Crissey observed, "During the twenty-one years since his retirement from the University he has led an active life, associating himself with educational and political groups, as well as with interests of local garden clubs."[1] His innate interest in all subjects was particularly apparent during his retirement, when he could pursue reading, hobbies, and various activities. The voluminous correspondence, reports, inquiries, and clippings in the Williamson Papers at Columbia represent his interests during the years from 1943 through 1965, when he read, studied, and collected vast amounts of material.

ACTIVITIES DURING RETIREMENT

Williamson's professional library career ended with his retirement from Columbia University. Interests in other fields of endeavor occupied his active retirement years. He approached these new interests with the same energy and zeal he showed during his professional career. In retirement he became less and less involved in matters pertaining to library work and gradually lost interest in library events and trends.

On September 12, 1945, Joseph T. Wheeler wrote to Williamson for some ideas in the field of library education which would or should be "done in the next ten years to put us a lot further ahead." Williamson replied that he had been out of library work for two years and really did not feel capable of answering the question. His interest in library work had ended, he stated. "After all my information and ideas are hopelessly out of date. I have not kept up with what has been going on or being written for two or three years."

In the years immediately following retirement he often was asked to speak on library matters, especially library education. He refused, since he felt his work in this field was finished and he was no longer aware of changes and developments.

Robert D. Leigh sent Williamson a copy of his *Major Problems in the Education of Librarians* in 1954. He wrote back on May 18, that in reading the introduction he had "the curious feeling of being looked upon as a kind of museum-piece dating from an earlier period of history and now being pointed out to the present generation as a time-worn milestone past which the world has marched into a new and better existence." He felt this picture corresponded "pretty closely to my actual feelings today about any part I ever had in library service and in education for librarianship."

He gave another indication of his attitude toward past accomplishments in a letter of February 28, 1949, to Alma C. Mitchill, Editor of *Special Libraries*. She had requested information about Williamson's most outstanding accomplishments during his presidency of the Special Libraries Association.

> I seem to be constitutionally unable to reconstruct from memory a realistic picture of any part of my past experience, especially of a past so remote as my presidency of the S.L.A. I can't even recall the dates! I am sure we had some "burning" questions and equally sure that we thought at the time we had accomplished something worthwhile. I doubt, however, that to the present generation of S.L.A.'ers our triumphs would seem to have any importance at all.

He commented further on his contributions.

> Some day I suppose a history of S.L.A. will be written. If, and when, it is, I shall be surprised (and gratified—assuming I am still alive) if my administration is even mentioned outside of the chronological list. Perhaps you will say I should make sure

of a place in history by taking advantage of this opportunity to put the future historian on the right track. But, alas! it can't be done.

Honors During Retirement

Further recognition of Williamson's work for the Special Libraries Association came in 1952, when honorary memberships were awarded to him and nine other people who "gave so loyally of their time and services in the early, formative years, so that those who came after them could reap the benefits of their untiring efforts."

Williamson always was a practical man. He revealed this quality, as well as his generosity, in the gift in 1947 of his personal set of the *Library of Congress Catalog* to the Union Catalog of the Westchester Library Association. He felt they needed the material. Isabel D. Clark, President of the association, thanked him for his "generous gift of the Library of Congress catalog," which was "appreciated very deeply."

The Alumni Association of the Columbia University School of Library Service selected Deane Keller, of the Yale University School of Fine Arts, to paint Williamson's portrait for the Library School. By December 1948, the portrait was finished and the formal dedication took place at a reception for Dr. and Mrs. Williamson held at 4 P.M. at Columbia in the Social Room. He wrote Dr. and Mrs. Carl M. White his thanks for the perfectly grand party and the chance to see so many old friends among the alumni and university people.

In 1954 Williamson worked as Consultant to the Connecticut State Educational Television Commission. In the report the commission expressed its thanks to Dr. Williamson.

> Shortly after the formation of the Commission, it was suggested to the Chairman that the work which was about to be undertaken might be expedited through contact with Dr. Charles C. Williamson of Greenwich. Dr. Williamson, former Director of Libraries at Columbia University, had been

retired for some time, and had become interested in recent years in the subject of educational television, and had acquired a large amount of material on the subject.

Dr. Williamson volunteered his services, without pay, and in due course was appointed Consultant to the Commission. His tireless energy in pursuit of the facts surrounding the whole subject of educational television has been of inestimable value, has saved the Commission members many weeks of work, and has enabled them to discharge their duties at a total cost of approximately one fourth of the appropriation provided under the act—a feat that under other circumstances would have been impossible.

Other groups which interested Williamson at this time were the Continuing Education Center and the Center for the Study of Liberal Education for Adults of Chicago. He also was interested in teacher training and efforts to introduce instruction in the American economic system into the secondary schools.

He found much to interest him locally in Connecticut, including his publication of *Who's Who in Connecticut*. In 1960 he was a judge of "Freedom Essays" prepared by students in the Greenwich Schools. Other associations which he joined included the Connecticut Audio-Visual Education Association, the National Association of Educational Broadcasters, the Association for Education by Radio-Television, and the Connecticut Citizens Committee for Educational Television, of which he was Chairman. He also was a member of the local Lions Club Foundation.

Mrs. Williamson stated he was

> On various committees, both civic and educational in connection with the Greenwich Garden Center. . . . His time was full. . . . Vitally interested in Educational TV. We took many trips thru the middle west as far as Wisconsin and New England, going to many colleges to interest them in educational TV. He was Consultant to Connecticut State Educational Television Commission. He was also president American Council for Better Broadcasts 1956-57.

Williamson found all this work exciting and challenging. He spoke of his interest in educational TV in a letter to A. J. Stoddard, of the Foundation for the Advancement of Education:

> Perhaps I should explain further that my interest is entirely nonprofessional—what you might call a hobby. I am a retired functionary of Columbia University. A glance at my entry in "Who's Who in America" will show that during a long life I have been engaged in a good many different things and I can truthfully say that in none of them have I found such a challenging complex of the known and the unknown.

His activities with the Greenwich Garden Center included his work in their library, where he helped catalog the books, build bookcases, and organize the work of the center.

He wrote to Ernest J. Reece on July 23, 1959, about his interests during retirement.

> I welcomed this Garden Center library responsibility, not beause it gave me something to do (already having enough), but because I can now turn over to the Center nearly all of my horticulture books, pamphlets, and clipping files, and that makes way on the shelves for books in new fields of interest.

Williamson's activities at the Greenwich Garden Center were best described in the article which appeared in *The Greenwich Social Review*. The article goes into detail of Williamson's education and training and is entitled "Distinguished Educator Serves Garden Center." He served as Treasurer and Librarian at the center. The library itself was not a research library, but "here we try to be of practical help in people's horticultural problems."

Williamson also revealed the range of his activities in retirement in a letter to Reece, written on July 19, 1957.

> I manage to keep busy with the activities of a number of organizations, national, state, and local, all of which interferes with a lot of reading I want to get ahead with. It would

be a godsend to have at hand a great library as yours at Urbana. Beyond the resources of our nice little public library I depend mainly on Yale, and the New York State Library, thanks to Gosnell and Mason Tolman. But I have to spend a good deal for books and periodicals that I have little room to house.

BETA PHI MU AWARD

On June 21, 1956, Williamson was elected a member of Beta Phi Mu National Library Science Honor Fraternity. In 1964 the American Library Association gave him the Beta Phi Mu Award for "distinguished service to education for librarianship." Williamson was unable to be present when the award was granted at the Annual Convention of the American Library Association at St. Louis, Missouri. When the award was announced he received a letter on June 16, 1964, from Ethel M. Fair, Interim Executive Secretary of the Library Education Division of the American Library Association.

> All who have been concerned abut the education of librarians are deeply indebted to you for your guidance in charting guide lines for education from the 1920's on. I may say that there is scarcely a week passes in this office when there is not some reference, direct or indirect, to your pronouncements of the 1920's and later.

His personal reaction to the Beta Phi Mu Award also reveals his personality. He wrote to the author on October 17, 1964: "Thank you for your reference to the Beta Phi Mu Award. I welcomed it, of course, but coming at this time in the autumn of my life, it did seem somewhat like the leaves that are falling at my doorstep."

PLANNING THE BIOGRAPHY

Dr. Charles C. Williamson discussed with the author plans for the writing of the biography and gave his approval on

Retirement and Death

November 2, 1964. Another meeting was arranged on November 22 to examine the "stuff" he had located and wanted the author to see. At that time he was alert, able to recall past events and discuss aspects of his life and work.

WILLIAMSON'S DEATH

On the Monday before his death he insisted on going to the Greenwich Garden Center but was persuaded to visit his doctor. He was immediately put in the Greenwich Hospital where he died of cancer at 8:55 P.M. on January 11, 1965. Services were held in Hartford, Connecticut, and burial was in the Village Cemetery at Wethersfield, Connecticut.

His death brought to a close "the career of a man of high standards, goals, and achievements"[2] as reflected in his many and varied interests. Certainly one of his great qualities was his innate interest in almost everything. With his passing, an era in the history of librarianship and library education came to an end.

NOTES

1. Lucy M. Crissey, "Charles C. Williamson, 1877-1965," *Library Service News* 26 (March 1965), 1.
2. Frank Bradway Rogers, *Librarianship in a World of Machines*, p. 1.

16
LIFE AND CONTRIBUTIONS IN RETROSPECT

A CAREER OF MANY FACETS

IN 1905 PRESIDENT THWING wrote to the young Williamson of his hopes for his future—"we expect great things, my friend." Williamson's long career is a testimony that "great things" were realized. The range and variety of his activities were evident in his work as a teacher, principal, secretary, economist, political scientist, college professor, librarian, library educator, administrator, director of libraries, dean, bibliographer, researcher, editor, compiler, foundation executive, consultant, and advisor—all part of his fruitful career.

This biography has tried to show that his life and work reflected his contributions to library education and librarianship in the change that he effected in the concept of library training. As the "librarian's librarian" he can be considered the father of modern professional library education. Although he was not professionally trained himself, Williamson developed the professional aspect of librarianship.

Training for Library Service will always be his major and most influential work. However, his contributions in other activities and interests also were significant. The sum total of his life and work touched a wide range of interests and a great variety of areas of study and investigation.

WILLIAMSON'S CONTRIBUTIONS TO LIBRARIANSHIP

Williamson came on the scene in the history of American librarianship at a time which destined him to play a major role in the historical development of the library profession.

Williamson's contribution must be considered in its historical context. The present work has discussed his strengths and weaknesses. They must be viewed, however, not as personal triumphs or failures but as part of the evolving development of the work which was Williamson's contribution to library service. His impact was contributory, not final. What he left undone—and he would be the first to admit that much was not done—others did after him, but what he accomplished lightened the work of those who followed. If Melvil Dewey was the pioneer in library training, Charles Williamson was the synthesizer of library education. He was and still is a force in the development of library education and librarianship. He certainly was a dominant figure in the historical development of librarianship and library education in the first half of the twentieth century in the United States.

Few major activities in library education and librarianship from 1923 to 1943 can be mentioned without including the name of C. C. Williamson. His work has endured because he was able to understand the real problem of librarianship and, with his clear thinking, frankness, and ability to synthesize, to suggest ways and means of resolving those problems. He was able to achieve only part of his goal of professional librarianship but he took a giant step forward. His colleagues in the second half of the twentieth century were able to carry his recommendations another step further along the way toward placing librarianship on a level with other scholarly, intellectual professions.

EVALUATION BY COLLEAGUES

Alice Jewett felt that Williamson's greatest contribution was the fact that, as a result of his work, there was a "gradual improvement in the acceptance of librarianship as a profession." This was "in no small part due to his prestige and influence." She also considered him responsible for alerting "educators, librarians in service, library school administrators and students to the dignity of librarians, the possibilities, the essential qualifications and rewards."[1]

According to Louis Round Wilson, Williamson

> made his principal contribution to librarianship as a leader in professional training. As an individual administrator of a university library, the librarian's primary work is to promote his institution's program of instruction, graduate and professional study, research, publication, and service. Of course he can participate in planning for organizations of librarians, and various library movements and activities. But as the dean of a library school he serves the profession of librarianship rather than a single institution. He trains librarians and teachers in library schools who carry the results of his planning, his teaching, his stimulation to other libraries and schools. If he at the same time is active in library association activities, if he promotes library legislation, if he writes for the profession and promotes publication, his contributions to the profession are correspondingly increased.[2]

Wilson believed that Williamson had a good concept of graduate education and made the best provisions he could to bring effective training into existence. Nevertheless, "like Moses, he had to let later leaders bring the School to its present stage. It has had to conform more to the setting and conditions in which it was placed. He had the proper concept, but not a free hand."[3] Unquestionably, the "conservative, gentlemanly instincts of the man also probably contributed to the outcome."[4]

In summarizing Williamson's contributions, Wilson maintained:

> His *Report* was outstanding. It changed the organization and support of education for librarianship. He established, through merger, a school organized on sound principles, which, in that respect, served as an example for other schools. He publicly supported research as a means of solving problems of librarianship and approved the idea of scientific procedures. He organized a curriculum that made possible, in a limited way, the realization of his concept. He gave dignity to the office of the librarian and dean which he filled, and

Life and Contributions in Retrospect

thereby increased the role of librarianship in American higher education.[5]

SUMMARY

Williamson instilled in his entire life a spirit, breadth, depth of interest, and understanding which was reflected in everything he did. This spirit gave meaning to the man and his work. His career, his activities, professional work, interests, personal life, writing, and relationships with friends and colleagues all revealed a constant and genuine interest in many things born of his curiosity in the myriad aspects of life. He gave to every task—noble and menial alike—the same concentration, vitality, energy, and perfection which were his own.

The prophecy of his teacher had been fulfilled: "I know you will not disappoint me in achieving the greatest of greatness."[6]

NOTES

1. Alice Jewett, statement to the author, June 16, 1966, p. 4.
2. Louis Round Wilson, statement for the author, July 13, 1966, p. 5.
3. *Ibid.*, p. 6.
4. *Loc. cit.*
5. *Ibid.*, p. 7.
6. Letter from C. S. Barnes to Charles C. Williamson, February 4, 1895.

PUBLISHED AND UNPUBLISHED WORKS OF CHARLES C. WILLIAMSON

As Author

Address at assembly of the School of Library Service, Columbia University. October 5, 1938. (Typewritten.) 8 pp.

Address at the opening of the School of Library Service. [1926]. (Typewritten.) 3 pp.

Address by Professor C. C. Williamson, Director of University Libraries and Dean of the School of Library Service, at the laying of the cornerstone of South Hall. October 3, 1932. (Typewritten.) 3 pp.

Address to members of the Music Library Association at Columbia University. June 22, 1937. (Typewritten.) 5 pp.

Address to Special Libraries Association (trip to Columbia University). June 19, 1937. (Typewritten.) 9 pp.

Address to the American Association of Law Libraries. N.d. (Typewritten.) 10 pp.

"Adult Education." N.d. (Typewritten.) 12 pp.

"Andrew Carnegie—His Contribution to the Public Library Movement: A Commemorative Address by Charles Clarence Williamson, Ph.D." Founder's Day Address, Delivered at the Library School, Western Reserve University, Cleveland. June 15, 1920. 14 pp.

"Can the Catalogue of the Bibliothèque Nationale Be Completed in Ten Years?" *American Library Association Bulletin* 22 (1928), 402-408; and *Library Journal* 53 (1928), 593-597.

"Carnegie Celebration Address" (holograph manuscript). November 25, 1935. 7 pp.

"Catalogue of the Bibliothèque Nationale." *Library Journal* 53 (September 1, 1934), 670.

"Charles Alexander Nelson." In *Dictionary of American Biography*, volume 3, 1934, pp. 413-414.

"Columbia University School of Library Service." *Library Journal* 62 (January 1, 1937), 14-16.

"The Comprehensive Examinations as Used in the Columbia University School of Library Service." N.d. (Typewritten.) 10 pp.

"Crawford's Administration of the Treasury." February 5, 1906. (Typewritten.) 50 pp.

"Creative Librarianship." Conference on School Library Service, Columbia University. June 28-July 3, 1939. (Typewritten.) New York: Columbia University School of Library Service. 6 pp.

"Discusses Municipal Reference Library." *American Library Association Bulletin* 10 (January 1916), 49.

"Donation Sent to England." *Library Journal* 66 (March 1, 1941), 186.

"The Education of the Library School Instructor." N.d. (Typewritten.) 10 pp.

"The Education of the Library School Instructor" (summary). *American Library Association Bulletin* 20 (1926), 535.

"Efficiency in Library Management." *Library Journal* 44 (February 1919), 67-77; and *Library Occurent* 5 (1919), 148-154.

"Essentials in the Training of Archivists." June 23, 1937. (Typewritten.) 8 pp.

"Essentials in the Training of University Librarians—III." *College and Research Libraries* 1 (December 1939), 30-32.

"The Establishment of New York City's Municipal Reference Library." A radio talk from WNYC. March 3, 1928, 9:50 to 10:00 P.M. (Typewritten.) 4 pp.

"Filing Methods in Public and Special Libraries." *Filing* 4 (February 1920), 576-577.

Finances of Cleveland. New York: Columbia University Press, 1907.

"For Better Librarians: Columbia Plans Library Service School on a Higher Professional Plane." *New York Times*, November 10, 1935, sec. 10, p. 10.

"General Report of P.A.I.S." January 20, 1920. (Typewritten.) 2 pp.

"An Historical Sketch of the Finances of Cleveland" (summary). (Typewritten.) 10 pp.

"The Importance of Special Libraries to the Public Library." *Special Libraries* 4 (June 1913), 115-116.

"Information for Public Officials." *Modern City* 1 (May 1917), 12-13.

"Japanese Culture Center at Columbia University." New York: Columbia University, 1931.

"The Librarian." N.d. (Typewritten.) 6 pp.
"Libraries." *Encyclopedia Americana* (1938).
"Libraries—Library Schools." *Encyclopaedia Britannica* (14th ed.), vol. 14, pp. 10-11.
"Libraries—The United States." *Encyclopaedia Britannica* (14th ed.), vol. 14, pp. 22-25.
"Libraries and Literature." N.d. (Typewritten.) 28 pp.
"The Library of the National Health Council." A report by C. C. Williamson. March 1925. (Typewritten.) 31 pp.
"Library Service." *Wisconsin Library Bulletin* 16 (June 1920), 90-92 (extracts from "Efficiency in Library Management").
"Library Service in a Machine Age." *Bulletin of the Randolph-Macon Woman's College* 16 (October-December 1929), 8-28 (address at the dedication of the new library).
"A Look Ahead for the Small Library." *Illinois Libraries* 1 (July 1919), 39-44; *Library Occurent* 5 (1919), 201-206; and *American Library Association Proceedings* (1919), 141-146.
"Melvil Dewey: Creative Librarian." In *Fifty Years of Education for Librarianship* (Urbana: University of Illinois Press, 1943), pp. 3-8.
"Memorandum for the Advisory Committee of the Public Affairs Information Service." October 30, 1918. (Typewritten.) 9 pp.
"Memorandum *in re* Plans for New Library Building of the University of Buffalo." August 11, 1933. (Typewritten.) 6 pp.
"Memory Tribute to Edward C. Williams, Negro Librarian." Address delivered at the Negro Library Conference, Nashville, North Carolina. November 1930. (Mimeographed.)
The Minimum Wage: A Preliminary List of Selected References. New York: The Public Library, 1913.
"Municipal Reference Libraries" (abstract). *Library Journal* 53 (1928), 320.
"Music Library Administration." *Library Journal* 63 (April 1, 1938), 275.
"My Contribution to the Special Library Movement: A Symposium." *Special Libraries* 23 (May-June 1932), 213.
"Need of a Plan for Library Development." *Library Journal* 43 (September 1918), 649-655.
"New York's Tax Report." *Survey* 36 (September 30, 1916), 643.
"Notes on the Aims, Scope, and Method of Study of Training for Library Service, for Discussion at the Meeting of the Advisory Committee to be held Wednesday, April 28, 1920." New York: Carnegie Corporation of New York, 1920. Prepared by C. C. Williamson, in charge of Study and

Training for Library Work. Advisory Committee: Wilson Farrand, James H. Kirkland, and Herbert Putnam. (Typewritten.) 16 pp.

"Open Letter: Regarding American Correspondence School of Librarianship." *Gaylord's Triangle* 7 (May 1, 1928), 35.

"Personnel Specifications for Library Work: A Project." *American Library Institute Papers and Proceedings* (1920), pp. 42-49; and *Public Libraries* 26 (1921), 297-301.

"The Place of Research in Library Service." *Library Quarterly* 1 (January 1931), 1-17.

"Plans for the Training of Law Librarians at Columbia University." *Law Library Journal* 30 (July 1937), 261-264.

"Presidential Address of Dr. C. C. Williamson: Louisville, Kentucky, June 25, 1917." *Special Libraries* 8 (September 1917), 100-102.

"Professional Standards." Presidential address delivered at the annual meeting of the New York Library Association, Ithaca, New York. September 12, 1921. (Typewritten.) 14 pp.

"The Progressive Librarian." Address at assembly of the School of Library Service, Columbia University. September 29, 1937. (Typewritten.) 9 pp.

"The Public Official and the Special Library." *Special Libraries* 7 (September 1916), 112-119.

A Reader's Guide to the Addresses and Proceedings of the Annual Conferences on State and Local Taxation. Madison, Wis.: National Tax Association, 1913. Vols. 1-4.

"Remembrance of Things Past." *Special Libraries* 40 (April 1949), 137-138.

"Report of the A.L.A. Committee on National Certification and Training." N.d. (Typewritten.) 23 pp.

"Report on P.A.I.S." May 3, 1921. (Typewritten.) 11 pp.

"Report on Plan for the Rapid Completion of the Catalogue Générale of the Bibliothèque Nationale to the Conference on Eastern College Librarians, December 1, 1928." Revised, January 1, 1929. (Typewritten.) 5 pp.

Reports of the Director of Libraries, 1936-1943. New York: Columbia University in the City of New York, annual.

Reports of the Director of the School of Library Service, 1927-1931; and *Reports of the Dean of the School of Library Service,* 1932-1942. New York: Columbia University in the City of New York, annual. (No report was issued in 1934.)

"Research Methods in Professional Library Training" (extract). *Agricultural Library Notes* 5 (1930), 89.

"Selected References on Markets and Marketing." *Special Libraries* 4 (March 1913), 49-52.
"Selection of Library Students." *Wilson Bulletin* 4 (January 1930), 203-206.
"Shall New York City Untax Buildings? A Review of the Report on Taxation." *Survey* 36 (June 24, 1916), 332-334.
"Some Aspects of the Work of the New York Municipal Reference Library." *Library Journal* 40 (October 1915), 714-715.
"Some Definitions of the Special Library." *Special Libraries* 6 (December 1915), 158.
"Some Newer Ideals of Library Service." Address delivered at the Jones Library, Amherst, Massachusetts. Fall 1928. (Typewritten.) 13 pp.
"Some Present-Day Aspects of Library Training." *Library Journal* 44 (September 1919), 563-568; and *American Library Association Bulletin* 13 (July 1919), 120-126.
"Some Unusual Features of South Hall" (abridged). *American Library Association Bulletin* 31 (October 15, 1937), 798-799.
"State Budget Reform." *Case and Comment* 23 (March 1917), 813-817.
Statement prepared for the Carnegie Corporation of New York, covering the work of the School of Library Service from its establishment in 1926 to date, its plans for the future, and its financial needs. New York: Columbia University, 1936.
"Suggestions for a Theory of Rent." N.d. (Typewritten.) 11 pp.
A Summary of the Market Situation in Boston. Preliminary report of the Market Advisory Committee, June 1915. The City Planning Board, Boston: MA. Printing Department, 1916.
"Summary of the Report on Training for Library Work." Prepared for the Carnegie Corporation of New York by C. C. Williamson, 1921. (Typewritten.) 16 pp.
"Survey of the Yonkers Public Library." By C. C. Williamson and the staff of the School of Library Service, Columbia University. February 2, 1933. (Typewritten.) 24 pp.
Talk to the alumni of the New York State Library School. Untitled and undated. (Typewritten.) 7 pp.
"The Theory of Authority and Its Significance in a Democracy." February 14, 1906. (Typewritten.) 16 pp.
Training for Library Service: A Report for the Carnegie Corporation of New York. New York: Carnegie Corporation of New York, 1923.
"Training for Library Work." Report prepared for the Carnegie Corporation of New York by C. C. Williamson. Advisory

Committee: Herbert Putnam, J. H. Kirkland, and Wilson Farrand. New York: Carnegie Corporation of New York, 1921. (Typewritten.) 276 pp.
"Trend of Professional Training for Library Service in the Last Twenty-five Years." Memorandum for Dean Russell, from C. C. Williamson. New York: Columbia University, School of Library Service, n.d. (Typewritten.)
"Types of Libraries." N.d. (Typewritten.) 16 pp.
"Typographic Library." *Columbia University Quarterly* 33 (December 1941), 299-303.
"Uniform Accounting in Ohio." N.d. (Typewritten.) 19 pp.
"Valuable Notes on the Peace Conference." *Library Journal* 54 (1929), 125.
"Various Organizations of Library Friends." *Library Journal* 58 (April 1, 1933), 315.

AS EDITOR

The Minutes of the Common Council of the City of New York, 1784-1831. 19 vols. New York: Published by the City of New York, 1917. (2-vol. index, 1930.)
Municipal Library Reference Notes. New York: Municipal Reference Library of the City of New York, 1914-1918.
Municipal Year Book of the City of New York. New York: City of New York, 1915, 1916.
"Public Finance, Banking, and Insurance." *American Yearbook, 1912-1916.* New York: D. Appleton, 1916.

COLLABORATIONS, ETC.

Williamson, Charles C., and Jewett, Alice, editors. *Who's Who in Library Service.* New York: H. W. Wilson, 1933.
———. *Who's Who in Library Service.* 2nd ed. New York: H. W. Wilson, 1943.
Williamson, Charles C., and Newman, O. P. "Herbert Putnam, Librarian." *Review of Reviews* 79 (February 1929), 64-66
Williamson, Charles C., et al. "Library Service." *Bulletin of the American Association of University Professors* 17 (1931), 205-213.

Williamson, Charles C. Emily Miller Danton, ed., "The Library of Tomorrow: A Symposium" (book review). *Journal of Higher Education* 11 (March 1940), 169-170.

———. M. Llewellyn Raney. "The University Libraries" (book review). *Journal of Higher Education* 4 (December 1933), 499-500.

———. H. B. Van Hoesen and F. K. Walter. "Bibliography: Practical, Enumerative, Historical. An Introductory Manual" (book review). *American Economic Review* 19 (June 1929), 335-336.

REPRINT

Williamson, Charles C. *The Williamson Reports of 1921 and 1923: Including "Training for Library Work" (1921) and "Training for Library Service" (1923)*. Metuchen, N.J.: Scarecrow Press, 1971.

BIBLIOGRAPHY

"Accredited Library School Histories: Columbia." *Library Journal* 62 (January 1, 1937), 25.
Adelbert College. *The Reserve, 1905*. Yearbook of Adelbert College. Cleveland: Western Reserve University, 1905.
American Library Association. "Proceedings." *Library Annual* 23 (August 1898), 123.
———. *Report of the Temporary Library Training Board*. Chicago: American Library Association, 1924.
———. *A Survey of Libraries in the United States*. 4 vols. Chicago: American Library Associaiton, 1926-1927.
American Library Association. Committee of Five on Library Service. "Report, 1919." *American Library Association Bulletin* 13 (July 1919), 327.
Anderson, Edwin H. "Training for Library Service." *Library Journal* 49 (May 15, 1924), 462-466.
Anderson, Florence. *Library Program, 1911-1961*. New York: Carnegie Corporation of New York, 1963.
Asheim, Lester. "Education for Librarianship." *Library Quarterly* 25 (January 1955), 76-79.
Association of American Library Schools. *New Frontiers in Librarianship*. Chicago: The Graduate Library School, University of Chicago, 1940.
Baldwin, Emma V. "The Education of Librarians." *American Library Institute Papers and Proceedings* (1919), pp. 226-232.
———. "The Training of Professional Librarians." *Library Journal* 44 (September 1919), 574-576.
Berelson, Bernard. *Graduate Education in the United States*. New York: McGraw-Hill, 1960.
———, editor. *Education for Librarianship*. Chicago: American Library Association, 1949.
Beust, Nora A. *Professional Library Education: Introducing the Library*. Washington: Government Printing Office, 1938.
Bevis, Dorothy. "Windows—Not Mirrors." *American Library Association Bulletin* 57 (January 1963), 47-52.

Bidlack, Russell E. "Accreditation of Library Education." In *Encyclopedia of Library and Information Science* (New York: Marcel Dekker, Inc., 1985), vol. 39, supplement 4, pp. 1-34.

Bishop, William Warner. *Carnegie Corporation and College Libraries, 1929-1938.* New York: Carnegie Corporation of New York, 1938.

———. "The Status of Library Schools in Universities." *Journal of the Proceedings and Addresses of the Association of American Universities.* 35th Annual Conference. Princeton University. October 1933.

Blauch, Lloyd E., editor. *Education for the Professions.* Washington: Government Printing Office, 1955.

Bobinski, George S. "Carnegie, Andrew (1835-1919)." In *ALA World Encyclopedia of Library and Information Services.* 2nd ed. (Chicago: American Library Association, 1986), pp. 166-167.

———. *Carnegie Libraries: Their History and Impact on American Public Library Development.* Chicago: American Library Association, 1969.

Bogle, Sarah C. N. "Trends and Tendencies in Education for Librarianship." *Library Journal* 56 (1931), 1029-1036.

Bone, Larry Earl, editor. *Library Education: An International Survey.* Urbana: University of Illinois, Graduate School of Library Science, 1968.

Bostwick, Arthur E. *The American Public Library.* 4th ed. New York: D. Appleton, 1929.

———. "The Meaning of the Library School." *Library Journal* 51 (March 15, 1929), 275-277.

Bramley, Gerald. *A History of Library Education.* Hamden, Conn.: Archon Books, 1969.

———. *World Trends in Library Education.* Hamden, Conn.: Linnet Books, 1975.

Brigham, Harold F., and Sherman, Clarence E. "The Training Class Is Passing; The Training Class Is Not Passing." *American Library Association Bulletin* 27 (January 1931), 23-33.

Brough, Kenneth. *Scholar's Workshop: Evolving Conceptions of Library Service.* Urbana: University of Illinois Press, 1953.

Bryan, Alice I. *The Public Librarian.* New York: Columbia University Press, 1952.

Burns, Allen T., editor. *Americanization Studies.* 10 volumes. New York: Harper and Brothers, 1920.

Butler, Pierce. *An Introduction to Library Science.* Chicago: University of Chicago Press, 1933; reprint, 1961.

Bibliography

Carnegie, Andrew. *Autobiography of Andrew Carnegie*. Boston: Houghton Mifflin, 1920.
Carnegie Corporation of New York. "Proposed Program in Library Service" (office memorandum). New York: Carnegie Corporation of New York. November 10, 1925.
———. "Report of Informal Conference on Library Interests." New York: Carnegie Corporation of New York. December 8, 1930; February 24, 1931; and April 27, 1931.
———. "Report of the Advisory Committee *In Re*: Survey of Dr. C. C. Williamson on Training for Library Work," to the Carnegie Corporation of New York. March 23, 1922. (Typewritten.)
———. "Study of the Methods of Americanization (leaflet)." New York: Carnegie Corporation of New York, 1918.
Carnegie Corporation to Study Trends in Education for Librarianship. *Report of the Committee Convened*. New York: Carnegie Corporation of New York. April 1933.
Carnovsky, Leon. "Changing Patterns in Librarianship: Implications for Library Education." *Wilson Library Bulletin* 41 (January 1967), 484-491.
———. "The Evaluation and Accreditation of Library Schools." *Library Quarterly* 37 (October 1967), 333-347.
———. "Preparation for the Librarian's Profession." *Library Quarterly* 12 (July 1942), 404-411.
———. "Why Graduate Study in Librarianship?" *Library Quarterly* 7 (April 1937), 246-261.
Carroll, C. Edward. *The Professionalization of Education for Librarianship: With Special Reference to the Years 1940-1960*. Metuchen, N.J.: Scarecrow Press, 1970.
Cassata, Mary B., and Totten, Herman L., editors. *The Administrative Aspects of Education for Librarianship: A Symposium*. Metuchen, N.J.: Scarecrow Press, 1975.
Charters, W. W. "Job Analysis in Education for Librarianship." *Libraries* 32 (January 1927), 7-10.
Child, James B. "Hasse, Adelaide Rosalia." In *Encyclopedia of Library and Information Science* (New York: Marcel Dekker, 1973), vol. 10; pp. 373-377.
Churchwell, Charles D. "Charles C. Williamson (1877-1965)." In *ALA World Encyclopedia of Library and Information Services*. 2nd ed. (Chicago: American Library Association, 1986), pp. 850-852.
———. *The Shaping of American Library Education*. Chicago: American Library Association, 1975.

"Columbia Library Named: Building Given by Harkness Will Be Called South Hall." *New York Times,* January 9, 1932, p. 19.

"Columbia Opens Its New Library: Buchan Outlines Role for Colleges—Ceremony Held in 1,000-Seat Reading Room of Structure Donated by Harkness—Briton Praises Fostering of Modesty in Politics and Learning." *New York Times,* December 1, 1934, p. 15.

"Columbia Plans Library Opening: Will Dedicate $4,000,000 South Hall, Harkness Gift on Nov. 30—Briton to Speak." *New York Times,* October 7, 1934, sec. 2, p. 1.

"Columbia to Mark Library's Opening: John Buchan, English Author, to Speak at Formal Exercises Friday Afternoon." *New York Times,* November 25, 1934, sec. 2, p. 3.

Columbia University. Charles C. Williamson Papers. Rare Book and Manuscript Library, Columbia University in the City of New York. (Extensive file of letters, notes, typewritten and holograph manuscripts, reports, newspaper clippings, scrapbooks, etc.)

———. *Honorary Degrees Awarded in the Years 1902-1945.* New York: Columbia University Press, 1946.

———. "Program of the One Hundred and Fifty-Third Annual Commencement." June 12, 1907.

———. School of Library Service. *School of Library Economy of Columbia College, 1887-1889: Documents for a History.* New York: School of Library Service, Columbia University, 1937.

———. The University Libraries. *Reports of the Librarian, 1921-1935.* New York: Columbia University, annual. (Dr. Williamson did not write the annual report until 1936.)

Connecticut State Commission on Educational Television. "Report of the Connecticut State Commission on Educational Television to the Honorable John Davis Lodge, Governor of Connecticut." May 1954.

Coon, Horace. *Columbia: Colossus on the Hudson.* New York: E. P. Dutton, 1947.

Crissey, Lucy M. "Charles C. Williamson, 1877-1965." *Library Service News* 26 (March 1965), 1.

Cutter, W. P. "A Graduate School for Librarians." *Special Libraries* 15 (1924), 81-82.

Dain, Phyllis. *History of the New York Public Library: A History of its Founding and Early Years.* New York: The New York Public Library, Astor, Lenox, and Tilden Foundations, 1972.

———. "Notes of a Taped Interview with Charles C. Williamson." October 28, 1964.

Bibliography

Danton, J. Periam. *Education for Librarianship: Criticisms, Dilemmas, and Proposals*. New York: School of Library Service, Columbia University, 1946.

Davis, Donald G., Jr. "AALS: The Lost Years, 1925-1928." *Journal of Education for Librarianship* 17 (Fall 1976), 98-105.

―――. *The Association of American Library Schools, 1915-1968: An Analytical History*. Metuchen, N.J.: Scarecrow Press, 1974.

―――. "Education for Librarianship." *Library Trends* 25 (July 1976), 113-134.

Davis, Donald G., Jr., and Dain, Phyllis, editors. "History of Library and Information Science Education." *Library Trends* 34 (Winter 1986).

Debons, Anthony. "Education in Library and Information Science: Education in Information Science." In *Encyclopedia of Library and Information Science* (New York: Marcel Dekker, 1972), vol. 7, pp. 465-474.

De Vane, William G. *Higher Education in Twentieth-century America*. Cambridge: Harvard University Press, 1965.

Dewey, Melvil. "Library Instruction: Summary of Plans Proposed to Aid in Educating Librarians." *Library Notes* 2 (March 1888), 286-306.

―――. "School of Library Economy." *Library Journal* 8 (1883), 285-291.

The Dictionary of American Biography. New York: Charles Scribner's Sons, 1958 (with supplements).

"Dr. John Shaw Billings." *Library Journal* 21 (February 1896), 63-65.

Downs, Robert B. "Education for Librarianship in the U.S. and Canada." In Larry Earl Bone, editor. *Library Education: An International Survey* (Urbana: University of Illinois, Graduate School of Library Science, 1968), pp. 1-20.

Eastman, Linda A. *Portrait of a Librarian: William Howard Brett*. Chicago: American Library Association, 1940.

Eaton, Thelma, editor. *Contributions to American Library History*. Champaign: Illini Union Bookstore, University of Illinois, 1961.

Elliott, Julia E. "Library Conditions Which Confront Library Schools." *American Library Association Bulletin* 3 (September 1909), 427-436.

Ennis, Philip H., and Winger, Howard E., editors. *Seven Questions about the Profession of Librarianship: The Twenty-sixth Annual Conference of the Graduate Library School, June 21-23, 1961*. Chicago: University of Chicago Press, 1962.

Fall, John. "PAIS: Fiftieth Anniversary." *Library Resources and Technical Services* 9 (Spring 1965), 231-234.

Fifty Years of Education for Librarianship: Papers Presented for Celebration of the Fiftieth Anniversary of the University of Illinois Library School, March 2, 1943. Urbana: University of Illinois Press, 1943.

Flexner, Abraham. *Universities: American, English, German.* New York: Oxford University Press, 1930.

Fosdick, Raymond B. *The Story of the Rockefeller Foundation.* New York: Harper and Brothers, 1952.

"France Honors Dr. C. C. Williamson." *New York Times*, November 17, 1929, p. 20.

Friedel, J. H. "Training for Librarianship." *Library Journal* 44 (September 1919), 569-574.

———. *Training for Librarianship.* Philadelphia: J. B. Lippincott, 1921.

Gardner, Richard K., editor. *Education of Library and Information Professionals: Present and Future Prospects.* Littleton, Colo.: Libraries Unlimited, 1987.

Garrison, Fielding H. *John Shaw Billings: A Memoir.* New York: G. P. Putnam's Sons, 1915.

Getchell, M. W. "The American Library Association and Training for Librarianship." *Library Journal* 51 (1926), 511-612; 770-774.

Gilchrist, Donald B. "The Evolution of College and University Libraries." *American Library Association Bulletin* 20 (October 1926), 293-299.

Goldhor, Herbert, editor. *Education for Librarianship: The Design of the Curriculum of Library Schools.* Urbana: University of Illinois, Graduate School of Library Science, 1971.

Gray, David. "A Modern Temple of Education: New York's New Public Library." *Harper's Monthly* 122 (March 1911), 562-576.

Gray, William S., and Munroe, Ruth. *The Reading Interests and Habits of Adults.* New York: Macmillan, 1929.

Hefferlin, JB Lon. "Accreditation of Library Education." In *Encyclopedia of Library and Information Science* (New York: Marcel Dekker, 1968), vol. 1, pp. 61-64.

Hendrick, Burton J. *The Life of Andrew Carnegie.* 2 vols. Garden City N.Y.: Doubleday, Doran, 1932.

Henry, W. E. "Certification of Librarians." *Library Journal* 44 (1919), 762-763.

Bibliography

———. "Librarianship as a Profession." *Library Journal* 42 (May 1917), 350-355.

Hessell, Alfred. *A History of Libraries*. Translated with supplementary material by Reuben Peiss. New Brunswick, N.J.: Scarecrow Press, 1955.

Hill, Frank P. *James Bertram: An Appreciation*. New York: Carnegie Corporation of New York, 1936.

A History of Columbia University, 1754-1904. Published in Commemoration of the 150th Anniversary of the Founding of King's College. New York: Columbia University Press, 1904.

History of Columbiana County, Ohio. Philadelphia: D. W. Ensign, 1879.

Horrocks, Norman. "Library Education: History." In *ALA World Encyclopedia of Library and Information Services*. 2nd ed. (Chicago: American Library Association, 1986), pp. 491-497.

———. "North American Trends in Library and Information Science." *Canadian Library Journal* 43 (October 1986), 293-296.

Horton, Marion. "Recent Developments in Correspondence Study." *Library Journal* 54 (1929), 1022-1023.

Hostetter, Anita M. *A Review of Studies and Projects in Education for Librarianship*. Chicago: American Library Association, 1939. (Mimeographed.)

Hostetter, Anita M. and University of Chicago Graduate Library School. "Education for Librarianship." *Year's Work in Librarianship* 4 (1931), 197-206.

Howe, Harriet. "The Library School Curriculum." *Library Quarterly* 1 (July 1931), 283-290.

———. "Two Decades in Education for Librarianship." *Library Quarterly* 12 (July 1942), 557-570.

Howe, Harriet, and Waples, Douglas. "Education for Librarianship: The United States." *Year's Work in Librarianship* 3 (1930), 159-168.

Howett, Thomas R., and Howett, Mary B., editors. *The Salem Story, 1806-1956*. Salem, Ohio: The Salem Sesquicentennial Committee, 1956.

Howson, Roger. "The Columbia Library System as a Research Laboratory." *Columbia Alumni News* 18 (October 30, 1925), 101-102.

———. "Editorial: The Erbs." *Columbia University Quarterly* 30 (June 1938), 148.

———. "Roger Howson, 79, Retired Librarian at Columbia

University, Served 22 Years" (obituary). *New York Times*, April 23, 1962, p. 29.
Hoxie, Ralph Gordon, et. al. *A History of the Faculty of Political Science, Columbia University*. New York: Columbia University Press, 1955.
Issues in Library Education. Conference on Library Education, Princeton University. Ann Arbor, Mich.: Edwards Brothers, 1949.
Joeckel, Carleton B. *The Government of the American Public Library*. Chicago: University of Chicago Press, 1935.
"John Shaw Billings." *Library Journal* 38 (April 1913), 212-213.
Johnson, Alvin Saunders. *A Report to Carnegie Corporation of New York on the Policy of Donations to Free Public Libraries*. New York: Carnegie Corporation of New York, n.d. (Submitted in accordance with authorization of Board of Trustees of Carnegie Corporation of New York, Resolution of November 18, 1915).
Johnson, Elmer D. *Communications: An Introduction to the History of Writing, Printing, Books, and Libraries*. 4th ed. New York: Scarecrow Press, 1973.
Jordan, Philip D. *Ohio Comes of Age, 1873-1900*. Columbus: Ohio State Archaeological and Historical Society, 1943.
Josephson, Aksel, G. S. "Is Librarianship a Learned Profession?" *Public Libraries* 1 (September 1896), 195-196.
———. "Preparation for Librarianship." *Library Journal* 25 (May 1900), 226-228.
———. "Training for Librarianship." *Public Libraries* 22 (June 1917), 223-224.
Keogh, Andrew. "Advanced Library Training for Research Workers." *American Library Association Bulletin* 13 (July 1919), 165-167.
Keppel, Frederick P. "The Carnegie Corporation and the Graduate Library School: A Historical Outline." *Library Quarterly* 1 (January 1931), 22-25.
———. *Columbia*. New York: Oxford University Press, 1914.
———. *Philanthropy and Learning*. New York: Columbia University Press, 1936.
Kerner, Robert J. "Essentials in the Training of University Librarians—IV." *College and Research Libraries* 1 (December 1939), 33-34.
Kitchen, Karl K. "Just Ask Dr. Williamson" (unidentified newspaper clipping), December 30, 1920.

Lancour, Harold, and Harrison, J. Clement. "Education for Librarianship Abroad and in Selected Countries." *Library Trends* 12 (October 1963).

Learned, William S. *The American Public Library and the Diffusion of Knowledge*. New York: Harcourt, Brace, 1924.

Leigh, Robert D. "The Education of Librarians." In Alice I. Bryan. *The Public Librarian* (New York: Columbia University Press, 1952), pp. 299-425.

———. *Major Problems in the Education of Librarians*. New York: Columbia University Press, 1954.

———. *The Public Library in the United States*. New York: Columbia University Press, 1950.

Lester, Robert M. *Forty Years of Carnegie Giving*. New York: Charles Scribner's Sons, 1941.

"Library Education." In Jean Key Gates. *Introduction to Librarianship*. 2nd ed. (New York: McGraw-Hill, 1976). pp. 89-103.

"The Library School of the New York Public Library." *Bulletin of the New York Public Library* 15 (June 1911), 349.

Lichtenstein, W. "The Question of a Graduate Library School." *Library Journal* 43 (1918), 233-235.

Linderman, Winifred B. "History of the Columbia University Library, 1876-1926" (unpublished doctoral dissertation, Columbia University), 1959.

Lussen, Helen L. "Developing Attitudes Toward Library Education, 1876-1950" (unpublished master's thesis, Kent State University), 1952.

Lydenberg, Harry Miller. *History of the New York Public Library: Astor, Lenox, and Tilden Foundations*. New York: The New York Public Library, 1923.

———. *John Shaw Billings*. Chicago: American Library Association, 1924.

McAneny, G. "Municipal Reference Library as an Aid in City Administration." *Library Journal* 38 (September 1913), 509-513.

McCord, William B. *A Souvenir History of ye Old Town of Salem, Ohio, with Some Pictures and Brief References to ye People and Things of ye Olden Times*. Salem, Ohio: Centennial Souvenir Committee, 1906.

McGrath, Earl J. *The Graduate School and the Decline of Liberal Education*. New York: Teachers College, Columbia University, 1959.

McMullen, Haynes. "The First Hundred Years—Library Education: A Mini-History—What Hath Dewey's Daring Venture Wrought?" *American Libraries* 17 (June 1986), 406-408.

Manley, Marian C. "Emma Baldwin." *Library Journal* 77 (March 15, 1952), 487.

———. "Personalities Behind the Development of Public Affairs Information Service." *College and Research Libraries* 15 (July 1954), 263-270ff.

———. "Personalities in the Fifty Years of Business Library Service." N.d. (Typewritten.)

Marshall, John David, compiler. *An American Library History Reader*. Hamden, Conn.: Shoe String Press, 1961.

Martin, Lowell A. "Research in Education for Librarianship." *Library Trends* 6 (October 1957), 207-218.

Mearns, David C. *The Story Up to Now: The Library of Congress, 1800-1946*. Washington: The Library of Congress, 1947.

Metcalf, Keyes D. "Charles C. Williamson." *Library Service News* 11 (November 1943), 23-24.

———. *Random Recollections of an Anachronism; or, Seventy-five Years of Library Work*. New York: Readex Books, 1980.

———. "Six Influential Academic and Research Librarians." *College and Research Libraries* 37 (July 1976), 332-345.

Metcalf, Keyes D., et. al. *The Program of Instruction in Library Schools*. Urbana: University of Illinois Press, 1943.

Miller, James M. *The Genesis of Western Culture: The Upper Ohio Valley, 1800-1825*. Columbus, Ohio: The Ohio State Archaeological and Historical Society, 1938.

Mishoff, Willard O. "Education for Library Service." In Lloyd E. Blauch, editor. *Education for the Professions* (Washington: Government Printing Office, 1955), pp. 121-129.

Mitchell, Sidney B. "Education for Librarianship: The Last Decade and the Next One." *American Library Association Bulletin* 29 (February 1935), 72-79.

———. "Essentials in the Training of University Librarians—II." *College and Research Libraries* 1 (December 1939), 22-29.

Mitchill, Alma C., editor. *Special Libraries Association: Its First Fifty Years, 1909-1959*. New York: Special Libraries Association, [1959].

Morris, Richard B., editor. *Encyclopedia of American History*. Rev. ed. New York: Harper and Row, 1961.

Morton, Florrinell. "Education for Librarians" (a Conference held April 22-23, 1960, at Kansas State Teachers College at Emporia). *Bulletin of Information* 41 (January 1961), 5-38.

Bibliography

Mudge, Isadore Gilbert. "The Development of the Reference Department of the Columbia University Libraries." New York: Columbia University, 1941. (Typewritten.)

"Municipal Reference Library." *City Record* (March 7, 1912), 2021-2022.

Municipal Reference Library of the City of New York. "Annual Statistics." New York: Municipal Reference Library, n.d. (Typewritten.)

———. "Budgets." New York: Municipal Reference Library, 1914-1918. (Typewritten.)

"The Municipal Reference Library of the City of New York." New York: The Municipal Reference Library. February 16, 1920. (Typewritten.)

Munn, Ralph. *Conditions and Trends in Education for Librarianship*. New York: Carnegie Corporation of New York, 1936.

Munthe, Wilhelm. *American Librarianship from a European Angle*. Chicago: American Library Association, 1939.

Nasri, William Z. "Education in Library and Information Science: Education for Librarianship." In *Encyclopedia of Library and Information Science* (New York: Marcel Dekker, 1972), vol. 7, pp. 414-465.

The National Cyclopaedia of American Biography. New York: James T. White, 1898 (with supplements).

"New Building of the New York Public Library." *Library Journal* 36 (May 1911), 221-232.

"New Library Stone Laid at Columbia." *New York Times*, October 4, 1932, p. 23.

"New York Municipal Reference Library." *Library Journal* 38 (May 1913), 270-272.

Ohio Wesleyan University. *Fifty-fifth Catalogue*. Delaware, Ohio: The University, 1899.

———. *Fifty-sixth Catalogue*. Delaware, Ohio: The University, 1900.

Pearson, F. B. and Harlor, J. D. *Ohio History Sketches*. Columbus, Ohio: Press of Fred J. Heer, 1903.

Pierce, Helen F. *Graduate Study in Librarianship in the United States*. (a report prepared for the Board of Education for Librarianship of the American Library Association). Chicago: American Library Association, 1941. (Mimeographed.)

Plummer, Mary Wright. "Evolution of the Library School Curriculum." *American Library Association Bulletin* 2 (1908), 203-205.

———. "Library Training." *Public Libraries* 7 (1901), 399-401.

———. "Pros and Cons of Training for Librarianship." *Public Libraries* 8 (1903), 208-220.

———. *Training for Librarianship*. 3rd edition. Rev. Frank K. Walter. Chicago: American Library Association, 1923.

———. "Value of a School for Library Training." *Library Journal* 16 (1891), 40-44.

Pomahac, Gertrude C., editor. "Education for Library Management." In *Workshop on Library Management*. (Occasional Paper Number 1.) (Red Deer: The Library Association of Alberta, 1969.)

Public Affairs Information Service. "Brochure." New York: Public Affairs Information Service, n.d.

———. "PAIS Fiftieth Anniversary, 1914-1964: A Selection from the Early Records of PAIS." New York: Public Affairs Information Service, 1964. (A selection of Xerox materials from the files.)

Putnam, Herbert. "Education for Library Work." *Iowa Library Commission Quarterly* 1 (1901), 17-19.

Rankin, Rebecca "Dr. C. C. Williamson: In Memoriam." *Special Libraries* 56 (February 1965), 120.

———. "Training for the Special Librarian." *Special Libraries* 19 (March 1928), 72-74.

Reece, Ernest J. "C. C. Williamson: A Record of Service to American Librarianship." *College and Research Libraries* 4 (September 1943), 306-308.

———. *The Curriculum in Library Schools*. New York: Columbia University Press, 1936.

———. *Programs for Library Schools*. New York: Columbia University Press, 1943.

———. *Some Possible Developments in Library Education*. Chicago: American Library Association, 1924.

———. *The Task and Training of Librarians*. New York: King's Crown Press, 1949.

Reed, Sarah R., editor. *Problems of Library School Administration: Report of an Institute, April 14-15, 1965*. Washington: U.S. Department of Health, Education, and Welfare, Office of Education, 1965.

Rice, Paul North. "Editorial Forum: Charles C. Williamson." *Library Journal* 68 (June 15, 1943), 522.

Rider, Fremont. *Melvil Dewey*. Chicago: American Library Association, 1944.

Bibliography

The Rise of a University. 2 vols. New York: Columbia University Press, 1937.

Robbins-Carter, Jane. "Library Education: Curriculum." In *ALA World Encyclopedia of Library and Information Services.* 2nd ed. (Chicago: American Library Association, 1986), pp. 484-488.

Rogers, Frank Bradway. "Librarianship in a World of Machines." Nashville, Tenn: Peabody Library School, George Peabody College for Teachers, 1966, (First annual C. C. Williamson Memorial Lecture, May 17, 1966).

Rudolph, Frederick. *The American College and University: A History.* New York: Alfred A. Knopf, 1962.

Russell, Trusten W. "A Library of the New Era." *New York Times,* July 8, 1934, Special Features Section, p. 6.

Salamanca, Lucy. *Fortress of Freedom: The Story of the Library of Congress.* Philadelphia: J. B. Lippincott, 1942.

Salem Area Industrial Development Corporation (brochure). *Salem, Ohio.* N.d.

Sawyer, Rollin A. "Success Story: The Public Affairs Information Service, 1910-1945." *Library Journal* 71 (January 15, 1946), 98-100.

Selden, William K. *Accreditation.* New York: Harper and Brothers, 1960.

Shearer, A. H. "Historical Sketch of the Library War Service." *American Library Association Bulletin* 13 (July 1919), 224-234.

Shera, Jesse H. *The Foundation of Education for Librarianship.* New York: Becker and Hayes, 1972.

Shores, Louis. *Library Education.* Littleton, Colo.: Libraries Unlimited, 1972.

———. *A Quiet World: A Librarian's Crusade for Destiny.* Hamden, Conn.: Linnet Books, 1975.

Stone, Elizabeth W. *American Library Development, 1600-1899.* New York: H. W. Wilson, 1977.

———. "Historical Approach to American Library Development: A Chronological Chart." *University of Illinois Graduate School of Library Science Occasional Papers* 83 (May 1967), 1-233.

Storr, Richard J. *The Beginnings of Graduate Education in America.* Chicago: University of Chicago Press, 1953.

Strohm, Adam J. "Do We Need a Post-Graduate Library School?" *Public Libraries* 15 (February 1910), 54-55.

———. "The Library Training Board." *American Library Association Bulletin* 18 (January 1924), 2-4.

———. "Why Educate for Librarianship?" *American Library Association Bulletin* 18 (1924), 167-170.

Sullivan, Peggy. *Carl H. Milam and the American Library Association*. New York: H. W. Wilson, 1976.

Tai, Tse-chien. *Professional Education for Librarianship*. New York: H. W. Wilson, 1925.

Tees, Miriam H. "Accreditation and Certification." In Richard K. Gardner, ed., *Education of Library and Information Professionals: Present and Future Prospects*. (Littleton, Colo.: Libraries Unlimited, Inc., 1987), Chapter 8, pp. 108-120.

Thompson, C. Seymour. "Do We Want a Library Science?" *Library Journal* 56 (July 1931), 581-587.

Thompson, Lawrence. "The Historical Background of Departmental and Collegiate Libraries." *Library Quarterly* 12 (January 1942), 49-74.

Tobitt, Edith. "The Essentials of a Good Library School." *American Library Association Bulletin* 4 (September 1910), 776-779.

"Training for Library Service." *Library Journal* 47 (September 1, 1923), 711-714 (an abridged version of the "Summary of Findings and Recommendations" of the Williamson Report).

Trautman, Ray. *A History of the School of Library Service, Columbia University*. New York: Columbia University Press, 1954.

Turner, Harold M. "The CECL's First Fifty Years." *College and Research Libraries* 26 (July 1965), 289-296.

Tyler, Alice S. "Education for Librarianship: As It Is and As It Might Be." *American Library Association Bulletin* 18 (1924), 161-166.

University of Wisconsin. *Catalogue, 1905-1906*. Madison: University of Wisconsin, 1906.

Utley, George B. "The American Library Institute: A Historical Sketch." *Library Quarterly* 16 (April 1946), 152-159.

———. "The Expanding Responsibilities of the American Library Association." *American Library Association Bulletin* 17 (July 1923), 107-112.

———. *Fifty Years of the American Library Association*. Chicago: American Library Association, 1926.

Bibliography

Vann, Sarah K. Letter from Dr. Charles C. Williamson, May 23, 1955.

———. "Statement Prepared for the Use of Miss Sarah K. Vann," by Charles C. Williamson. June 27, 1955. 9 pp.

———. *Training for Librarianship Before 1923; Education for Librarianship Prior to the Publication of Williamson's Report on Training for Library Service.* Chicago: American Library Association, 1961.

———. *The Williamson Reports: A Study.* Metuchen, N.J.: Scarecrow Press, 1971.

Walter, Frank K. "A Dynamic Report." *Library Journal* 48 (September 1, 1923), 709-711.

Walters, Everett. *Graduate Education Today.* Washington: American Council on Education, 1965.

Waples, Douglas. "The Graduate Library School at Chicago." *Library Quarterly* 1 (January 1931), 26-36.

Wheeler, Joseph L. *Progress and Problems in Education for Librarianship.* New York: Carnegie Corporation of New York, 1946.

White, Carl M. *Developing the School of Library Service.* New York: Columbia University Press, 1957.

———. *A Historical Introduction to Library Education: Problems and Progress to 1951.* Metuchen, N.J.: Scarecrow Press, 1976.

———. *The Origins of the American Library School.* New York: Scarecrow Press, 1961.

White, Herbert S., editor. *Education for Professional Librarians.* White Plains, N.Y.: Knowledge Industry Publications, 1986.

White, Theodore H. "Scholarly Impact on the Nation's Past." *Life*, June 16, 1967, pp. 56ff.

Wickizer, Alice F. "Education for Librarianship: A Brief History, 1886-1953." (unpublished master's thesis, Western Reserve University), 1953.

"Williamson Report: Comment from Librarians." *Library Journal* 48 (December 1, 1923), 999-1006.

"Williamson Report: Comment from the Library Schools." *Library Journal* 48 (November 1, 1923), 899-910.

Williamson, Charles C. (awards). "ALA Awards and Citations for 1964—Beta Phi Mu Award." *Library Journal* 89 (August 1964), 2938.

———. "Awards—Dr. Charles C. Williamson . . . Received the

Beta Phi Mu Award." *Wilson Library Bulletin* 39 (September 1964), 31.

———. "The 1964 ALA Awards Winners—The Beta Phi Mu Award." *American Library Association Bulletin* 58 (September 1964), 726.

Williamson, Charles C. (biographical sketch). "Charles C. Williamson, 1877-1965." *Public Affairs Information Service Bulletin*, 1965.

———. "Distinguished Educator Serves Garden Center." *Greenwich Social Review* 13 (March 1960), 31.

———. In *Leaders in Education*, ed. Jacques Cattell and E. E. Ross. 3rd ed. (Lancaster, Pa.: Science Press, 1948), p. 1158.

———. "The Literary Month." *Wilson Bulletin* 4 (January 1930), 210.

———. In *Who's Who in America* (Chicago: A. N. Marquis, various editions).

———. In *Who's Who in Library Service* (New York: H. W. Wilson, 1st ed., 1933, p. 443; and 2nd ed., 1943, p. 594.)

———. In Louis Round Wilson and Maurice F. Tauber. *The University Library*. (New York; Columbia University Press, 1956), pp. 543-546.

Williamson, Charles C. (Obituary). "About People." *Library Journal* 90 (February 1, 1965), 612.

———. "C. C. Williamson Dies at 88: Was Noted Librarian." *Greenwich* [Connecticut] *Times*, January 12, 1965, p. 2.

———. "C.C. Williamson Ran Libraries at Columbia." *New York Herald-Tribune*, January 13, 1965, p. 14.

———. "Charles Williamson, 87, Dies: Directed Libraries at Columbia." *New York Times*, January 13, 1965, p. 25.

———. "Charles Williamson, Educator, Librarian." *Newsday*, January 13, 1965, p. 48.

———. "Charles C. Williamson." *New York Post*, January 13, 1965, p. 33.

———. "Charles C. Williamson Dies at 88." *Hartford* [Connecticut] *Courant*, January 13, 1965, p. 4.

———. "Charles G. [*sic*] Williamson, 87, Ex-Dean Rites Tomorrow." *New York World-Telegram and Sun*, January 13, 1965, p. 31.

———. "Dr. C. C. Williamson." *Salem* [Ohio] *News*. January 12, 1965, p. 8.

———. "Necrology." *College and Research Libraries*, 26 (July 1965), 352.

———. "People: Charles Williamson." *Wilson Library Bulletin* 39 (February 1965), 439.
Williamson, William L. "A Century of Students." *Library Trends* 34 (Winter 1986), 433-449.
Wilson, Louis Round. "The American Library School Today." *Library Quarterly* 7 (April 1937), 211-245.
———. "Aspects of Education for Librarianship in America." *Library Quarterly* 2 (January 1932), 1-10.
———. "The Board of Education for Librarianship." *American Library Association Bulletin* 25 (January 1931), 5-11.
———. *Education and Libraries: Selected Papers by Louis Round Wilson*, ed. Maurice F. Tauber and Jerrold Orne. Hamden, Conn.: Shoe String Press, 1966.
———. "Essentials in the Training of University Librarians—I." *College and Research Libraries* 1 (December 1939), 13-21.
———. "Historical Development of Education for Librarianship in the United States." In Bernard Berelson, editor. *Education for Librarianship* (Chicago: American Library Association, 1949), pp. 44-65.
———. "The Role of the Library in Higher Education." *School and Society* 47 (May 7, 1938), 585-592.
Wilson, Louis Round and Tauber, Maurice F. *The University Library*. 2nd ed. (New York: Columbia University Press, 1956), pp. 543-546.
Winckler, Paul A. "Charles Clarence Williamson (1877-1965): His Professional Life and Work in Librarianship and Library Education in the United States" (unpublished doctoral dissertation, New York University), 1968.
———. "Charles C. Williamson." In *Dictionary of American Library Biography* (Littleton, Colo.: Libraries Unlimited, 1978), pp. 553-558.
———. "Charles C. Williamson, 1877-1965." In *Encyclopedia of Library and Information Science* (New York: Marcel Dekker, 1982), vol. 30, pp. 147-159.
———. "Letter: Reader's Voice." *Library Journal* 90 (February 15, 1965), 798.
Windsor, Phineas L. "The Association of American Library Schools." *American Library Association Bulletin* 11 (July 1917), 160-162.
Winger, Howard W. "Aspects of Librarianship: A Tracework of History." *Library Quarterly* 31 (October 1961), 321-335.

Works, G. A. "Research and Graduate Library School." *Libraries* 33 (1928), 100-103.

Wyer, James I. "Factors in the Development of the Library School Curriculum." *American Library Association Bulletin* 2 (1908), 205-206.

CHRONOLOGY OF WILLIAMSON'S LIFE AND CAREER

1877	Born on January 26 at Salem, Ohio.
1897	Graduated from Salem High School, June 17.
1897-1898	Teacher in the elementary school of Mahoning County, Ohio.
1898-1899	Student at Ohio Wesleyan University.
1899-1900	Teacher in the Salem Public Schools.
1900-1901	Principal in the Salem Public Schools.
1901-1904	Student at Adelbert College of Western Reserve University.
1901-1905	Secretary to President Charles F. Thwing of Western Reserve University.
1904	Granted Bachelor of Arts degree from Adelbert College of Western Reserve University.
1904	Elected to Phi Beta Kappa.
1905-1906	Graduate student in economics at the University of Wisconsin; personal secretary to Professor Richard T. Ely.
1906-1907	Transferred to Columbia University, School of Political Science, as a graduate student and candidate for the Ph.D.

1907	Awarded Ph.D. on June 12 from Columbia University; doctoral dissertation entitled "The Finances of Cleveland."
1907	Married Bertha L. Torrey on June 22.
1907-1911	Associate Professor and Head of the Department of Economics and Sociology at Bryn Mawr College, Pennsylvania.
1911-1914	Chief of the Economics Division of the New York Public Library.
1912-1916	Tax and Finance Editor of the *American Yearbook*.
1913	Daughter, Cornelia, born on August 15.
1913-1917	Member of Council of the American Library Association; also served as a Member of Council from 1919-1923 and again from 1927-1931.
1914-1918	Librarian of the Municipal Reference Library of the City of New York.
1914-1918	Editor of *Municipal Reference Library Notes*.
1914-1918	Associate Editor of the *American Political Science Review* and the *National Municipal Review*.
1915-1917	President of the New York Chapter of the Special Libraries Association.
1915-1916	Wrote and edited the *Municipal Year Book of the City of New York*.

1916	Member of Committee for New Sources of Revenue of the National Municipal League; Chairman of its Committee on Municipal Reference Libraries.
1916-1917	Vice-President of Special Libraries Association.
1916-1917	Member of the Board of Administration of the Marquand School for Boys, Brooklyn, New York.
1917	Secretary of the Publications Committee of the *Minutes of the Common Council of the City of New York, 1784-1831*.
1917-1918	President of Special Libraries Association.
1918-1919	Worked as statistician in the Advertising Bureau of the Liberty Loan Organization.
1918-1921	Chairman of the Publications Committee of the Public Affairs Information Service.
1918-1919	Published three articles in *Library Journal* on library training: "The Need of a Plan for Library Development," "Efficiency in Library Management," and "Some Present-Day Aspects of Library Training."
1918-1919	Statistician for the Americanization Study of the Carnegie Corporation of New York.
1919	Gave Asbury Park Address on June 26 at the Annual Convention of the American Library Association ("Some Present-Day Aspects of Library Training").

1919	On March 28 the Carnegie Corporation of New York authorized an inquiry into library training. The Advisory Committee consisted of Herbert Putnam, James H. Kirkland, and Wilson Farrand, with C. C. Williamson in charge. The survey was entitled "Study of Training for Library Work."
1919	Appointed Member of the Committee of Five on Library Service of the American Library Association.
1919-1921	Returned as Chief of the Economics Division of the New York Public Library.
1920	Gave the Founder's Day Address at the Library School of Western Reserve University ("Andrew Carnegie: His Contribution to the Public Library Movement").
1920	Member of the Committee of Five on Standardization, Certification, and Library Training of the American Library Association.
1920	Chairman of the new Committee of Nine on National Certification and Training of the American Library Association.
1920-1921	President of the New York Library Association.
1920-1921	Undertook visits to library schools for the survey commissioned by the Carnegie Corporation.
1921-1926	Director of Information Service of the Rockefeller Foundation.
1923	Publication of *Training for Library Service* by the Carnegie Corporation of New York.

Chronology

1926	Merger of the New York State Library School and the Library School of the New York Public Library with Columbia University to form the new School of Library Service. He served as Director until 1931 and then as Dean until his retirement in 1943.
1926-1943	Director of Libraries and of the School of Library Service of Columbia University in the City of New York.
1926-1927	Chairman of the Committee on Study and Development of Reading Habits of the American Library Association; also served on this committee from 1928-1931.
1927-1929	Chairman and Member of the Committee on Journal of Discussion of the American Library Association; also served 1932-1934 and 1936-1938.
1928	Member of the Committee on Academic and Professional Higher Degrees of the Association of American Universities.
1928	Member of the Century Club until 1944.
1928	Prime mover in marshaling support in the United States for the completion of the printed catalog of the Bibliothèque Nationale of France. For this work he was named a Chevalier of the Legion of Honor by the French government on August 6.
1929	Received honorary degree of Litt.D., from Columbia University.
1929	Gave Dedication Address at the new library of

Randolph-Macon Women's College ("Library Service in a Machine Age").

1929 — Associate Editor of the *Journal of Higher Education* until 1949; also served as Editorial Consultant to the journal from 1958.

1929 — Established *Library Service News* at Columbia University.

1929-1931 — President of the Association of American Library Schools (AALS).

1929-1943 — In charge of the Annual Conference of Eastern College Librarians held at Columbia University.

1930 — Member of the Committee on Coordination of Conference Programs of the American Library Association.

1930 — Involved in the move to publish a supplement to Cannons, *Bibliography of Library Economy, 1876-1920*, which resulted in the publication of *Library Literature, 1921-1932*, by the American Library Association. He felt the urgent need for an index to professional library literature and urged that an index be compiled and published.

1930 — Gave Founder's Day Address at the Library School of Western Reserve University ("The Place of Research in Library Service").

1930-1931 — Member of the Committee on Recruiting for Library Service of the American Library Association.

1931 — Served for many years as Associate Editor of the *Library Quarterly*. His article, "The Place

	of Research in Library Service," was the first article in volume 1 of this new library journal.
1933	Board Member of the American Library Institute.
1933	Co-editor with Alice L. Jewett of the first edition of *Who's Who in Library Service*.
1934	Started Columbia University Studies in Library Service series.
1934	Member of the American Friends of Lafayette.
1935	Opening of the new library (South Hall) at Columbia University (now called Butler Library). He was involved in the planning and work on this new library building.
1937	Editor of *School of Library Economy of Columbia College, 1887-1889*.
1938	Ran for the elected position of Vice-President (President-elect) of the American Library Association, but was defeated by Ralph Munn.
1939	Bertha L. Williamson died on September 16.
1939	Served on the Committee of the Herbert Putnam Honor Fund of the American Library Association.
1940	Married Genevieve Austen Hodge on August 26.
1940	Appointed to Advisory Board for the Study of Special Projects of the American Library Association.
1940-1941	Member of the Committee on Tests and Meas-

	urements of the Association of American Library Schools.
1941	Served as Advisor to Facts on File until 1965.
1943	Co-editor with Alice L. Jewett of the second edition of *Who's Who in Library Service*.
1943	Retired on June 30 from Columbia University.
1943	Named Director of Libraries Emeritus of Columbia University.
1952	Made Honorary Member of Special Libraries Association.
1954	Consultant to the Connecticut State Commission on Educational Television.
1956-1957	President of the American Council for Better Broadcasting.
1957-1958	President of the Lions Club Foundation of Greenwich, Connecticut.
1958-1965	Board Member, Treasurer, and Librarian of the Greenwich (Connecticut) Garden Center.
1959-1965	Treasurer of the Greenwich (Connecticut) Association for the Public Schools.
1964	Awarded the Beta Phi Mu Award for his outstanding contribution to education for librarianship by the American Library Association.
1965	Died on January 11 in Greenwich, Connecticut. Buried in Wethersfield, Connecticut.

INDEX

Academy of Political Science in the City of New York   253
Adams, James   6, 8
Adams, Jane   6, 8
Adelbert College (Western Reserve University)   24, 29–30, 32–33, 48, 66–67
Adler, Elmer   285
Ahern, Mary Eileen   134
Alumni Association of the Columbia University School of Library Service   291
American Association for Adult Education   270
American Association of University Professors   253
American Council for Better Broadcasts   253, 286, 292
American Economic Association   253
American Humanist Association   253
American Library Association   111–116, 119–125, 127, 129, 131, 133, 141, 146, 150, 167, 173, 240, 242, 245–246, 253–256, 262, 265–266, 268, 270, 294
  Asbury Park Convention   111, 113–115, 122
  Association of College and Research Libraries   253
  Board of Education for Librarianship   120–121, 123, 125, 141, 168, 242
  Buffalo Convention   129
  Chautauqua Conference   132
  Committee of Five on Library Service   121
  Committee of Five on Standardization, Certification, and Library Training   112, 122
  Committee of Nine on National Certification and Training   122
  Committee on Accreditation   121, 125
  Committee on an Enlarged Program for American Library Service   115, 122
  Committee on Library Examinations and Credentials   133
  Committee on Library Schools   132
  Committee on Library Survey   122
  Committee on Library Training   120, 132–134
  Committee on Professional Instruction and Bibliography   133

Committee on Professional Training for Librarianship 133
Committee on the Library School 132
Committee on the Library School and Training Classes 132
Council 125, 167, 254, 265
Office of Library Education 121, 170
Round Table of Library School Instructors 132–133
Saratoga Springs Convention 139–140
Special Committee of Certification 120
Temporary Library Training Board 120, 122–125
American Library Institute 253, 264–266
American Political Science Association 253
American Political Science Review 91
American Society for Information Science 268
American Society of Mechanical Engineers 254
American Sociological Society 253
American Statistical Society 253
American Yearbook 81
Americanization Study. See Carnegie Corporation's Study of the Methods of Americanization, or Fusion of Native and Foreign Born
Amherst Summer School of Library Economy 67, 130
Anderson, Edwin Hatfield 62, 67, 71–72, 74, 77, 82–85, 93, 105, 107, 176, 232, 254, 285
Anderson, Florence 139
Angell, James R. 270
Appleton, D., and Company 81
Arbuthnot, C. C. 28, 37, 60, 62, 68, 72
Armour Institute (Chicago, Illinois) 130, 134
Ash, Lee 268
Asheim, Lester 170
Association for Education by Radio-Television 292
Association for Library and Information Science Education 133
Association of American Library Schools (later called Association for Library and Information Science Education) 110, 113, 120, 132–133, 146, 253, 256
Association of American Universities 270
Association of College and Research Libraries. *See under* American Library Association
Association of the Columbia School of Library Service and Its Predecessors 234–235
Atlanta (Georgia) Public Library 131
Atlanta (Georgia) University 270

Index

Bacon, Corinne 167
Badalic, Josip 242
Baker, Newton D. 45
Baldwin, Emma V. 120, 134, 236
Barker, Tommie Dora 163
Barkley, Alben W. 246
Barnes, C. S. 14
Benton, Elbert 190
Bertram, James 110, 116, 139–140, 144–145, 150, 153
Beta Phi Mu 254, 294
Beta Phi Mu Award 294
Bevis, Dorothy 169
Bibliographical Society of America 253
Bibliography of Library Economy, 1876–1920 262
Bibliothèque Nationale (France) 196, 253, 257–261, 284
Billings, John Shaw 67, 70–72, 74–80, 178
Bishop, William Warner 112, 114, 121, 159, 186, 189–190, 245, 256, 264
Black, William 266
Boas, Franz 273
Bobinski, George 138, 141
Bockman, Eugene 98–99
Bodleian Library (England) 283–284
Bogle, Sarah C. N. 115, 150
Book Table 285
Borba de Moraes, Rubens 242
Bostwick, Arthur E. 121–122, 150
Bowdoin College 55–61
Bowerman, George F. 117–118, 162, 165
Bowker, Richard R. 66, 161–162, 232, 262
Bowker, R. R. (company) 285
Brett, William Howard 47–48, 63, 134
Brewster, William K. 270
Brigham, Herbert B. 265
British Museum (England) 284
Brooklyn (New York) College Library 246, 261
Brooklyn (New York) Public Library 114, 134
Brooks, John Graham 103
Brown University 146, 152, 190
Bruere, Henry 84–85
Bruni, Gerardo 242
Bryan, Alice I. 279
Bryn Mawr College 43, 47–49, 51–58, 60–64, 67–68, 70–73, 178, 275

Buffalo, University of 271
Burns, Allan T. 103, 105
Burris, W. P. 23
Butler, Nicholas Murray 186–188, 191, 193–194, 201, 203, 208–210, 214–215, 219–222, 224–227, 229, 231–232, 237–238, 248, 272
Butler Library. *See* South Hall

California State Library 165
California, University of (at Berkeley) 170
  Courses in Library Science 144
Campbell, Robert 82, 84, 99
Cannons, C. L. 167
Cannons, Harry G. T. 262
Carnegie, Andrew 63, 77–78, 137, 266
Carnegie Corporation of New York 98, 102–103, 105, 110, 112, 116, 124, 131, 135, 137–142, 144, 146–147, 149, 151–154, 159, 161, 166–171, 173, 179–180, 184, 191, 200, 210, 215, 217, 226, 229–230, 236, 241, 246–247, 270
Carnegie Corporation's Study of the Methods of Americanization, or Fusion of Native and Foreign Born 98, 102–105, 108, 139
Carnegie Foundation for the Advancement of Teaching 285
Carnegie Libraries 128, 130, 137–138, 166
Carnegie Library of Pittsburgh 254
Carnegie Library School
  at Atlanta 130, 143, 163
  at Pittsburgh 130, 143, 150
Carnegie Library Training School for Children's Librarians 132
Carnovsky, Leon 170, 254
Carpenter, William Henry 46, 209–211
Carré, M. 258
Carroll, C. Edward 128
Center for the Study of Liberal Education for Adults (Chicago, Illinois) 292
Century Club 285
Cessna, Joseph 14
Charters, W. W. 270
Chautauqua (New York) Summer School 23
Chevalier de la Légion d'Honneur 28, 257–260
Chicago (Illinois) Public Library 165
Chicago, University of 141, 161, 170, 270
Child, James 80
Churchwell, Charles D. 120
City Club of New York 285

Index

Clark, Isabel D.   291
Clark, John B.   47
Cleveland (Ohio) Public Library   42, 47–48, 63, 131, 134, 270
Clevinger, John S.   231
Clift, David H.   197, 208, 225, 250, 280–281
Coker, Frances W.   261
Cole, Dorothy   268
Columbia College School of Library Economy   127, 129, 134, 230
Columbia University   33, 41–47, 62, 65, 67, 109, 129, 145, 161, 183–191, 194–201, 203–208, 210–211, 216–219, 225, 227–231, 233–235, 237–244, 248–250, 267, 270, 272–273, 275, 278, 282–285, 288–289, 291, 293
  Libraries   183, 185, 187, 191–200, 203–208, 211–214, 216–220, 224, 227–228, 240, 249
  Press   235, 271
  School of Library Service   170–171, 183, 185, 187, 191–194, 197–199, 206, 212, 216, 220, 224–226, 228–234, 238–240, 243–244, 249–250, 280
"Columbia University Studies in Library Service" (series)   235
Columbian University (Washington, D.C.)   130
Commission on the Library and Adult Education   270
Conference of Eastern College Librarians   263–264
Conference of Negro Librarians   234
Connecticut Audio-Visual Education Association   292
Connecticut State Educational Television Commission   286, 291–292
Continuing Education Center (Chicago, Illinois)   292
Cook, Grace   190
Cook, Jacob   2
Cook, Lavina   7, 9
Cornell University   264
Coss, John J.   145, 231
Coykendall, Frederick   186, 231
Crissey, Lucy M.   277–278, 289
Cyclopedia of Education   118

Dana, John Cotton   114
Dana report   132
Danton, J. Periam   170
Darrow, Whitney   285
Davis, Donald G., Jr.   132
Davis, Elmer   261, 285
Denver (Colorado) Public Library   131
Detroit (Michigan) Public Library   124

Dewey, Emily   237
Dewey, John   23, 118, 273
Dewey, Melvil   119, 123, 127, 129, 133–134, 192–193, 230, 232, 237, 271, 297
Dick, J., Publishing Research Publications   268
Dickinson, Asa D.   246
District of Columbia Public Library   117, 165
District of Columbia Training Center for Professional Librarians   134
Dix, John A.   77
Doctor of Letters (*honoris causa*) (Columbia University)   273
Downs, Robert B.   133, 170, 196, 280
Drexel Institute Library School   130, 167
Drury, F. W. K.   146–147

Eastman, Linda   121
Eckelberry, R. H.   271–272
"Efficiency in Library Management" (journal article)   109, 111
Eliot, Edward Charles   273
Elliott, Julia   131–132
Ely, Richard T.   25, 28, 32–38, 40–41, 43, 46, 52–57, 60, 63, 68, 71–74
Embree, Edwin R.   85, 91–93, 102, 105, 109, 177–180, 267
Emerson, Haven   178
Epstein, Howard M.   261–262
"Essentials in the Training of University Librarians—III" (journal article)   195

Fackenthal, Frank D.   186, 193–194, 211, 222, 226, 231
Facts on File   261–262
Fair, Ethel M.   237, 294
Fairchild, Milton   232
Fairchild, Salome Cutler   134
Fall, John   96, 260
Fargo, Lucile F.   235
Farrand, Wilson   142
Fay, Lucy E.   231, 237
Federal Reserve Bank   103
Ferguson, Milton J.   165, 245–247, 285
Fife, Robert H.   231
"The Finances of Cleveland" (doctoral dissertation)   44
Fisher, Dorothy Canfield   273
Fisk University   67
Fosdick, Raymond B.   179

Index

Foundation for the Advancement of Education   293
French government   28, 257, 259
Frick, Bertha   243
Friends of the Bibliothèque Nationale and of the Great Libraries of France. *See* Société des Amis de la Bibliothèque Nationale et des Grandes Bibliothèques de France
Friends of the Columbia University Libraries   205
Furst, Clyde   285

Gavit, John Palmer   105
Gaynor, William J.   77
Gerlach, Margaret (Williamson)   6, 9
Gerould, James Thayer   190
Gideonse, Harry D.   261
Giordani, Igino   242
Glenn, John   62, 64, 103
Godard, George S.   94
Gosnell, Charles   294
Gracia-Peña, Idilio   99
Graff, Robert de   285
Grand Bienfaiteurs de la Bibliothèque Nationale   260
Gray, William S.   270
Greenwich (Connecticut) Association for the Public Schools   286
Greenwich (Connecticut) Garden Center   283, 287–288, 292–293, 295
Grolier Society, The   268
Gunther, John   261

Hadley, Arthur T.   98
Haines, Helen E.   235
Hamlin, T. F.   235
Hard, Myron E.   15, 18–19, 21–23
Haring, Harry W.   25
Harkness, Edward S.   201, 204
Harper and Company (publisher)   105
Harvard Faculty Club   266
Harvard University   23, 86, 204–205, 264
Hasse, Adelaide R.   70, 78–80
Hazeltine, Alice I.   238, 243, 278
Health Department (City of New York)   178
Heinmiller, W. H.   30
Henry, William E.   164
Herbert Putnam Honor Fund   256
Hitchler, Theresa   114

Hodge, Genevieve (Austen). *See* Williamson, Genevieve (Austen Hodge)
Honorable Charter Revision Commission   83
Hope, John   270
Hopper, Franklin E.   285
Horrocks, Norman   125, 133, 173
Howe, Frederic C.   42
Howson, Roger   188, 191, 209–214, 218–219, 222–229, 231
Hyde, William de Witt   56–59
Hyland, John F.   97

Illinois, University of   151
  Library School   130, 132, 143, 151, 170
Indiana Library Association   111
Indiana Library Trustees' Association   111
International Health Bureau   181
Ivy Lee Associates   184

Jennings, Judson T.   167
Jewett, Alice L.   267–269, 280, 297
Johns Hopkins University   264
Johnson, Alvin S.   137–138
Johnson, Elmer   129, 160–161
Johnson report   137–138
Johnston, William D.   62–63, 67, 263
Jones, Thomas J.   166
Jones Library (Amherst, Massachusetts)   266
Josephson, Aksel G. S.   133–134
Journal of Higher Education   270–272

Kaiser, John B.   116, 118
Kaltenborn, H. V.   261
Keller, Deane   291
Keogh, Andrew   151, 180, 264
Keppel, Frederick E.   153, 167, 173, 216
Kinkeldey, Otto   264
Kirk, Grayson   192
Kirkland, James H.   142
Kirtlan, W. H.   22
Knopf, Alfred A.   285
Koopman, H. L.   152, 190

Lake Placid Club (Florida)   192–193
Lapp, John   95–96

Index

Learned, William S.   140, 149, 151, 153
Legion of Honor. *See* Chevalier de la Légion d'Honneur
Leigh, Robert D.   159, 169–170, 290
Leonard, Robert E.   231
Liberty Loan Campaign   102–103, 108
Librarian of Congress   142, 245–246, 256, 280
Library Council of São Paulo   242
Library Literature (index)   262
Library Literature: A Supplement to Cannons, 1921–1932 (index)   262
Library Quarterly   271
Library Service News (Columbia University)   234
Library Worker's Association   120
Lions Club Foundation   292
Lockwood, P.   209
Lord, Milton E.   247, 264
Los Angeles (California) Public Library   114, 181
   Library School   144
   Training Class   130
Low Memorial Library   201–204, 248, 263
Lydenberg, Harry Miller   73–74, 264, 285, 287

McCarthy, Charles   42
McCarthy, Joseph   286
McCoombs, Charles   189, 287
McDonald, Eliza   6, 8
McIver, Robert Morison   273
McKinnie, Adele   103
McLeish, Archibald   244–246
MacPherson, Harriet D.   224, 238
Maine State College of Agriculture and Mechanical Art   130
Manhattan Special Libraries Association   253
Manley, Marian C.   95, 134
Marcel, Roland   257
Marquand School for Boys   285
Martin, Lowell A.   171
Massachusetts Institute of Technology   271
Mather, Benjamin   7, 9
Mather Family Genealogy   6, 7, 9
Maurer, W. H.   18–19
Melcher, Frederic G.   285
Melvil Dewey Professorship of Library Service   236–237, 241
Merchant's Association of New York   83
Merrymount Press   153–154

Metcalf, Keyes D.   78, 86, 107, 109, 185, 204, 241, 264, 273, 287
Michigan, University of   186, 190, 264
Middle West   1
Milam, Carl   115, 121–122, 150, 255, 262
Miller, Eunice H.   107
Minutes of the Common Council of the City of New York, 1784–1831   91–92
Mitchel, John Purroy   92, 97
Mitchill, Alma C.   290
Mixer, Charles W.   205
Monroe, Paul   273
Moore, John Bassett   279
Morton, F. N.   96
Morton, Florrinell   120, 168
"The Mountaineers"   287
Mudge, Isadore G.   190
Mulvaney, Helen   153
Mumford, L. Quincy   280
Municipal Reference and Research Center. *See* Municipal Reference Library of the City of New York
Municipal Reference Library Notes (periodical)   87–89, 99
Municipal Reference Library of the City of New York (later called Municipal Reference and Research Center)   82–88, 90–91, 93, 95, 96–99, 102–103, 109, 139, 178, 185
Municipal Year Book of the City of New York   90–91
Munn, Ralph   246, 254–255
Munroe, Ruth   270

National Arts Club   253
National Association for Educational Broadcasters   292
National Examining Body   125
National Glass Blower's Association   104
National Library of Peking   242
National Municipal League   91, 253
National Municipal Review   91
National Tax Association   81
"The Need of a Plan for Library Development" (journal article)   109, 111, 139
New Jersey College for Women   237
New Jersey State Education Department   134
New York City Board of Estimate   84, 86
New York City Department of Records and Information Services   99
New York Library Association   145, 253–254

Index

New York Library Club   253
New York Public Library   43, 46, 62, 67–68, 70–78, 80–86, 94–96, 105, 107–109, 116, 145, 167, 176, 178–181, 185, 229, 232, 254, 264, 285
   Library School   77–78, 131, 143, 151, 187, 210, 230–231, 233, 241
New York State Library   129, 294
   Bulletin   63
   Library School (Albany, N.Y.)   67, 131, 143, 162, 187, 210, 230–232, 241
New York Times Index   82, 261
Newark Academy   142
Nutwood Farm (Salem, Ohio)   10, 13

Oberlin, Jonathan F.   30
Oberlin College   134
Ohio Wesleyan University   20–22

Painter, Jacob   2
Patton, Robert   272
Pegram, George P.   219–222
Perry, Everett R.   114, 181
Phelps-Stokes Fund   166
Phi Beta Kappa   29, 253
Phi Gamma Delta   30, 253–254
Pittsburgh (Pennsylvania) Public Library   131
Plum, Dorothy A.   231
Plummer, Mary Wright   134
Portland (Oregon) Library School   270
Power, Effie   270
Pratt Institute Library School   130, 132, 134, 143, 162
Prendergast, William A.   83, 87, 92
Prentice, Noyes   30
Price, Miles   276
Princeton (New Jersey) University Libraries   166–167, 190
Pritchett, Henry S.   142, 153
Providence (Rhode Island) Public Library   164
Public Affairs Information Service   92–96, 260
Public Libraries   134
Public Library Inquiry   141, 169
Public Library Standards   141
Purdue University   273
Putnam, Herbert   142, 147, 149, 171, 256

Quakers. *See* Society of Friends

Randolph-Macon Women's College   266
Raney, Mark L.   264
Rankin, Rebecca B.   85, 88, 95, 99
Rathbone, Josephine Adams   150, 162
Rational Free Press of London   253
A Reader's Guide to the Addresses and Proceedings of the Annual Conferences on State and Local Taxation (pamphlet)   81
Reece, Ernest J.   116, 150–151, 161–163, 197, 231, 235, 253, 279, 293
Reed College Library   204
Regents of the University of the State of New York   232
"Report of A.L.A. Committee on National Certification"   149
"Report of the Special A.L.A. Committee on Certification, Standardization, and Library Training"   149
"A Report to Carnegie Corporation of New York on the Policy of Donations to Free Public Libraries" (Johnson report)   137
Rhodes, Isabella K.   231, 243, 281
Rice, Paul North   86, 196–197, 204, 240–241, 254, 264, 287
Richards, Daniel I.   13–14, 20
Richards, Emma F.   13–14, 20
Richards, Grace   11, 13–14, 19, 23
Richards, Herbert   13
Richards, Lewis   13
Richards, Lola   13
Richards, Samuel   13
Richards, Thomas   13
Richardson, Ernest C.   166
Rider, Fremont   264
Riverside (California) Library Service School   131, 144
Roanoke (Virginia) Public Library   134
Rochester (New York) Public Library   152, 163
Rockefeller Foundation   85, 91, 118, 145, 172, 176–184, 187, 257, 267
Roden, C. B.   165
Roosevelt, Franklin D.   245–246
Roosevelt, Theodore   104
Root, Azariah Smith   121–122, 134
Rothrock, Mary U.   247
Rouncevel, Elizabeth   6, 8
Ruggles, Melville J.   235
Rumford Press   182
Rush, Charles E.   247

Index

Russell Sage Foundation   62, 64, 104
Russell, Trusten W.   202
Rutgers, The State University of New Jersey   171

Saginaw (Michigan) Public Library   231
St. Louis (Missouri) Public Library—Library School   131, 144
St. Nicholas Magazine   11
Salem (North Carolina) College   271
Salem (Ohio) High School   15–16
Salem (Ohio) Public Library   11, 16
Sanderson, Edna M.   231, 234, 237
Sawyer, Rollin A.   95–96
Scarecrow Press, Inc.   160
Schneider, Georg   235
School of Library Economy of Columbia College, 1887–1889   271
Schooley, Elisha   2
Schwab, John C.   98
Seager, Henry R.   41–42
Seaver, William N.   271
Selden, William K.   135
Seligman, Edwin R.   64, 67, 83
Sharp, Katherine L.   134
Shaver-Brown, Mary   238
Shaw, Albert   179
Shaw, Ralph R.   235
Sherman, Clarence E.   164
Shirer, William L.   261
Shoe String Press, Inc.   268
Shores, Louis   233–234
Siewers, Grace   271
Simmons College School of Library Science   130, 143
Smith, David Eugene   205
Smith College   238
Social Science Research Council   141
Société des Amis de la Bibliothèque Nationale et des Grandes Bibliothèques de France   260
Society of Friends (Quakers)   2–5
"Some Present-Day Aspects of Library Training" (journal article)   109, 112, 114–115, 149
South Hall (later called Butler Library)   195, 198, 201–204, 235, 241, 277
Special Libraries (journal)   97
Special Libraries Association   96–97, 139, 253, 268, 290–291
Stoddard, A. J.   293

Straughan, John 2
Street, John 3
Street, Zadok 2
Strohm, Adam 124
Strong, F. R. 182
Study of the Methods of Americanization. *See* Carnegie Corporation's Study of the Methods of Americanization, or Fusion of Native and Foreign Born
"Study of Training for Library Work" (survey) 142
A Survey of Libraries in the United States 122
Sutliff, Mary L. 231
Suzzallo, Henry 270
Syracuse (New York) University Library School 132, 143, 163

Taft, William Howard 77
Tai, Tse-chien 264
Tannenbaum, Frank 261
Taube, Mortimer 235
Tauber, Maurice F. 91, 93, 104, 184, 235, 241, 257, 269
Thomas, Martha Carey 47, 49, 51–61, 65
Thompson, C. Seymour 122
Thorndike, E. L. 270
Thorne, Elisabeth G. 163–164
Thorpe, Gertrude P. 231
Thwing, Charles F. 24–30, 35–36, 42, 48–49, 66, 72–73, 149, 260, 296
Tisserant, Eugene 242
Tolman, Mason 294
Tompkins, Miriam D. 244, 281
Torrey, Bertha. *See* Williamson, Bertha (Torrey)
Training for Library Service (Williamson report) 112, 116, 123–125, 135, 141–142, 153, 160–173, 180, 185, 189, 250, 267, 296, 298
  Recommendations 154–159
"Training for Library Work: A Report Prepared for the Carnegie Corporation of New York" 144, 147, 149–150, 153, 160, 229
Trautman, Ray 238–240
Turner, Harold M. 263
Tyler, Alice S. 110, 122

Ungar, Nell A. 204
Updike, Daniel Berkeley 153–154
Updike Press. *See* Merrymount Press
Utley, George 113–114, 247, 265–266

Index

Vanderbilt University 142
Van Doren, Carl 285
Vann, Sarah K. 113, 116, 123–124, 131, 139–140, 144, 153, 166
Van Vechten, Carl 285
Vatican Library 242
Vincent, George E. 177, 180–181, 183
Vitz, Carl 30
Voll, John A. 104

Wagner, Robert F. 286
Waite, Frank 287
Walter, Frank K. 122, 159
Walters, Everett 272
War Department (United States) 98
Warrington, Abram 2
Washington, University of (Library School) 144, 164
Watson, Charles S. 276
Watson, Cornelia (Williamson) 276
Watson, Derrick S. 276
Watson, Edward Stiles 276
Watson, Martha Torrey 276
Welles, Jessie 115
Wesleyan University 264
Westchester (New York) Library Association 291
Western Reserve University (Cleveland, Ohio) 24–31, 32, 37, 63, 66, 97, 190, 234, 266–267, 276, 279
  Hatch Library 63, 66
  Library School 63, 130, 134, 143, 266
Wheeler, Joseph T. 289
White, Carl M. 132, 197–199, 204, 228, 291
Whitlock, W. F. 22
Who's Who in Library Service 261, 267–269, 282
Williams, Edward C. 63, 66, 234
Williams, Margaret S. 231
Williamson, Alfred 5, 7, 10–12, 275
Williamson, Bertha (Torrey) 27, 46, 52, 193
Williamson, Clarence 6–8, 11
Williamson, Cornelia. *See* Watson, Cornelia (Williamson)
Williamson, Effie 6
Williamson, Elaner 6
Williamson, Florence 6
Williamson, Genevieve (Austen Hodge) 275–276, 282–284, 287, 291–292
Williamson, Gilbert 6, 8

Williamson, Herbert 6
Williamson, Lambert 6
Williamson, Lavina 6
Williamson, Lewis 6, 8
Williamson, Lizzie 6
Williamson, Lizzie (Keturah Mather) 7, 9, 11
Williamson, Loanda 6
Williamson, Mahlon 6
Williamson, Mary 7, 10–11
Williamson, Nora 6
Williamson, Zorenda 6
Williamson Family Genealogy 6–8
Williamson report. *See Training for Library Service*
Wilson, H. W. 93
Wilson, H. W. (company) 93–94, 96, 262, 267
Wilson, Louis Round 91, 93, 96, 104, 112, 171–173, 184, 200, 235, 241, 244, 248–249, 257, 269, 298
Windsor, Phineas L. 132, 151
Winterich, John T. 285
Wisconsin, University of 25, 28, 32–35, 37–41, 43–44, 47, 63, 109
  Library School 130, 143
Wisconsin State Historical Society 63
Wyer, James I. 232

Yale University 98, 151, 180, 206, 261, 264, 294
  School of Fine Arts 291
Young, A. A. 33
Young Men's Christian Association 285
Youth's Companion 11
Yuan, T. L. 242
Yugoslavia, University of 242
Yust, William F. 152–153, 163

Zechert, Adeline B. 122